S0-BZU-429

THE LAWS OF COOKING*

*and
how
to
break
them

JUSTIN WARNER
THE LAWS OF COOKING*

PHOTOGRAPHY BY DANIEL KRIEGER

*and
how
to
break
them

FLATIRON
BOOKS
NEW YORK

OCT 0 7 2015

THE LAWS OF COOKING . . . AND HOW TO BREAK THEM.
Copyright © 2015 by Justin Warner. Photography © 2015 by Daniel Krieger.
All rights reserved. Printed in China. For information, address Flatiron Books,
175 Fifth Avenue, New York, N.Y. 10010.

www.flatironbooks.com

Photos on pages 11, 12, 17, 18, 19, 21, and 22 courtesy of the author.

Project Manager: Elinor Hutton
Culinary Assistant: Erin Barnhart
Illustrations by Justin Warner
Designed by Elizabeth Van Itallie

The Library of Congress Cataloging-in-Publication Data is available upon request.

ISBN 978-1-250-06513-1 (hardcover)
ISBN 978-1-250-06514-8 (e-book)

Flatiron books may be purchased for educational, business, or promotional use.
For information on bulk purchases, please contact the Macmillan Corporate and
Premium Sales Department at 1-800-221-7945, extension 5442, or write to
specialmarkets@macmillan.com.

First Edition: October 2015

10 9 8 7 6 5 4 3 2 1

DAD-ICATION

CONTENTS

LAW OF THE HOT DOG

LAW OF THE WEDGE SALAD

LAW OF GUACAMOLE

LAW OF CHEESE FRIES

LAW OF LEMONADE

LAW OF PESTO

LAW OF GENERAL TSO'S CHICKEN

LAW OF GIN AND TONIC

APPENDICES

FOREWORD

By the time Justin Warner walked into my studio, I was already grouchy and burned. Grouchy because I'd been auditioning cooks all day for my *Food Network Star* team without a lot of luck and burned because what I wanted was teachers and had assumed the best way to find them would be to have candidates teach me to make a dish, literally talking me through the paces while I did the cooking. For some reason I'd chosen Bananas Foster and after following ten sets of faulty instructions, my arms had been flambéed to the elbows.

Then, in walks this scrawny kid with Clutch Cargo lips wearing a flat-brim cap jutting off-angle like a rapper, which it turns out he actually was. He looked fifteen but when he spoke there was a smooth confidence in his voice that told me he'd seen some stuff, yo. Sure, he knew the whys, whats, and hows of the dish, but he also understood what actually mattered. Like a hacker, he'd considered the laws of Bananas Foster and had decided which of these laws were going to pertain to him and which weren't. When we were done, a perfect Bananas Foster had been prepared without sacrificing a single arm hair or eyebrow. As Warner's bright red clogs walked out of the room I remember thinking, *The (culinary) force is strong with that one.*

Justin Warner made it onto my team, and with each challenge he displayed a rebellious legerdemain that continuously beamed out one message loud and clear: I know the rules and I know exactly how and when to break them. His kitchen chops, specifically his ability to create and combine unexpected flavors, gave him the edge, but I think it was his experience as a fine dining waiter that provided the crux around which the contest turned. He won the competition with style and (although he might argue the point) ease.

With the competition over, I was finally able to visit Justin in his restaurant, Do or Dine, in the Bedford-Stuyvesant neighborhood of Brooklyn. Although his Foie Gras Doughnuts and Lamb Breast with Coriander, Cumin, and Lime were already famous, it was his Cold Cantaloupe Soup that made me realize this kid had a touch of Mozart, a kind of crazy genius that doesn't come around very often and when it does it often takes decades to find its proper expression.

But not for Justin.

The Laws of Cooking . . . and How to Break Them is exactly what I expected . . . the unexpected. From its playful but totally rational organization (by Law rather than simply ingredient or course) to its playfully mouthwatering photos to Justin's proselike recipes, stories, and explanations, this is a cookbook unlike any other. This kid may be an outlaw but, like I said, the culinary force is strong with this one. And now he's sharing a bit of that crazy magic with us all. So hang on, kids, it's going to be a tasty ride.

—Alton Brown

Painting by Alex Paozols

First taste of choc. '85

Thanks for my first chocolate, GMA!

INTRODUCTION

Our first interactions with food, from baby mouthfuls of mushy peas to little slurps of apple juice, are characterized by likes and dislikes. Every person I know loves some foods and is not so crazy about others. But why do certain dishes almost always inspire wild amounts of pleasure while others are pretty much guaranteed to be disappointing? As with Legos, Social Security, and the Genetic Sequence, there is a system that governs what makes food tasty. In fact, there are *laws*. These laws have been around for as long as cooking itself.

We know that rich, salty peanut butter (a fat) is complemented by grape jelly (sweet and fruity), and the combination is best experienced when spread evenly between two pieces of bread (the canvas). This primal truth is the Law of Peanut Butter and Jelly. We know that a mixture of lemon juice (something sour) and sugar (something sweet) becomes refreshing lemonade, after being diluted with water to make it palatable. This primal truth is the Law of Lemonade. Even those who don't feel confident in the kitchen know how to make a PB&J sandwich or a pitcher of lemonade. These aren't just a lunch and a drink: they are archetypes. And, as such, they provide a path to create countless recipes. As just one example: What's Peking Duck if not a PB&J? The fatty duck is the peanut butter; the sweet bean sauce is the grape jelly; the pancake or bun is the bread.

I considered other classic and beloved combinations, and came up with eleven powerful flavor systems, each of which serves as a law. I discovered that by following these eleven laws, I could create an endless number of things people would love to eat. The trick was simply to substitute and riff on ingredients and components within the recipes to create new and tasty dishes. Suddenly, ingredients and techniques that were previously intimidating became a piece of cake (or, in this case, a piece of a PB&J).

Working for years as a server in restaurants taught me what people want to eat, and how often they're drawn to the same familiar dishes over and over again. But what if we could convince even the most unadventuresome diner to try Escolar with Strawberry Salsa (page 43) by tapping into a collective culinary consciousness formed by the Skippy and Smucker's jars from our early childhood? What if we could confidently combine foods we've never paired or even cooked before, knowing that *by law* they will taste delicious? This is what this book is about.

THE ELEVEN LAWS

- **LAW OF PEANUT BUTTER AND JELLY:** *Fat meets Fruit*
- **LAW OF COFFEE, CREAM, AND SUGAR:** *Bitter meets Fat and Sweet*
- **LAW OF BAGEL AND LOX:** *Smoked meets Acid and Fat*
- **LAW OF THE HOT DOG:** *Salt meets World*
- **LAW OF THE WEDGE SALAD:** *Funky meets Fresh*
- **LAW OF GUACAMOLE:** *Meet Vegan Fats!*
- **LAW OF CHEESE FRIES:** *Sharp meets Mellow*
- **LAW OF LEMONADE:** *Sour meets Sweet*
- **LAW OF PESTO:** *Herbs meet Fat*
- **LAW OF GENERAL TSO'S CHICKEN:** *Spicy meets Sweet*
- **LAW OF GIN AND TONIC:** *Aromatic meets Aromatic*

HOW TO USE THIS BOOK

Each chapter of this book is named for a law, and each law is named for a dish we all know and can easily prepare or acquire. I trust that I don't need to tell anyone how to make a gin and tonic, or order General Tso's chicken from the local Chinese restaurant. These eleven archetypal dishes each represent the clearest articulation of the flavor combination that defines a particular law. In the chapter introduction for each law, I explain exactly why these iconic dishes taste the way they taste. Then, in the recipes that follow, we explore the power of each law in action, showing how eleven seemingly different dishes have the same familiar flavor backbone. Each chapter begins with canapés, and ends with dessert, with eight courses in between.

The dishes in each chapter are presented to stand alone. It's a cookbook—make any dish you like from any chapter. Or you can build a square meal out of a few recipes from one chapter, or one each from different chapters, which will put more variety on the plate. If you are feeling ambitious, each chapter can be its own ten-course feast. If you are feeling incredibly ambitious, you can create a multicourse menu with one dish from each chapter, for a choose-your-own-adventure ride through all eleven laws.

I don't want to eat foams and microgreens for every meal, and I do not want to eat three bowls of mac and cheese every day either—but there are dishes on both ends of the complexity spectrum in terms of both preparation and flavor. Context is the key to enjoying a great meal. The food in this book is not restaurant food, but I'm hoping it will be as delightful to eat as anything you'll get outside your home. Actually, I'm hoping it will be more so.

While I wholeheartedly believe in these laws, I do ask that you take them with a grain of salt. These are not hard and fast; they are a flexible system that I created to show you some interesting patterns in food and cooking. For example, you might notice recipes under one law that could be categorized under the jurisdiction of another law, but I chose each recipe for each law for a reason. It seems like the Apricot and Habanero Wings (page 44)—which fall under the Law of Peanut Butter and Jelly— could instead be an example of the General Tso's Chicken Law, because the wings are both spicy and sweet. But the Law of PB&J better high- lights why the recipe works: the most important thing about that recipe is not the hot and sweet interplay, but the comingling of the butter (fat) and the apricot (fruit). The habanero (also a fruit) is a spicy bonus in this recipe—it's not the focus.

Also, these laws are not all-encompassing. You might have had some dish prepared by a monk in Bhutan that doesn't follow any of the laws covered here. (Congratulations!)

These laws simply show you the underlying mechanics of these recipes. Further, by following the laws, you can construct your own variations and create original recipes. You may have to experiment to get a dish you love, but this is the creative part. Enjoy the experimentation: it's what cooking is all about.

Of course (knowing me), after I named these laws and immersed myself within them, I wanted to break them. Not all the time; just occasion- ally. What if you don't feel like following a law? This is where my rebel- lious sensibility, which certainly shows up in my restaurant's food, comes through. I realized that by combining elements of one law with another, I could "break" the law and create even more complex dishes. For example, introducing a sharp or funky flavor into a recipe that was designed to take advantage of the play between fat and fruit (the Law of PB&J) has the effect of disrupting the combo, but in a good way. At the bottom of each recipe, I give my advice and guidance on how to break the law that governs that dish, but my goal is to get you to eventually feel confident enough to level up on your own.

In a restaurant, all of the components of a dish are "mised out," which is kitchen jargon for the fancy French *mise en place,* meaning "held in place." To help you fit cooking into your daily life, you'll see that I've provided a note in just about every recipe showing when and how you can "HOLD IT?" Most dishes you eat in a restaurant are not prepared from scratch the second the order hits the kitchen. Some components may have been made days in advance. If you apply this logic to your kitchen, you can prepare components of a dish in advance and hold them until it's time to finish the food and serve it. The great thing about this is that if life happens, you don't have to scrap your plans for dinner. The vast majority of these recipes can be prepared a day in advance and cooked "on the fly" (quickly) when the situation demands it. There are, however, a few that need to be prepared and cooked straight from start to finish. (In professional kitchens, this is called *à la minute*.) There's no "HOLD IT?" note for these. Of course, you can cook every recipe in the book start to finish and skip the "HOLD IT?" note.

Hendrix wouldn't take the stage without his Strat, so you'll need some gear. You'll find a list of exactly what gear you will need for each recipe at the beginning of that recipe. I assume you have a chef's knife, cutting board, fridge, freezer, stove, oven, basic utensils, a wooden spoon, plastic wrap, aluminum foil, and paper towels. The list is a guide to let you know what other implements you'll need. When possible, I list substitutions and also let you know what's optional. If there's no substitution and it's not listed as optional, it's because I think the juice won't be worth the squeeze with anything else. In the back, you can find an Appendix on Gear (page 311) with a list of tools that I think are worthwhile investments to step your game up.

Most of the food in this book—from the fancier Sardines, Their Skeletons, and Sumac (page 150) to the modest Adzuki Bean and Kale Soup (page 66)—are just as good for a family dinner as a dinner party. You'll find tips on cooking for parties in the entertaining appendix (page 312). It's common knowledge that all good parties end up in the kitchen, so I see no problem with cooking in spurts, hanging out, and cooking some more. Your dishes will become a set list, and your friends and acquaintances will become your *fans*. Nothing beats the rush of feeding someone something tasty from your very hands, and having them make the "dude-are-you-magic-or-whut" face. When you find yourself in this situation, like a culinary Hendrix, take a bow.

There are a couple of other appendices at the end of this book: one of them concerns texture (page 318). Texture is a big deal in cooking, but I would never put it above flavor. If you find a recipe that you like, and can execute it with confidence, I would certainly hope that you would customize it. The texture appendix deals with various techniques for transforming the size, shape, and even sound of the components of a dish. For example, you could make the escolar with the salsa as listed on page 43, or you could turn the salsa into a gel, which could be applied to each bite with laser precision. For that matter, you could also turn it into a foam, which would provide the opposite sensation. You could even dehydrate it, to make crispy shards of salsa. The texture appendix is the game after the game, an epilogue that doesn't end. If you find yourself there, congratulations—you are the most curious of all, and I've done my job.

Finally, here's a secret: all of the recipes in the chapter called the Law of Guacamole are vegan. There are other vegan recipes throughout the book, as well as easy ways to transform many of the rest of the recipes so that they become vegan or vegetarian. The vegetarian/vegan appendix (page 321) lists all the vegan recipes and explains how to turn various other recipes vegan.

HELP, I'M IN A NUTSHELL

By all means, feel free to skip ahead to page 27 if you just want to get on your way. I would.

Peanut Butter and Jelly is the first law I learned to follow, because a parent showed me how to follow it. Cliché as it may be, I owe most of my relationship with food to my mom. I had a weird family. My dad was born in 1927, my mother in 1951, and myself in 1984. Dad used to chew on tar when he couldn't afford gum. Mom hid under her desk during fallout drills. I remember the day we got cable TV. Mom didn't toil in the kitchen as much as some, but whatever she didn't do in the kitchen, she exposed me to outside our home. When I was three, I summoned a waiter to order some calamari for myself; far from telling me to pipe down, my mother let me. When I was around five, I was impressed (as I now recall) when she read the riot act to a guy who didn't have lox at his bagel shop (see page 83). Instead of taking me for McDonald's after a doctor's appointment in Baltimore, my mother (and father) splurged and introduced me to sushi.

By the time I was six, my mother had taught me to set a table, which is really the only truly marketable

Left to right: my first cookout; my second birthday; calling home from Pike's Peak on a giant cell phone.

skill I have. My mom told me that to do most anything, you just have to read and follow instructions and be willing to learn along the way.

With this in mind, I applied for a work permit around the age of fifteen, and began working at Oliver's Pub, in Hagerstown, Maryland, as a dishwasher. I intentionally failed at dishwashing in order to get redeployed as a busser, which was much more exciting to me, as I could interact with guests and not have to listen to the senior dishwasher's *KISS* album on repeat. Plus, I knew how to set a table, which set me apart from most of my colleagues (to this day!). I got addicted to the hustle of service. I loved walking home with a wad of singles, which I would use to buy big packs of gum from Sam's Club, only to resell the sticks to boys at school or give them away to girls. Around that time I competed in the National Spelling Bee in Washington, D.C. I bombed in the first round, but conned my dad into taking me to extraordinary chef Michel Richard's restaurant Citronelle. I had read a review in the paper and was intrigued by the descriptions of squab, and a "mood wall" that changed colors as the dining room bustled. The servers treated me like an adult.

In high school, I hung out with a couple of dudes (the lamb guys, page 45) at a coffee and bagel joint called Bentley's from time to time before school. We'd get jacked up on forty ounces of sugar-laden coffee and subject our first-period teachers to the secondhand effects of caffeination. Eventually, I started working at Bentley's, which was owned by a dude named Bill Eichelberger, and staffed by his family. Bill used to say that we were "there to make friends, not money," which has been a motto I still try to apply to all aspects of life. One day I got a wild hair and decided I wanted to work in the kitchen, making sandwiches. It wasn't anything too heady, but the boss always let me experiment and try new combinations. I even launched an ad campaign to sell scones: "Everybody must get sconed." That was risqué as heck for a business across from the County Courthouse, let me tell you. Then I moonlit at a joint called Roccoco [*sic*], where I had the privilege of serving the nightly canapé, a snack they offered for people to enjoy while they pondered the menu. I wore a tie, which was a very big deal to me. As a server, I got to see what people ate while also broadening my own palate. The kitchen served me kidneys and sweetbreads once, half-snickering in anticipation of my revulsion. Instead, I couldn't fathom that something so "weird" could be so tender and full of flavor. I'll never forget that bowl of guts.

During this whole time, I was kind of a hellion. All through high school, I was in and out of detention, "borrowing" chemistry equipment, building fermenters in the back of class, and making my first mojitos (page 222). It didn't help that my father's health was declining; had he been in his prime, he could have smacked some sense into me. My uncle (see page 209) lived in Estes Park, Colorado, and housed me for a few summers before I graduated, just to get me out of my mom's hair. I bussed at a sweet little Italian joint called the Dunraven Inn. I fell in love with the open-mindedness, the blue skies, and the general "high" associated with the Rockies. When my dad died, the decision to move there was pretty simple. I was nineteen.

I plunked myself down in Fort Collins, Colorado, and set out with a resumé. As you enter Old Town Fort Collins from the south, on College Avenue, the largest patio is attached to Sushi JeJu; I walked in and gave them my paperwork. By the time I got home, they had called. I was to be a full-fledged waiter! Within a few months, most of the senior staff was gone. Brian Yoo, the boss, made me the general manager before I could legally drink. I hustled the heck out of every college kid in that town. Pretty girls got free sushi rolls, which I would buy with my discount. They'd tip more, and I'd make a profit and get requested the next time they came in. The head chef, Masa Suzuki, tasked me with articulating the nightly specials, which were generally pretty tough to sell to guys who had just rolled into town from a two-week gig on a rig in North Dakota. I learned that with the right descriptive words, any muddy boot could appreciate monkfish liver, salmon roe, or sea urchin. Masa ended up rooming with me, and I learned more about Japanese and Korean foods than I ever thought possible. One day he slipped me a nugget of something yellowish and green to try. He wouldn't tell me what it was. Without looking up from the Nintendo, I told him it was mustard, miso, and a tiny eggplant. His reaction of "Whoa. You are good!" put the idea in my head that I had a working palate. Around then, I met George McNeese, who would become my drinking buddy, grilling companion, future business partner, and all-around friend.

It was during this time in Colorado that I read an article in *Esquire* about a dude in New York City named Danny Meyer, who made his fame and fortune as a restaurateur. I knew there were famous chefs, but Danny became a legend, and not for lifting the pan. He'd even written a book about restaurants, service, and life. I bought a copy and gulped furiously at the Kool-Aid within it. I applied his teachings to another management gig, at Sushi Tora in Boulder, where I curated the wine and special fish list. In its heyday, Sushi Tora would have twenty to thirty kinds of sea creatures on the menu. I maintain to this day that I've eaten more kinds of sushi than most Japanese people. Cod milt. Enough said!

I moved on to a pretheater fine dining gig with Kevin Taylor's group in Denver. It was nice to "just" wait tables again, and to help build a new restaurant. It was also really refreshing to experience all the fun things

that "New American" food was doing (that was a buzzword back then). I ate my first medium-rare pork chop, first finger of béarnaise, and first taste of truffle oil there under the hand of Dave Boehm. Somehow, I ended up serving Lori Midson, the critic for the *Rocky Mountain News*. In her review, she liked the food, but was in love with my service. When I read the review, I couldn't believe it. Kevin Taylor gave me a free plate of lamb chops as a thank-you.

With my newly inflated head, I decided that I had mined all the hospitality gold in the West, and wanted a challenge. The girl I was chasing at the time was headed to New York for art school, so I made it my goal to work at one of Danny Meyer's restaurants. I worked two very bad jobs in New York for a month before I got a call from Graceanne Jordan, the general manager of the Modern, Danny's restaurant attached to the Museum of Modern Art. I was nervous as hell. I don't know what Graceanne saw in me, other than a desire to learn, because I was absolutely not qualified to represent the caliber of service and hospitality that she, Chef Gabriel Kreuther, and Pastry Chef Marc Aumont were putting out. I trailed in the dining room that night, and watched as suited waiters and sommeliers tasted and decanted wine over a candle. They served the food simultaneously, like synchronized swimming with plates. Some dishes were carved before the guest. There was a cheese cart with thirty varieties. Busboys wore tunics and were called server assistants. There wasn't just one table setting; there were three forks, three spoons, four knives, and a spork. I had never seen such splendor.

I made friends quickly, and was mentored by some of the best in the business. Eventually I was promoted to captain, which is basically a "boss waiter." It was a lot of work, but I loved this job. Chef Gabriel and Chef Marc opened my mind to flavors, techniques, and possibilities I didn't know could exist. It was my duty to articulate these flavors to the guests in a way that made sense. Lobster and chamomile might sound like a pretty bizarre combination at first, but once I realized that chamomile is soft and round and almost buttery, and thus could explain to guests that this dish was really a riff on the most traditional way of serving lobster, even the most skeptical diners would take the bait. George from Fort Collins joined me at the Modern. It was nice to have an old friend, but it was even better to introduce him to all the people I had met, most notably Luke Jackson. Luke and I were always paired up as captain and waiter in the back section of the dining room. It was like a Good Cop/Bad Cop routine with us, as generally the guests found one of us to be abrasive or annoying. George and Luke and I would get beers after the shift, hang out, and eat stuff, as we all ended up living on the same block on Madison Street in Bed-Stuy, Brooklyn.

One morning, I was hungover, and lying next to one of my colleagues in her bed. She was working in the restaurant while trying to make it as an actress, and got casting notices in her inbox every morning. A Food Network show was casting a block away. On a whim, we decided to give it a whirl. The premise was simple—two people would build a restaurant in twenty-four hours, competing against another team of two. Possibly the only reason we were cast is because I had never cooked in a commercial kitchen—aside from making those scones and sandwiches at Bentley's in Hagerstown, Maryland. I guess the producers thought we would provide some entertainment. We *did* practice before the taping, but not enough to bring us to the skill level of the other team. What we had, though, that the other team didn't was a knack for interesting flavor combinations. We won the show by launching a glorified pancake restaurant.

Now, I was somewhat hooked. While still waiting tables, I rigged up a little cart to make my pancakes on the street from time to time. My first gig was for an event at Luke's friend Perry's jewelry shop. I stood outside and made the pancakes, giving them away for free, and cleared $300 just from tips. You don't have to be a fiscal gastronomist to understand the insane amount of profit I was making on flour, eggs, milk, and baking powder. The people liked the crazy jellies I would make from agar agar, and the interesting compound butters that I'd churn to complement them. Perry got a kick out of the pancakes, and must have confused me with someone who could actually cook. Many beers were had, and from this humble success, Luke, Perry, George and I decided to open up our own restaurant in Bed-Stuy, called Do or Dine, after the (un)official neighborhood motto of "Do or Die."

George and I would cook, Luke would make drinks and take care of paperwork, and Perry would fund, design, and build the project. We wanted to make a nice dive bar with a few snacks. Maybe a special quesadilla, some good wings, and maybe some fun grilled meats. All we wanted was a place where we could eat, drink, have some fun, and then walk home. The concept snowballed, and before we knew it, we were open with a full menu (well . . . about nine items!) and a blurb in the *New York Times*. George and I had a license to ill, concocting whatever we wanted, largely food based around puns or awkward situations. We were fortunate enough to hire some folks who knew the technical aspects of cooking on a line, while we continued absorbing, reading, and learning about interesting flavors and ingredients. The *New York Times* followed the blurb with a glowing, albeit tiny, review, Michelin nodded, and we were swamped for months. Not bad for four dudes who had never cooked professionally.

During the build-out of the restaurant, I liquidated most of my posses-

@itsmeanne and I "working" a brunch shift

That feeling when you are in a trailer about to compete on *Cutthroat Kitchen.*

sions, and was crashing at my current GF's apartment night after night. I had holes in my socks, but I had a restaurant to show for it. On the busiest night we had ever seen, Do or Dine was raided by all of the city offices that can raid a restaurant. They thought we were a front. While we weren't peddling contraband, we were "operating an unlicensed bottle club" (read: BYOB, read also: BS). We were horrified. We shut the doors to the restaurant, unsure of our fate. I lay in my GF's bed while she was at work, feeling horribly sorry for myself. That's when the phone rang. It was one of the casting directors from *24 Hour Restaurant Battle,* asking me if I wanted to try out for a television show called *Food Network Star.* I tried out. Two days later, we reopened the restaurant. Six months later, in 2012, I won *Food Network Star.*

On *Food Network Star,* I was mentored by Alton Brown. His style of mentorship was to "get out of the way" but to encourage me to do my best. His confidence in my abilities is the reason I won the show with so little training. He gave me the paternal push that I hadn't felt for years. If it weren't for Alton Brown, I couldn't have even written this book. He and I cook different food, and cook it very differently, but what we have in common is curiosity and no fear of failure. He remains a huge influence and a good friend. I have a painting of him in my kitchen.

I also have a kegerator. I recommend you get both.

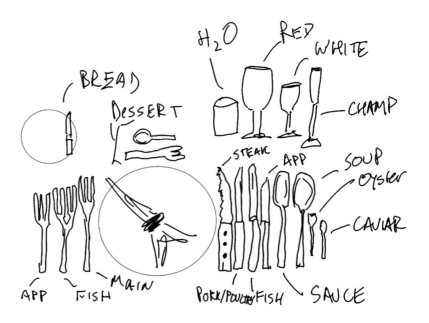

THE INSPIRING CAT POSTER SPEECH

Curiosity and lack of fear are the rules of my kitchen, if I had any. They lead to positive experimentation, which is how one learns. We do something, record the results in our mind, and if it works, we do it again. If it fails, we try something else. If you wanted to dabble in automechanics, you would need a serious garage. Whether training Pokémon or conducting an orchestra, you need a dedicated space. Cooking is no different, but I'm guessing your domicile already has a built-in laboratory/stadium/rehearsal studio for you to continue down the path of experimenting with food—your kitchen! Everyone should learn how to play the stove. It's not expensive, and what you produce keeps you alive.

Recipes show you how to achieve a particular result in the kitchen. They are just sheet music, which you can use simply for inspiration or choose to play note-for-note, as if for a recital. Sometimes I like to riff and freestyle in the kitchen, but there is also a certain Zen about following a recipe exactly. It's like putting together Ikea furniture, solving a puzzle, or building a Lego castle. The world outside of our kitchens can be pretty crazy; inside, it's often nice to have one road to follow.

That said, I cut any corners I can, but preserve the corners that might otherwise compromise the end result. If I can make a machine do something, I'm going to. If someone else can make a component better than I can, I use what they make. Cooking shouldn't be a schlep or an exercise in tedium. Don't kill yourself to follow a recipe. Cheat where you can!

Every now and then you'll play a sour note and stuff will get weird, burned, wrong, off, or just generally gross. The hardest part of cooking is not burning toast. I say this because flavors can be corrected, whereas if anything is cooked past its optimal point, it can't go back. Metaphorically, if you keep an eye on the toast, you'll be just fine.

Taste everything that goes into a recipe; this way you'll know what it is that you don't like or what it is that you love for the next time. If something is too *something* there is always something you can do to make that *something* shut up a little. Every basic taste sensation—salty, sweet, sour, bitter, and savory—can be foiled by adjusting fats and acidity. I always try to eat my mistakes. I try to find the one thing I did right in that pile of burned disaster, pat myself on the back for that, and return to the drawing board. The kitchen should be a place of discovery, not stress. Shit happens. Neither one of us is Wolfgang Puck, and even he scraps stuff and orders pizza.

Now, venture forth, and cook like nobody's eating.

LAW OF PEANUT BUTTER AND JELLY

fat meets fruit

The peanut butter and jelly sandwich is one of the first dishes many Americans learn to "cook." I think we take for granted just how complex the play is between its simple components. Jelly, jam, or preserves are generally made from foods that contain seeds (fruits!), so most jams and jellies are sweet and fruity. Peanut butter is salty and rich due to the lipids (fats) in the nuts. Fats and sugars contain the most caloric bang for the buck, and our taste buds have evolved to help us find them. Consider also that wild nuts and berries were probably what we ate before we developed tools to kill animals. The bread serves as a vessel, but I like to call it a canvas. We enjoy peanut butter and jelly more on a canvas because its flavor is spread out, essentially diluting it to make it a more pleasant, if not prolonged, eating experience. Pizza, with its fruit sauce, cheese, fat, and crusty canvas, would fall under the law of PB&J, but because all of the components of pizza must be cooked, I believe the PB&J to be a more primal articulation of the law. The subsequent ten recipes are proof that fruit, fat, and a canvas are all you need for a composed dish.

fat meets fruit

HAZELNUT BUTTER	HAZELNUT BUTTER TOASTS WITH BACON 'N JAM	JAM
BACON		
DUCK BREAST	ARUGULA SALAD WITH PAN-ROASTED DUCK BREAST AND FIGS	FIGS
POPPERS	JALAPEÑO POPPERS WITH BLUEBERRY DIPPIN' SAUCE	BLUEBERRY SAUCE
FRIED CHICKEN	CHILLED RED PEPPER SOUP WITH COLD FRIED CHICKEN AND GOAT CHEESE	RED PEPPER SOUP
GOAT CHEESE		
GRILLED CHEESE	TOMATO SOUP WITH "GRILLED CHEESE" RAVIOLI	TOMATO SOUP
HALIBUT	HALIBUT CEVICHE IN MINI MANGO "TACOS"	MANGO
ESCOLAR	ESCOLAR WITH STRAWBERRY SALSA	STRAWBERRY SALSA
		HABANERO
WINGS	APRICOT AND HABANERO WINGS	APRICOT
LAMB SHANKS	LAMB SHANKS WITH CUMBERLAND SAUCE	CUMBERLAND SAUCE
FOIE GRAS DOUGHNUT	FOIE GRAS DOUGHNUTS	GRAPE JELLY

YIELD Makes about 1 cup
hazelnut butter; enough for
about 60 bite-size toasts

PREP TIME 10 minutes

COOK TIME 30 minutes

gear

sheet pan

tongs

large skillet

food processor

ingredients

1 pound bacon

HAZELNUT BUTTER

6 tablespoons olive oil

½ pound raw hazelnuts

1 teaspoon kosher salt

1 loaf sourdough bread, sliced

8 ounces raspberry jam (see
page 31), for every single recipe
of nut butter

hazelnut butter toasts with bacon 'n jam

(CANAPÉ/SNACK)

Elvis has touched many lives with his music, but it was his contribution to gastronomy that touched me. My grandfather first served me the King's combo of peanut butter, banana, and bacon when I was in the second grade. He rolled it up in a flour tortilla, which I had never previously experienced independently from its role in a microwavable burrito. My grandfather is a master teller of tall tales, legally blind, and not generally known for his culinary prowess. For these reasons, I was legitimately nervous about the combination, and feared it was retribution for the hair brush I snuck into his bed every night. But I took a bite and was blown away. Until I realized that this was Elvis's combo, Gramps might as well have been Brillat-Savarin. The combo of nuts, bacon, and fruit is always a smash.

Cook the bacon. Preheat the oven to 400°F. Lay the bacon, without overlapping, on a sheet pan. Cook it until crispy, 15 to 30 minutes, checking periodically after the 15-minute mark, and using tongs to transfer the individual strips to a paper towel–covered plate as they crisp.

Make the hazelnut butter. Heat 2 tablespoons of the oil in a large skillet over medium-high heat, then add the hazelnuts in a single layer. Toast the nuts, tossing or stirring often, until they are audibly hissing, golden brown, and giving off a nutty smell, 4 to 6 minutes.

Once the nuts are toasted, carefully add them to a food processor and blend on high until pasty, scraping down the sides every few minutes, about 5 minutes. With the food processor running, gradually add the remaining 4 tablespoons oil and the salt and continue blending until combined. (The texture will be a bit looser than commercial nut butters, but this will show that you made it yourself.)

Make the toasts. Preheat the broiler. Cut off the crusts of your bread slices. Cut the bread into smaller, bite-size pieces.

HOLD IT? Keep your nut butters and jams, covered, in the fridge for up to a month. Cooked bacon can be wrapped in paper towels and then in plastic wrap and stored in the fridge for 2 days, but make sure it returns to room temperature before serving. The prepared bread can be held, untoasted and covered, for up to 6 hours.

Place the breads in a single layer on a sheet pan. Put the pan under the broiler and, keeping a constant eye on it, broil for 3 to 5 minutes, flipping once, until both sides are golden brown and toasty. (Don't do this after even one cocktail.) If you mix types of bread, don't toast on the same sheet pan because different breads cook at different speeds; toast in batches if needed.

PLATE IT! Cut the room-temperature bacon into 1-inch pieces. With the bread still on the warm sheet pan, smear a bit of the hazelnut butter and the jam on each piece of toast. Add a strip of bacon on top. Transfer the warm toasts to a platter and serve.

BREAK IT: Instead of bacon, top these with bonito flakes and seaweed! The fresh fruity flavors in the jam will balance the funky fishy flavors.

STEP YOUR GAME UP

If you have disposable pastry bags, you can put the jam in those to allow for laser accuracy. You might want more or less jam depending on your preference. You can also use the pastry bags or corner-snipped zip-top bags to scribble a letter or symbol on each toast.

For even more visual appeal, when cutting up your bread for party toast, cut the bread into different shapes—diamonds, circles, or whatever you like—or use cookie cutters. Birthday party for Susan? Cut out some S's and make her day. Bon voyage? I have a sweet palm tree cookie cutter. With a very small amount of effort, this simple setup can make you into a human Pinterest board at any shindig.

alternative nut butters and jams

I created this recipe to be flexible, so you could serve a few friends or a crowd. Make one nut butter, or make a few and present your guests with a bunch of combinations. Once you factor in the jam and bread options (for the jam, try tomato, gooseberry, cloudberry, lingonberry, orange-elderflower, guava, or mango; for the bread, consider rye, pumpernickel, focaccia, or ciabatta), you have endless possibilities for toasts. Jams generally offer the most fruit flavor and the most appealing texture, so I avoid jellies and preserves. Here are some of my favorite combinations, but be sure to experiment on your own as well:

- Mixed nut butter with grape jam and bacon on white toast (instantly conjures images of PB&J, but one taste reveals much more)
- Pistachio butter with hot pepper jelly and bacon on rye toast
- Pecan butter with apple jam and bacon on wheat toast
- Cashew butter with passion-fruit jam and bacon on pumpernickel toast

FOR A MIXED NUT BUTTER
½ pound roasted, salted mixed nuts
¼ teaspoon kosher salt

FOR A PISTACHIO BUTTER
1 tablespoon olive oil, for toasting, plus an additional 3 tablespoons
½ pound raw shelled pistachios
1 teaspoon kosher salt

FOR A PECAN BUTTER
2 tablespoons olive oil, for toasting, plus an additional 1 tablespoon
½ pound raw pecans
½ teaspoon kosher salt

FOR A CASHEW NUT BUTTER
2 tablespoons olive oil, for toasting, plus an additional 2 tablespoons
½ pound raw cashews
1 teaspoon kosher salt

Heat the specified amount of toasting oil in a large skillet over medium-high heat, then add the nuts in a single layer. (Skip this step for the already roasted mixed nuts.) Toast the nuts, tossing or stirring often, until they are audibly hissing, golden brown, and giving off a nutty smell, 2 to 8 minutes depending on the nut. Continue to make the nut butter per the main recipe on page 28.

Adjust the recipe's directions to accommodate your bread, jam, and bacon.

YIELD Makes 2 servings

PREP TIME 5 minutes

COOK TIME 15 minutes

gear

very sharp knife (see Tip)

cast-iron skillet

tongs

probe thermometer (optional)

mixing bowl

ingredients

DUCK BREAST

One 8-ounce duck breast

Kosher salt

Freshly ground black pepper

FIGS

2 tablespoons balsamic vinegar

4 ounces fresh figs, halved (about 4)

½ teaspoon kosher salt

SALAD

2 handfuls (about 2 ounces) washed arugula

½ lemon

Extra-virgin olive oil

Pinch of kosher salt

Freshly ground black pepper

arugula salad with pan-roasted duck breast and figs

(Cold app)

Is this something you'd find at a fancy French joint? Yes. Does it require an entire brigade of French chefs to make? *Non!* In fact, this meal masquerading as salad is prepared entirely *à la minute*, so you can really impress with your ability to go from raw ingredients to plated dish in just 20 minutes. The key to understanding how duck breasts cook is to imagine a chicken breast with bacon glued onto one side. The meat itself is very lean, so you don't want to overcook it (in fact, duck breast should be eaten medium rare), but you do want to crisp up that baconlike skin by rendering out a lot of the fat over a medium-low flame, then finish the cooking in the oven. Arugula makes one of my favorite salads of all time because it doesn't need a fancy-pants dressing—you can just add a pinch of salt, a squeeze of lemon, and a drizzle of olive oil. Although the arugula is the canvas for the plate, its bite and freshness balance the rich duck (fat) and sweet figs (fruit). Pair this dish with a candle, some red wine, and someone you are trying to woo.

Cook the duck breast. Preheat the oven to 475°F.

Score the skin of the duck breast in a ¼-inch crosshatch pattern, being careful not cut through to the flesh of the duck. Liberally season both sides of the duck breast with salt and pepper.

Place the breast, skin side down, in a cast-iron skillet, then place the cold pan over medium-low heat. Let the fat render out of the skin until it's pooling all around, looking like underdone bacon, 6 to 7 minutes. Increase the heat to high, and immediately flip the duck breast. Sear the flesh side for 2 minutes. Then flip the duck again to skin side down and transfer the entire skillet to the oven for 5 to 7 minutes until the duck is cooked just to medium rare. Use my nifty doneness chart (see below) or use a thermometer; for me, 130° to 135°F

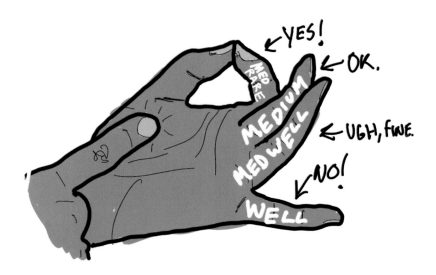

Confucius liked chopsticks because he thought knives had no place at an honorable table. Sometimes it is nice to slice meats in the kitchen.

☞ **Tip**

When scoring the skin of the duck breasts, using a never-used-for-anything-other-than-cooking adjustable X-Acto knife is even better than a chef's knife. Set on the shortest blade length, it will ensure that you don't cut into the flesh beneath the skin.

does nicely. (Bear in mind that the folks at the USDA don't think you should eat medium-rare duck, and specify 165°F.) Carefully remove the skillet from the oven and transfer the duck breast, skin side up, to a cutting board and let rest for 5 minutes. (It's important that the duck rests skin side up so as not to steam the crisp skin.) Set the skillet aside.

Make the figs. While the skillet from the duck breast is still hot, carefully add the vinegar and, using a wooden spoon, scrape the magic delicious bits from the bottom. Add the halved figs and salt, and toss gently. The residual heat in the skillet will warm up the figs, and also shellac them with a nice duck-fat sheen.

Dress the arugula. Put the arugula in a mixing bowl, add a squeeze of lemon juice, and toss. Add a drizzle of oil, a pinch of salt, and a few grinds of black pepper. Using your clean hands, swirl this around to coat the arugula. Give it a taste, and doctor the ratio of lemon, oil, salt, and pepper to what tastes good to you.

PLATE IT! Flip the rested duck breast skin side down onto the cutting board and, using a sharp knife, slice as thinly as possible.

Take half of the slices of duck and fan them out on each plate, skin side up. When fanning things, it's nice to have the piece closest to the front of the plate as the top piece of the fan.

Add the figs to the arugula and, using your clean hands, gently toss them around, then place a handful at the base of the fanned duck breast on each plate.

BREAK IT: Get herbaceous with some sage. The deep flavor of the figs and duck will be put in check by sage's piney astringency.

YIELD Makes about a dozen poppers

PREP TIME 20 minutes

COOK TIME 20 minutes

INACTIVE TIME 10 minutes

gear

1-quart saucepan

paring knife

chopstick

sheet pans lined with paper towels

3 shallow bowls

Dutch oven or heavy-bottomed pot

candy thermometer

slotted spoon or spider

ingredients

SAUCE

1 pint blueberries

½ cup light-colored beer (I use a pilsner, or a lager, or a wheat beer for extra fruitiness)

2 tablespoons balsamic vinegar

1 teaspoon onion powder

PEPPERS

One 26- or 28-ounce can whole pickled jalapeño peppers

FILLING

12 ounces cold cream cheese, cubed

BREADING

¼ cup cornstarch

4 egg whites, lightly beaten

½ cup unseasoned bread crumbs

½ cup panko bread crumbs

2 teaspoons kosher salt

Vegetable oil, for frying

jalapeño poppers with blueberry dippin' sauce

(HOT APP)

Before my GF was my GF, we bonded as friends over a road trip from Fort Collins, Colorado (where I was slinging sushi to college kids), to her hometown of Rapid City, South Dakota. Whoever was driving controlled the playlist. She was blasting Modest Mouse, the Misfits, and Murder City Devils. I was bumping Young Jeezy, Kanye West, and Lupe Fiasco. While we couldn't agree on music, we found that we shared a love of road food. One of our favorite stops, Arby's, has a very addictive, rich, cream cheese–stuffed jalapeño popper, with "fruity" Bronco Berry sauce. As Bronco Berries are rarely in season, I developed the following with blueberries.

Make the sauce. In a 1-quart saucepan over medium heat, combine all of the ingredients for the sauce and bring to a boil. Reduce the heat to low and simmer until the blueberries have burst and the sauce is shiny, 15 to 20 minutes. Set aside to cool.

Prep the peppers. Drain the peppers, saving the liquid because it is awesome. (More on that on the next page.) If you are lucky enough to find the kind of canned jalapeños that contain carrots, congrats—reserve the carrots for sandwiches or snacking.

Using a paring knife, lop off the tops of the peppers. Then use the skinny end of a chopstick to remove the seeds and membrane from the inside of the peppers. Generally a few circular scrapes will pop them right out. Rinse the peppers under water to remove any remaining seeds. Set the hollowed peppers upside down on paper towels, to dry off.

Using your fingers, stuff each pepper with the cubes of cream cheese.

Line a sheet pan with paper towels. Set up a dredging station: Place the cornstarch in a shallow bowl, the egg whites in a separate shallow bowl, and both bread crumbs and the salt in a third shallow bowl. Give the bread crumbs and salt a little mix with your fingers.

Dredge a stuffed pepper in the cornstarch, then in the egg white, then in the bread crumbs, then in the egg white again, and then bread crumbs again. (This double egg-white action seals the whole kit together nicely.) Make sure you don't miss the tops of the peppers! Place the breaded peppers on the lined sheet pan.

HOLD IT? Once assembled, and before frying, you could individually wrap the peppers in plastic wrap and freeze them for up to a week. You could also wrap the pan in plastic wrap and refrigerate them in anticipation of your awesome party later that same day. The sauce can be made and refrigerated for a week, or frozen indefinitely; allow it to come to room temperature before serving. Either way, don't fry these peppers until you are ready to eat them.

Fry the peppers. Preheat the oven to 225°F. Fill a Dutch oven only halfway with oil, clip on a candy thermometer, and bring the oil to 375°F over medium-high heat. Line a sheet pan with paper towels.

Brine There, Done That

Pickling liquid, or brine, is amazing stuff and should never be discarded. Regardless of whether the pickled vegetables are fermented or not, the tangy, seasoned liquid can be the missing link in a chain of deliciousness. The liquid has three main components, all of which are vital to a good dish; acid (vinegar or lactic acid), herbs and spices (dill, coriander, etc.), and salt. Using this liquid to make a vinaigrette is always a good idea, and it can be used any time a recipe calls for vinegar or lemon or lime juice. It's also a hell of a chaser to a shot of whiskey—this is called a "pickleback."

Using a slotted spoon, carefully lower 2 or 3 of the breaded peppers into the oil. Keeping an eye on the thermometer, throttle up the heat to high to get that oil back up to 375°F but no higher. Fry the peppers until they are dark golden brown, 4 to 5 minutes. Using a slotted spoon or spider, fish them out, and transfer them to the lined sheet pan to drain; store the pan in the warm oven. Repeat the process until all of the peppers are fried and hanging out in the warm oven.

PLATE IT! You could pile all these guys on a plate and put the room-temperature sauce in a bowl on the side. You could put the sauce in a zip-top bag, snip a tiny corner off, and pipe the sauce all over the peppers. You could spoon swoosh (drop a spoonful and swoosh it with the back of a spoon) the sauce onto a plate, slice the peppers in half along their equator, and place the peppers over the sauce. This is ideal for individual plating.

BREAK IT: Add some smoke to this by mixing some chipotle adobo with the cream cheese. The acidity of the pickled jalapeños along with the richness and smoke of the cream will make these almost like little barbecue bombs.

STEP YOUR GAME UP

 I like to use this semi-industrial technique both to make less of a mess when filling the peppers and also to guarantee cream cheese in every cranny. Almost magically, when the poppers are fried, the cream cheese returns to the gooey state we crave.

½ cup heavy cream
2 teaspoons agar agar (or 2 teaspoons gelatin, though note it's not vegetarian)
1 teaspoon kosher salt
8 ounces cream cheese, at room temperature, cubed

Pour the heavy cream into a saucepan, then add the agar agar (or gelatin) and salt; allow them to marry for a few minutes. Then place the pan over medium heat and slowly whisk in the cubes of cream cheese. Continue whisking until the mixture bubbles and there are more bubbles than you can easily count, about 5 minutes. Remove the filling from the heat and pour it onto a sheet pan. Carefully place the sheet pan in the refrigerator. In about 15 minutes (or 2 hours if using gelatin), you'll see that your filling is now the texture of American cheese. Don't be alarmed!

Using an offset spatula or dull knife, cut the filling into ¼-inch strips. Using the fat end of your chopstick, shove as many strips as you can into the cavity of each pepper. Be amazed at how much filling you can fit in, and how little mess is created! (If there is any filling left over, save it for adding to sandwiches—super on a hot dog with some sriracha!)

YIELD Makes 6 to 8 servings

PREP TIME 20 minutes

COOK TIME 25 minutes

INACTIVE TIME 2 hours

gear

blender

rubber spatula

fine-mesh strainer or chinois
(see sidebar opposite)

Dutch oven or heavy-bottomed
pot

candy thermometer

3 shallow bowls

slotted spoon or spider

chopsticks or tongs

small bowl

whisk

ingredients

SOUP

10 red bell peppers (4 pounds),
seeds and ribs removed,
chopped

3 celery ribs, roughly chopped

3 carrots, peeled and roughly
chopped

4 garlic cloves, peeled

1 quart vegetable stock (or
vegetable broth, and cut the
finishing salt by half)

CHICKEN

Vegetable oil, for frying

1 cup whole wheat flour

2 teaspoons cracked black
pepper

1 tablespoon kosher salt

1 tablespoon smoked paprika

1 large egg, beaten

½ cup cultured buttermilk

4 boneless, skinless chicken
thighs (about 1 pound)

chilled red pepper soup with cold fried chicken and goat cheese

(COLD SOUP)

One of the most memorable brunches I've ever had was at a joint called Fort Defiance in Red Hook, Brooklyn. It was a blisteringly hot day, and I had just cruised over on my (now stolen, RIP) moped because I was en route to Ikea. I smelled like a weed whacker, was hungover, and had helmet hair. On the menu was a dish of "cold fried chicken." It was served with red pepper jam and an oyster. The heavens opened. I now know that cold fried chicken in the summer or after a long night is a very smart move. This cold red pepper soup provides a refreshing fruity counterweight to the fried chicken thighs. The carrots, celery, and vegetable stock do what they do best: provide a canvas for other flavors.

I BELIEVE I CAN FRY

You could go buy a FryDaddy, but you can do a better job with a deep cast-iron Dutch oven and a candy thermometer. You see, most home fryers are made with aluminum and an electric heating element and thermostat.

Before we get into the gear, we'll talk about how frying things works. Think of a big glass of room-temperature soda. When you add ice, the ice melts (as its temperature increases due to the warmer soda) and the temperature of the soda decreases (because of the introduction of ice). Eventually, these two will reach a sweet spot wherein the soda is at its coldest, before it warms again. When you add food to hot oil in a fryer, it works just like an ice cube in a soda. The oil temperature drops, and the temperature of the food increases. Of course, increasing the temperature of the food is the desired effect (cooking). Unfortunately, as the oil gets colder, it slows the cook time, which means overly oily, soggy food. Electric fryers counteract this by increasing the heat flow once a change is registered in the thermostat. It's anyone's guess how quickly this takes place. On a stove top, you can be the thermostat. Before you add food to the oil, "throttle up" the flame or burner in advance, keeping an eye on the thermometer, throttling down as needed to keep the oil at the appropriate temperature.

Lastly, cast-iron retains more heat than aluminum, so the vessel itself works to keep the heat more constant. In the case of the soda, cast-iron is a coozie, while aluminum is just a naked can.

Make the soup. Working in batches, add the vegetables and the vegetable stock to a blender and blend until very smooth. Using a rubber spatula, push the soup through a fine-mesh strainer into a storage container. Cover and refrigerate until chilled.

Make the chicken. Fill a Dutch oven halfway with vegetable oil, clip on a candy thermometer, and bring the oil to 350°F over medium heat. Line a plate with paper towels to create a landing strip for your fried chicken.

Set up a dredging station: In a shallow bowl, mix together the flour, black pepper, salt, and paprika; place half of this mixture in the second bowl. In a third shallow bowl, gently beat the egg and buttermilk together with a fork.

TOPPING

4 ounces goat cheese, at room temperature

½ cup cultured buttermilk

FINISHING

½ cup olive oil

2 teaspoons kosher salt

Finely chopped fresh basil (optional)

Emulsifications

Emulsifications are basically just a riff on a game of "Come over, Red Rover" between two substances. Imagine team soup and team olive oil in the recipe above. The blender calls the team members back and forth, until you can't tell who was on the original teams. Some fancy people might call it a gentle dispersion of one substance into another.

Chin-wha?

The chinois is a workhorse in my kitchen. The word means "Chinese" because its shape was said to resemble Chinese hats. Regardless, its fine mesh does a great job of acting as a colander, a *tamis* (that's a fancy word for sieve), and a strainer.

Cut the chicken into approximately 1 x 1-inch pieces; about 6 pieces per thigh.

Working in dry-wet-dry order, dredge a handful of chicken pieces in the peppered flour mixture, then the buttermilk mixture, and then the second flour mixture. Continue until all the chicken has been dredged.

Fry the dredged chicken in batches, carefully lowering a few pieces at a time into the hot oil, using a slotted spoon or a spider. Once in the oil, use chopsticks (or tongs, if you prefer) to separate the pieces and keep them from sticking together. Don't forget to keep an eye on the thermometer and throttle the heat accordingly (see page 36) to keep the oil at temperature. Cook until the outside of the chicken is crunchy and the inside is cooked through, 4 to 5 minutes. Using a slotted spoon or spider, transfer the cooked chicken from the oil to the lined plate.

Immediately refrigerate the chicken, uncovered, on the towel-lined plate until chilled, at least 2 hours.

Make the goat cheese topping. In a small bowl, whisk together the goat cheese and buttermilk.

HOLD IT? You can keep the all your components refrigerated and separate for up to 2 days.

Finish the soup. Place the cold soup, oil, salt, and basil, if using, into a blender and blend on high until incorporated. (You want the oil to emulsify, so do not do this step ahead of time; see sidebar at left.)

PLATE IT! Serve tableside, with a couple spoonfuls of goat cheese topping and a nice pile of chicken pieces set in individual bowls and the soup in a chilled pitcher to be poured around the chicken at the last minute.

PARTY ON! Alternatively, you could make a little soup shooter in a Dixie cup, topped with some goat cheese and a bite of chicken. Yeah, party on!

BREAK IT: Sea-funk it out. Mix the minted sake from page 142 with the goat cheese. Then add the uni, salmon roe, and oyster to the soup. It'll be somewhere between a Bloody Mary and a cold bouillabaisse.

---

tomato soup with "grilled cheese" ravioli

(HOT SOUP)

YIELD Makes 4 servings

PREP TIME 20 minutes

COOK TIME 45 minutes

gear

medium stockpot

large pot

slotted spoon

blender

medium nonstick pan

sheet pan

ingredients

SOUP

2 tablespoons olive oil

1 yellow onion, diced

2 carrots, peeled and thinly sliced

4 garlic cloves, minced

4 tablespoons tomato paste

4 tablespoons Worcestershire sauce

12 vine-ripened tomatoes, cored and chopped

2 cups vegetable stock (or vegetable broth, and cut the salt by half)

20 fresh basil leaves

2 teaspoons kosher salt

2 tablespoons packed light brown sugar

"GRILLED CHEESE" RAVIOLI

2 tablespoons unsalted butter, plus more for buttering the plate

16 wonton wrappers

8 slices American cheese

¼ cup finely grated Parmesan cheese

Folks ask me all the time, especially around Independence Day, what I believe to be the quintessential American foods. Corn is my first answer, followed by tomato (fruit) soup with grilled cheese (fat). My first memory of having enjoyed this combo was with my mother at Peoples Drug Store. While my mother's prescriptions were being filled, we'd often have a bite at the counter. Yes, this was when the drugstore lunch counter was still clinging to the last scuds of existence. I remember how gooey the American cheese was, and how it rubberized when it cooled. I'd warm it back up in the soup, which retained much more heat and made the cheese pliable once more. I couldn't have been more than four years old when I learned this trick, and I've applied this pre-school logic to my version below, which amalgamates the two in one hot bowl of Americana.

Make the soup. In a medium stockpot, heat the oil over low heat. Add the onion and carrots and sauté until tender, about 8 minutes. Add the garlic and cook for 2 minutes, then add the tomato paste and cook, stirring, until it is the color of dark rust, about 3 minutes. Add the Worcestershire to the pot, scraping any bits stuck to the bottom of the pot with a wooden spoon. Add the chopped tomatoes and stock, bring to a boil, then reduce the heat and simmer until the soup has thickened and tomatoes are falling apart, about 30 minutes.

Make the "grilled cheese" ravioli. Butter a plate and set aside. Bring a large pot of water to a boil. Fill a small bowl with room-temperature water.

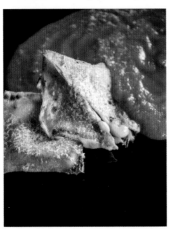

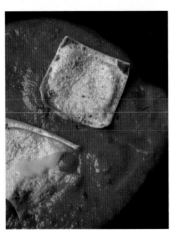

Place one wonton wrapper on a clean dry work surface. Break one American cheese slice into 4 squares. Lay the 4 squares in the middle of the wrapper so they overlap and are ½ inch from edge of the wrapper. Dip your finger in the bowl of water and paint the wonton wrapper's edges lightly to moisten them, then top with a second wonton wrapper, and press the edges together to seal. Repeat this process to make rest of the ravioli.

Reduce the heat to a simmer (so the ravioli don't get tossed around too much). Carefully drop the ravioli in the simmering water and cook just until they float to the top, 4 to 6 minutes, then remove them with a slotted spoon. Set aside on the buttered plate in a single layer.

HOLD IT? Boiled ravioli can be refrigerated in a single layer on a buttered plate, wrapped with plastic wrap, for up to a day. The soup can be made in advance and held in the refrigerator for up to a week, or frozen for up to a month.

Finish the soup and ravioli. Working in batches, add the soup to a blender and blend until smooth. Tear in the basil, add the salt and brown sugar, and blend again until incorporated. Return the soup to the pot and, if necessary, reheat over medium heat until piping hot, stirring occasionally.

Turn the broiler on high.

Melt the 2 tablespoons butter in a nonstick pan over medium heat. Working in batches, sear a few ravioli in the butter until browned and blistered, flipping once, 2 to 3 minutes per side. Transfer the seared ravioli to a sheet pan. Continue until all the ravioli are seared.

Sprinkle the grated Parmesan evenly on top of the ravioli. When the soup is hot, carefully transfer the sheet pan to the broiler, and broil the ravioli until the Parmesan has melted and turns golden brown, 1 to 3 minutes.

PLATE IT! Place 2 ravioli in each bowl. Transfer the soup to a tureen or similar serving vessel. At the table, ladle or pour the soup around the ravioli.

BREAK IT: Sharpen this up with a dash of horseradish in the soup, and sharp cheddar in the wonton skins.

YIELD Makes about 20 bite-size tacos

PREP TIME 20 minutes

COOK/INACTIVE TIME 1 to 6 hours

gear

nonreactive bowl

slotted spoon

mandoline (optional but strongly recommended)

ingredients

CEVICHE

1 Fresno chile

8 ounces very fresh halibut or other firm white-fleshed fish, skin discarded, flesh cut into ¼-inch pieces

½ cup strained fresh lime juice (about 5 limes)

½ shallot, finely diced

¼ cup loosely packed fresh cilantro leaves, roughly chopped

½ teaspoon kosher salt

"TACOS"

2 peeled mangos

¼ small head red cabbage

1 avocado

Reactive versus Nonreactive

Aluminum, cast-iron, and some copper pots can make your food weird in the presence of highly acidic foods (citrus, tomatoes). Generally the results are a little discoloration and a minimal metallic flavor. I'm not too terribly threatened by that, but maybe you are.

☞ Tip

Before you do anything with hot peppers, put your latex gloves on.

halibut ceviche in mini mango "tacos"

(COLD FISH)

On my season of *Food Network Star,* the show took us to Miami for the last few emotional episodes. As the cast was being whittled down to the final four, tensions were high. Finally, the shooting wrapped, and we were cut loose. I was like a feral animal released from the cage of "reality." This altered beast ran to the bar with his $10k of Discover card prize money and pounded mojito (recipe page 222) after mojito and scarfed a ton of ceviche, the dish of raw diced fish "cooked" only by the acid in its marinade. We had been living on catering, delivery, and craft services, so the fresh, citrusy fish with cubes of sweet mango was like making out with a mermaid. Turns out it wasn't just drunken lust—I craved more of it when I got back to NYC. Under the law of PB&J, the mild fruit is also the vessel, thin sheets perfect to fold into taco-shaped parcels, ideal for dropping directly into a mojito-moistened mouth.

Make the ceviche. Finely dice the chile, removing and discarding the seeds if you want less heat.

Toss all the ingredients for the ceviche in a nonreactive bowl (see sidebar). Cover and allow to marinate ("cook") in the refrigerator for at least 1 hour and up to 6 hours, stirring occasionally.

Make the "tacos." Starting on the widest side of the mango, and using a mandoline or a sharp knife, carefully slice the mangos as thinly as possible. Discard or snack on the first few slices, as they will be too small. Each mango will yield 5 to 8 nice big slices per side.

HOLD IT? The ceviche can be refrigerated for up to 6 hours in a covered container. The mango slices will keep for 6 hours stacked on top of each other, wrapped in plastic wrap, and refrigerated.

Just before serving, shred the cabbage very thinly, using a mandoline or a sharp knife, discarding any big chunks. (The cabbage must be sliced immediately before serving or it will wilt.) Dice the avocado.

PLATE IT! Using a slotted spoon, scoop up a bit of ceviche, letting the liquid drain off, and place it on a mango slice. Top with a bit of avocado and a pinch of cabbage. Continue constructing the mango "tacos" until all of the mango and ceviche are used. Serve immediately on a long platter and instruct folks to pick them up like tacos.

PARTY ON! This is an ideal party snack. If you are really looking to rage, challenge your friends to drink shots of the marinating liquid, also known as *leche de tigre*. This could be a wicked chaser to a shot of chilled dark rum, but maybe you don't party like that.

BREAK IT: Add a bitter component to this dish in the form of toasted walnuts sprinkled on top; this will also bump up the textural juxtaposition. Also, if you're not into eating raw fish or even fish "cooked" in acid, you could heat up the lime juice mixture and pour it over the top of the fish to cook it.

YIELD Makes exactly 6 servings for exactly 6 people

PREP TIME 15 minutes

COOK TIME 15 minutes

INACTIVE TIME 2 minutes

gear

medium nonreactive bowl (see page 40)

cast-iron skillet

spatula or fish spatula (see sidebar, page 99)

slotted spoon

ingredients

STRAWBERRY SALSA

1 pint strawberries, hulled and diced

¼ red onion, finely diced

½ jalapeño pepper, seeds and ribs removed, finely diced

Juice of ½ lime

¼ cup loosely packed fresh cilantro, roughly chopped

1 teaspoon kosher salt

½ teaspoon sugar

½ teaspoon ground cumin

FISH

2¼ pounds escolar fillets

Kosher salt

☞ **Tip**

Before you do anything with hot peppers, put your latex gloves on.

escolar with strawberry salsa

(HOT FISH)

Escolar is a very rich fish, so rich in fact that one should not consume more than 6 ounces of it in a sitting—or tummy trouble will follow. But that shouldn't stop you from trying this mild, buttery fish. Emeril Lagasse, Charlie Trotter, and Eric Ripert serve escolar to great fanfare and the rationale is simple. When it's cooked correctly—over a low flame to render out oils, like bacon—it tastes really good. The fish is both mild and oily, so it serves as both fat and canvas. Now you, too, can be one of these chefs, flying a beautiful strawberry-red and escolar-white flag at your dinner table.

Make the strawberry salsa. Place all of the ingredients for the salsa in a nonreactive bowl. Toss to combine, and chill until ready to serve.

HOLD IT? The salsa can be held for up to 3 days in the refrigerator.

Make the fish. Pat the fish dry with a paper towel. Cut the fish into 18 equal pieces, each about 1 inch thick. Liberally salt both sides of each piece.

Place the fish in a large dry cast-iron skillet over low heat. The fish is so oily that it is best to cook it slowly to render out the fat, just like cooking bacon. Cook the pieces on one side until barely golden, about 7 minutes, then flip using a spatula or fish spatula and cook for an additional 7 minutes on the opposite side. Transfer the fish to a cutting board and let rest for 2 minutes.

PLATE IT! Place 3 cut pieces of fish on each plate. Using a slotted spoon, place a scoop of salsa on top of the fish.

BREAK IT: Once the rich escolar is cooked, dust it with a little unsweetened cocoa powder. The bitterness of the cocoa will be tempered by the rich fish and the sweet strawberries. That's chocolate fish, for the record.

YIELD Makes about 50 wings

PREP TIME 10 minutes

COOK TIME 1 hour

INACTIVE TIME 1 hour

gear

10-quart pot with lid, and a colander to fit inside

sheet pan lined with paper towels

kitchen shears

2-quart pot

rack that fits the sheet pan

large mixing bowl

ingredients

CHICKEN

5 pounds chicken wings

Kosher salt

SAUCE

8 tablespoons (1 stick) unsalted butter

1 habanero pepper, seeded and minced

1⅓ cups apricot preserves

1 teaspoon kosher salt

½ teaspoon fresh lemon juice

☞ **Tip**
Before you do anything with hot peppers, put your latex gloves on.

apricot and habanero wings

(LIGHT MEAT)

When I was a little kid I couldn't hear the word *nifty* without thinking of candy canes. My dad, a psychologist, got a huge kick out of playing "word association games" with me, as the results were pretty bizarre. I think part of my culinary synesthesia can be attributed to the similar flesh tones and fruity nature of the apricot and the habanero, which is actually a fruit, spicy as it may be. Just like "nifty" is to candy canes, habanero is to stone fruits, and the combination works nicely within the fat and fruit law. I hope you think this recipe is totally ~~candy canes~~ nifty. You may wonder why I steam and chill the wings before baking. It renders out some excess fat from the skin and makes them extra crispy—this small step ensures you don't have gummy wings.

Make the wings. Fill a 10-quart pot halfway with heavily salted water and bring to a boil. Set a colander in the pot so that it does not touch the water.

If your wings are still whole, use kitchen shears to snip them at the joints; discard the tips (or reserve them for stock!).

Place the butchered wings in the colander and cover them with the pot lid. Steam the wings for 15 minutes, tossing them once halfway through. You're looking for opaque, sweaty-looking wings that are almost cooked through. Once they're almost cooked through, "shock" the wings by rinsing them under cold water to stop them from cooking more, then drain. Lay the parcooked wings on the lined sheet pan, pat them dry, and refrigerate until thoroughly chilled, about 1 hour. Meanwhile, make the sauce.

Make the sauce. Combine the butter and the minced habanero pepper in a 2-quart pot and cook over low heat until the butter begins to foam and is infused and spicy. Add the preserves and simmer over low heat until thickened, uniform, and glossy, about 4 minutes. Add the salt and lemon juice and remove from the heat. Put the sauce in a covered container and refrigerate.

HOLD IT? Hold the sauce and chicken in the fridge until ready to finish cooking; up to 2 days.

Finish the wings. Preheat oven to 450°F. Bring the sauce to room temperature.

Place the wings on a rack, discard the paper towels from the sheet pan, then place the rack back on the sheet pan. Roast the wings for 20 minutes, then rotate the pan and flip the wings. Roast for another 20 minutes or until the skin is looking crisp and bubbly.

In a large mixing bowl, toss the hot wings with a hefty pinch of salt while adding the room-temperature sauce, a little at a time, just until the wings are glazed. (Overly sauced wings can be messy and soggy.)

PLATE IT! Wings must be piled. If the pyramids were made of wings I would have visited already.

BREAK IT: Instead of steaming the wings to parcook and render their fat, smoke them at 225°F! Now you have smoked, fruited, and spiced-up wings!

YIELD Makes 4 servings

PREP TIME 20 minutes

COOK TIME 6 hours 15 minutes

gear

medium pan

slow cooker (at least 8-quart capacity)

ingredients

LAMB SHANKS

4 lamb shanks (about 4 pounds total)

1 teaspoon kosher salt, plus more for seasoning

Freshly ground black pepper

2 tablespoons olive oil

1 pound baby carrots

1½ cups vegetable stock (or vegetable broth, and cut the salt by half)

1½ cups dry red wine (I use a Merlot)

8 garlic cloves, peeled and crushed

½ cup (about 20) fresh sage leaves

CUMBERLAND SAUCE

2 tablespoons unsalted butter

3 shallots, finely diced

2 cups dry red wine (I use a Merlot)

½ cup dried currants

1 tablespoon Dijon mustard

lamb shanks with cumberland sauce

(DARK MEAT)

Two of my oldest friends, nicknamed Erk and Ern (Eric and Aaron), are the Rembrandt and Caravaggio of BS artists. Factor me in—more of the Dalí, I'd say—and you have a trifecta. When Ern was going to law school (talk about BS!) and lived in a tiny apartment in Philadelphia, Erk and I paid him a visit. It was decided that I should cook, and that lamb was in order. But this was long before I owned a restaurant, and I had no idea what I was doing. So I got the first lamb cut I found—shanks—and because I wanted to out-fancy the boys, some dried currants to make Cumberland sauce—an obscure (in America) sauce of English origin used to complement game. They could smell my ineptitude and promptly unleashed a torrent of thinly veiled insults and questions of my competency, assuming I was BSing because there is a town not far from where we grew up named Cumberland. But this time, the very tasty joke was on them. The currant-laden sauce serves as the jelly to the rich, fatty lamb's peanut butter, with the carrots as the canvas for both the PB&J and my BS artistry.

Make the lamb shanks. Season the shanks liberally with salt and pepper. In a medium pan over medium-high heat, heat the oil and sear the shanks until they're golden brown on all sides, about 8 minutes total. Add to slow cooker with the carrots. Set the pan aside.

Add the stock, wine, garlic, sage, and 1 teaspoon salt to the slow cooker. Cover and cook on low until the meat is fork-tender, about 6 hours.

Make the Cumberland sauce. Meanwhile, in the same pan that the lamb was seared, melt the butter with the drippings over low heat until foamy. Add the shallots and cook until both the butter and shallots are browned, stirring occasionally, about 5 minutes. Add the wine, currants, and mustard and bring to a boil. Reduce the heat to low and simmer, uncovered, until reduced by about half and the fruit is tender, about 40 minutes. Remove from the heat and allow the sauce to cool in the pan. Refrigerate the sauce until the lamb is done.

HOLD IT? The sauce will keep in the fridge, covered, for up to 2 days. The cooked lamb could be cooled and stored in the cooking liquid in the covered slow cooker insert in the fridge for up to 2 days. Transfer the lamb mixture to a pot and reheat until the braising liquid is bubbling before proceeding with the recipe.

Remove the hot lamb and carrots and transfer them to a platter. Allow them to rest while you reheat the sauce.

Add ¼ cup braising liquid from the slow cooker to the sauce, and warm over medium heat.

PLATE IT! Divide the carrots among four plates and place a shank on top of each. Distribute the hot Cumberland sauce evenly over the shanks.

BREAK IT: Follow the recipe as you would, but triple the Dijon. This supersharp sauce will be just like black-currant Dijon, which is a popular mustard variant in France. I'd then eat the entire dish cold, with a loaf of bread.

STEP YOUR GAME UP

If you want to put a little more work into the presentation, you can "lollipop" the lamb shanks and cut the carrots into what I call "fake baby carrots." The former makes for a dramatic presentation, while the latter makes your guests wonder where you procured such perfect, but oddly sized carrots.

"Lollipop" the shanks. Starting at the narrow end, working parallel with the bone, use kitchen shears to cut a slit on all four sides of the bone, as if you were slicing the skin of a banana to peel it three-quarters of the way. Continue cutting about three-quarters of the way down the shank. Liberally season any visible meat surface with salt and pepper. Pull the sections of meat from the bone down to the thick part of the shank and tie with butcher's twine—the idea is you want a "lollipop" effect. Depending on the size of the shanks, this might take two ties.

Carve fake baby carrots (easy). Trim the carrots, cut them into two pieces, and then use the vegetable peeler to round out the sharp edges, fashioning extra-large "fake" baby carrots. Add to one side of the slow cooker so they are easier to retrieve later.

Continue with the rest of the directions as is. When plating, cut and remove the kitchen twine from the shanks and stand each one up on a plate with the bone sticking straight up. Stack the carrots on the side and distribute the hot Cumberland sauce evenly over the shanks.

gear

skillet

blender

vessel for chilling the mousse

pastry bags or zip-top bags

stand mixer with dough hook attachment

small pot

rubber spatula

medium bowl, buttered

heating pad

Dutch oven or heavy-bottomed pot

candy thermometer

sheet pans

rolling pin

4-inch ring cutter or pint-size glass

spider or tongs

chopstick (optional)

fine-mesh sieve

ingredients

FOIE GRAS MOUSSE

8 ounces foie gras grade B, roughly chopped

About 15 green seedless grapes

2 shallots, finely diced

1 tablespoon Cointreau, or other orange liqueur

2 teaspoons kosher salt

¼ cup heavy cream

foie gras doughnuts

(DESSERT)

If I'm to be remembered for anything past my expiration, I think the foie gras doughnut might be my greatest accomplishment. It all started when I was seeing a girl who worked in the pastry department of a restaurant. We would have little tiffs about food and cooking. One of these was over which bread is "the king of breads." She argued for brioche, while I said fry breads. She temporarily won, citing that brioche accompanies the king of meats, foie gras. I swore that if I ever figured out how to make doughnuts, I'd put foie gras in a doughnut and serve it, proving once and for all that fry breads are the king of breads.

Some time and some girlfriends later, I opened Do or Dine. At that time, there was one person on the floor and two people in the kitchen. I was running food as I cooked it. I ran out to a silver-haired man and his beautiful wife and daughter, put the food down, my apron a mess, and explained the dish. In a Jean Reno accent, he asked me what my plans were for zis kitchen. I said I wanted to do a lot of things, but mostly I wanted to get the recently opened doughnut shop up the street (called Dough) to make me blank doughnuts that I could fill with foie gras. The man asked me what I would do wif zis. I said I'd sell them. He said, "Well, I am Dough." I couldn't believe how happily the fates smiled on me. I shook his hand, took his number, and before I could call, he was bringing me samples of hole-less doughnuts to fill. The problem was, I had never cooked with foie, only eaten it, so I didn't have any idea where to begin. I went to a specialty store and purchased some foie gras mousse. I ran back to the restaurant to pipe it into the blank doughnuts. I knew it needed a fruity jam to balance the richness and savoriness, but because I was impatient, I sent someone to get it for me. They came back with Welch's grape jelly, which I piped in right away, planning on substituting a fancy jam down the road. I salted the top of the doughnut, then hid the salt in confectioners' sugar. It looked like a normal jelly doughnut. I bit into it. The rich foie was put into overdrive by the sweetness, but tempered by the slight tang of the Concord grape jelly. The dough was light and fluffy. It was a four-star dish disguised as a jelly doughnut. I finally won the fight, at least in my own mind.

Some people came to take the doughnut's picture. Then some people claimed they invented the foie gras doughnut first. Then some people protested online. But it wasn't just some people, it was hundreds. Somehow we got an e-mail every time someone signed the petition, so we were missing e-mails from suppliers and employees with our inboxes flooded. I set up a filter to collect the protest e-mails. Eventually we had well over a thousand e-mails. I took a screen shot and sent it to the press. A war began. Everyone wanted to know why thousands of people were up in arms over a little doughnut. We made international news, and the little joint, cobbled together by and for friends in Bed-Stuy, cemented its tiny place in New York City dining history. Here you can make your own controversy, homemade, or you can just go buy the components and assemble them like I do at the restaurant.

DOUGH

½ cup very warm water

¼ cup granulated sugar

2 teaspoons active dry yeast

4 tablespoons (½ stick) unsalted butter

3 cups all-purpose flour, plus more for dusting

1 teaspoon kosher salt

¼ teaspoon ground cinnamon

2 large eggs, lightly beaten

DOUGHNUTS

Vegetable oil, for frying

½ cup grape jelly

1 tablespoon kosher salt, for sprinkling

¼ cup confectioners' sugar, for dusting

Make the foie gras mousse. Put the foie in a skillet over very low heat. Once some fat has rendered and pooled, about 3 minutes, add the grapes and shallots to the skillet. Cook until the shallots soften and the foie begins to melt and darken in color, about 5 minutes. Add the Cointreau and cook for 1 minute more.

Carefully pour the hot mixture into a blender with the salt. Then, with the blender running on the lowest speed, very carefully and slowly pour in the cream and increase the speed to high until combined. (The mousse at this stage will be very loose—it will set when refrigerated.)

Transfer the mousse to another vessel and chill in the fridge, uncovered, until cool to the touch. Pour or scrape the chilled mousse into a plastic bag or disposable pastry bag with no tip. Tie or seal the bag and allow to chill in the refrigerator until completely cool, at least 1 hour.

Make the dough. Activate the yeast by adding the sugar and warm water to the bowl of a stand mixer fitted with the dough hook attachment, then sprinkle in the yeast. Cover the bowl with a towel and let sit until the yeast has foamed up, about 10 minutes.

Meanwhile, in a small pot over low heat, melt the butter, then set aside to cool slightly.

In a separate bowl, whisk together the remaining dry ingredients.

Once the yeast has foamed up, add the dry ingredients to the stand mixer bowl and slowly combine with the dough hook. Using a rubber spatula, scrape down the sides. Continue kneading the dough on low, then gradually add the butter, then add the beaten eggs one-half at a time. Once the dough is uniform, turn it out onto a clean, floured work surface and knead just until smooth, about 10 turns, but not too much, or it will begin to toughen.

Place the dough in a buttered bowl and cover with plastic wrap. Let rise in the bowl on a heating pad set to low until doubled in size, about 1 hour.

Flip the risen dough out onto a floured surface, knead once, and regrease the bowl. Flip the dough back into the regreased bowl and cover with plastic wrap. Let the dough rise on the heating pad once again until doubled, about 1 hour more.

Make the doughnuts. Fill a Dutch oven halfway with vegetable oil, clip on a candy thermometer, and bring the oil to 350°F over medium heat. Lightly flour a sheet pan. Line another sheet pan (or plate) with paper towels or use a cooling rack.

Place the dough on a clean floured work surface. Using a rolling pin, very gently roll out the dough to a thickness of ½ inch. Cut out circles of the dough with a pint-size glass or ring cutter. (You might be inclined to reroll the scraps, but the doughnuts produced from rerolled dough will be tough.) Place the circles onto the floured sheet pan, cover with a clean kitchen towel, and let rise for at least 10 minutes. Make sure to monitor your oil so that it does not overheat.

When the oil is to temperature, and working in batches, drop the doughnuts into the hot oil and fry until risen on one side, about 1 minute, then flip and cook the other side for another minute. Use a spider to remove them from the hot oil, then land on the paper towel– or rack-lined sheet pan (or plate). Allow to cool slightly.

Bag it up! Transfer the jelly to a pastry bag or zip-top bag.

Fill the doughnuts. If your doughnuts are hot, use a twice-folded paper towel to hold the doughnut, then stick a knife or chopstick in the side of the doughnut to create a tunnel. Cut the tip of the bag and pipe the foie gras mousse into the hole until the doughnut feels full and heavy. Next, pipe in some of the jelly, allowing it to dribble out of the doughnut. Set the doughnut back on the rack, sprinkle with a tiny pinch of salt, and, using a fine-mesh sieve or shaker, dust with confectioners' sugar.

LAW
OF COFFEE,
CREAM,
AND SUGAR

bitter meets fat and sweet

I f you drink coffee, there's a good chance you've put cream and sugar in it at some time. That's because coffee—like some fruits and veggies and a lot of roasty, toasty things—is bitter. Cream (or any fat, for that matter) allows for a little dilution of the concentrated flavor of coffee. Dilution has a negative connotation when it comes to food, but in the case of coffee, fats act like the CliffsNotes. It makes coffee taste "nutty" as opposed to "the slightly torched skin of an unripe walnut," or "chocolatey" as opposed to "criollo cacao." I'm not saying fats dumb down bitter flavors—they actually let us appreciate them more. So if fats are the CliffsNotes of a bitter

ingredient's potable Ph.D. thesis, sugar is the Pixar movie version. You know when you watch a Pixar movie and you are "LOLing" at the very adult joke that went right over the heads of the kids? Sugar lets even those who can't read CliffsNotes enjoy bitter things. Don't believe me? Kids will eat the heck out of coffee ice cream or even one of those blendery drinks from your locally owned and operated coffee bar. Why do you think that is? Because bitter + fat + sweet is a law. Ahead, you'll get acquainted with all sorts of bitter things, and by the end of this chapter, you'll know how to deal with them. Unfortunately the law only applies to foods, not people.

bitter meets fat and sweet

Bitter	Dish	Fat	Sweet
PUMPERNICKEL	"TWO-PUMP" CROSTINI	CREAM	PUMPKIN
RADISH	RADISH CAPRESE	MOZZARELLA	CHERRY TOMATOES
ENDIVE	ENDIVE GRATIN WITH TALEGGIO AND RAISINS	TALEGGIO	RAISINS
TURMERIC	CHILLED YELLOW BEET AND WATERMELON SOUP WITH TURMERIC CREAM	CREAM	YELLOW BEETS
			WATERMELON
KALE	ADZUKI BEAN AND KALE SOUP	SHORTENING	APPLE JUICE
ARUGULA	OCTOPUS TIRADITO	AVOCADO OIL	OCTOPUS
BLACK SESAME SEEDS	SCALLOPS WITH BLACK SESAME AND CHERRY	BUTTER	SCALLOPS
			CHERRIES
MOLÉ	PORK TENDERLOIN MOLÉ DONBURI	BUTTER	NILLA WAFERS
COFFEE	COFFEE-RUBBED FLANK STEAK WITH CAULIFLOWER PURÉE	YOGURT	MAPLE SYRUP
DARK CHOCOLATE	MILK AND DARK CHOCOLATE DACQUOISE	HAZELNUTS	MILK CHOCOLATE

gear

stand mixer with whisk attachment

colander

large bowl

sheet pan

ingredients

PUMPKIN BUTTER

1 quart heavy cream (see Tip)

One 15-ounce can pumpkin pie filling

1½ teaspoons kosher salt

CROSTINI

Pumpernickel bread, sliced "sandwich style" (not that hard stuff for people who need fiber)

Olive oil

☞ **Tip**

For the biggest impact, use organic or farmer's market cream.

"two-pump" crostini

(Canapé/snack)

You know what's fancy? Pumpernickel. You know what's cool? Wordplay. With these pumpernickel (the bitter component) and pumpkin butter (the cream and sugar component) crostini, you can be both fancy and cool all night. Oh yeah, and as a bonus, you get to make your own butter. You don't even need a churn or an old lady to get it done. See, once upon a time I somehow ended up with a cookbook called *Another Blue Strawberry,* by James Haller. It was about cooking without recipes, and if memory serves, one of the first nonrecipes is about making butter. Adding pumpkin pie filling makes this taste just like the butter at Texas Roadhouse, the restaurant chain oddly based in Kentucky, which is delicious and addictive. Now that you know that you can combine canned pie filling with homemade butter, I fully expect you to put cherry butter (same technique but with cherry pie filling) on chocolate chip pancakes.

Make the butter. Add the cream to the bowl of a stand mixer fitted with the whisk attachment. If you have a splash guard, use it; otherwise you can drape the edge of the bowl with plastic wrap. Start the mixer on the slowest speed, then gradually increase the speed to the highest setting. Whisk the cream until peppercorn-size or larger bits of butter are floating in the milk, about 5 minutes.

Line a colander with a clean dish towel and place it over a large mixing bowl. Pour the contents of the mixer bowl into the colander. Reserve the milk for drinking because it's rad. Place the butter back in the bowl of the stand mixer. Add the pumpkin pie filling and salt and mix until combined, about 1 minute.

HOLD IT? Store the pumpkin butter in a covered container in the fridge until ready to use; it will keep for up to a week, or can be frozen for up to a month. You can also cut your bread ahead of time and store in an airtight container, ready to brush and toast (see next step).

PLATE IT! Preheat the oven to 350°F. Cut your bread into whatever shape you like. Drizzle or lightly brush the bread with olive oil on both sides. Place in a single layer on a sheet pan and bake, flipping once halfway through the baking, until crispy, 6 to 10 minutes.

Allow the bread to cool slightly so the butter doesn't melt everywhere. Place a chilled rosette of butter on each piece of bread, or simply smear heavily with the pumpkin butter. Serve.

CHEAT IT! If you don't have the time or energy to make your own butter, you can always replace the homemade butter with store-bought softened unsalted butter and mix it with the pumpkin pie filling and salt per above.

BREAK IT: Some curry heat (1 to 2 tablespoons of curry powder) added to the mix would take this over the top.

STEP YOUR GAME UP

If you want to get real fancy, you could put the freshly made butter in a pastry bag with a fluted tip, and pipe it into toast-size rosettes on a parchment paper–lined sheet pan. Refrigerate until ready for use, or freeze indefinitely. Feel free to cut your bread into unusual shapes, or even to use cookie cutters—this would be a great use for a pumpkin-shaped cookie cutter.

YIELD Makes 4 servings

PREP TIME 10 minutes

gear

vegetable peeler

bowl

ingredients

12 small red radishes (about 2 bunches)

8 ounces (about 16) *ciliegine,* or small mozzarella balls, drained

12 ounces cherry tomatoes

1 cup lightly packed fresh basil leaves

2 tablespoons olive oil

½ teaspoon fleur de sel

Freshly ground black pepper

Finishing Salt

Salt comes in a variety of shapes and colors, derived from different methods, all with a different flavor profile. Finishing salts are the "Maserati" of salts. They are generally coarse, and designed to look, feel, and taste different than the stuff in the shaker. My favorite is fleur de sel from France, which is moist, coarse, and mouthwatering. Maldon, from England, is another great option.

Chiffonade

Chiffonade is just a fancy French term for cutting leafy things into very thin ribbons. Stack and roll up whatever leaves you want to cut into chiffonade into a cigar shape. Slice crosswise in the direction you rolled.

radish caprese

(Cold app)

I'm totally obsessed with using the phrase "trompe l'oeil" at every opportunity. It's a ten-dollar word that refers to a particular style of painting that makes the depicted subject matter look real, deliberately creating an optical illusion. I first learned about it in Frederick, Maryland, where an artist named William Cochran had painted a series of trompe l'oeil images—fountains, windows, doorways—on and around a bridge downtown. The windows looked like they were built there, with shutters you could close, and an angelic figure seemed to leap from the walls, almost suspended in space. This was before 3D IMAX, so seeing it blew my ten-year-old mind. This dish offers its own "trickery of the eye" by disguising the crunchy, innately bitter radishes as their neighbor and foil, the supple, creamy mozzarella balls known as *ciliegine* (literally, "cherry-sized"). Throw in some sweet cherry tomatoes and you've fulfilled the Law of Coffee, Cream, and Sugar. A good magician doesn't reveal any secrets, so don't tell your guests, and watch them get tricked with every surprising bite of their first trompe l'oeil salad.

Carefully peel the radishes, carving them into the same size and shape as the mozzarella balls and removing any trace of red or pink. Transfer to a serving bowl. (You can snack on the trimmings.)

Add the cheese and tomatoes to the radishes.

Cut the basil into chiffonade (see sidebar) by stacking the leaves one on top of another and rolling them up like a cigar. Cut very thin crosswise slices of the rolled-up basil. This makes long threads of basil, which are easier to evenly distribute. Add these to the salad.

Drizzle the oil over the salad. Add some fleur de sel and freshly ground black pepper to taste and gently toss to coat.

PLATE IT! This is the kind of salad you serve in individual bowls. I find that bowls make the tomatoes and radishes easier to stab, whereas a plate allows them to slide around.

PARTY ON! You could leave the basil in its whole state and skewer one basil leaf, a radish ball, a mozzarella ball, and a tomato with a fancy toothpick, and serve them as an hors d'oeuvre.

BREAK IT: Sweeten the deal even more with some watermelon balls. Now there are two trompe l'oeil, and the sweetness of the watermelon will foil the radish even more.

gear

10-inch cast-iron skillet

tongs

trivet (see sidebar below)

ingredients

TOPPING

6 slices (about 4 ounces) white Italian bread, cubed

¼ cup loosely packed fresh flat-leaf parsley leaves

2 tablespoons olive oil

1 teaspoon crushed red pepper flakes

½ teaspoon kosher salt

½ teaspoon freshly ground black pepper

ENDIVE

2 tablespoons unsalted butter

2 Belgian endives, split lengthwise

2 garlic cloves, minced

1 cup sweet German Riesling

½ cup golden raisins

2 teaspoons kosher salt

4 ounces Taleggio cheese, thinly sliced

Trivets!

I can't tell you how many of my friends have ringed their countertops or tables because they put a hot pot of mac and cheese down to answer the phone. Trivets are a device used to elevate a hot plate or pan from a surface, so as not to scorch it. Trivets also allow you to serve food directly from the cooking vessel at the table, which makes for a nice home-style feeling.

endive gratin with taleggio and raisins

(HOT APP)

There is a scene in the movie *Amelie* wherein the character Lucien listens to an endive, because to him, it is precious. When that movie came out, I was just a lowly waiter with no knowledge of the world. That scene made me seek out an endive—the leafy, gently bitter vegetable—just so I could listen to it. To this day, I still like to listen to my ingredients. I understand that ingredients don't make noise on their own, but out of respect, I like to pay at least a little attention with every sense I have. This homey dish uses sweet raisins and rich Taleggio to offset the bitterness of the endive. For textural juxtaposition (more on textures on page 318), we build a crunchy top of bread cubes and parsley.

Make the topping. Preheat the oven to 350°F.

Combine all the ingredients for the topping together in a cast-iron skillet. Place the skillet over medium heat and cook, tossing the ingredients with a wooden spoon, until golden brown, 6 to 8 minutes. Transfer the topping to a lined plate and set aside.

Cook the endive. Put the butter in the same cast-iron skillet—unwashed is fine—and place over medium heat. Once the butter foams, add the endive, cut side down. When the endive begins to develop some distinct color, about 5 minutes, using tongs, remove the endive and reserve on a cutting board.

Add the garlic to the leftover butter in the skillet and sauté until just light golden, about 2 minutes. (Don't burn the garlic—endive is bitter enough as is. If you do, don't freak out; just throw it away, rinse out the skillet, and add some more butter and garlic.)

Add the wine and raisins to the skillet and scrape up the brown bits from the bottom with a wooden spoon. Sprinkle in 1 teaspoon of the salt. Return the endive to the skillet, placing it cut side up. Add the remaining 1 teaspoon salt, being sure to get some in between the leaves of the endive. Place the skillet of endive in the preheated oven and bake for 15 minutes. Remove the skillet from the oven, and turn the oven to broil.

Distribute the Taleggio cheese evenly on top of each endive and top with the toasted bread mixture. Broil for 2 to 3 minutes, checking every minute, until the top is golden brown and bubbly and the bread is extra toasty.

PLATE IT! You could put each endive on a plate and spoon over the raisins and sauce, but I'd prefer for you to get yourself a trivet and serve it directly from the cast-iron skillet.

BREAK IT: If you soaked some chamomile tea bags in the wine for a day before adding it to the mix, you would give it a floral bump.

YIELD Makes 4 servings

PREP TIME 15 minutes

COOK TIME 40 minutes

INACTIVE TIME 3 hours

gear

gallon-size zip-top bag

medium pot

blender

small pot

strainer

small bowl

colander or paper towel–lined plate

whisk, egg beater, hand or stand mixer, or cream whipper with N_2O cartridge

ingredients

WATERMELON

½ mini seedless watermelon, rind removed (about 12 ounces), cut into bite-size shapes

SOUP

3 cups vegetable stock (or vegetable broth, and cut the salt by half)

3 yellow beets, peeled and chopped

½ yellow onion, chopped

1 carrot, peeled and chopped

2 teaspoons kosher salt

TURMERIC WHIPPED CREAM

½ cup heavy cream

One 1-inch piece minced fresh turmeric, or 2 teaspoons ground turmeric

¼ teaspoon kosher salt

chilled yellow beet and watermelon soup with turmeric cream

(COLD SOUP)

The first borscht I ever liked was made with red beets and watermelon. The watermelon lightened up the intense earthy flavors of the beet. My only qualm was that I couldn't tell that there was watermelon in the soup aside from the text on a placard in front of me. I immediately thought of the yellow beet, which would allow me to take advantage of the striking difference in color. This recipe is like the Beastie Boys' lyric: "I like my sugar [beets and watermelons] with coffee [turmeric] and cream."

Why Freeze the Watermelon?

It's the poor man's version of "compressed" watermelon, a fancy thing chefs do with a vacuum sealer to remove all the wasted space in watermelon. Think of the watermelon as an apartment building. Certain cells are like rooms, other cells are like big plumbing pipes containing all that yummy watermelon juice. By freezing the watermelon we cause the pipes to burst and flood the apartments next door. In the bag, there's little space to allow for expansion, which makes for compression, leaving juicy, less grainy watermelon.

☞ Tip

I'm in love with my cream whipper. It makes perfect, fluffy whipped cream that can be refrigerated in the container in which it was made. One of the N_2O cartridges costs less than a can of the ready-made stuff, there is considerably less waste, and you can flavor the cream to your liking. Of course, you could just whip the cream by hand, but because a cream whipper uses nitrous oxide (which mingles with cream better than the air around us) you get almost twice the volume of whipped cream, and no tired arms.

Make the watermelon. Put the cut watermelon in a freezer bag. Fill a sink with cold water and slowly push the bottom of the unsealed bag into the water to push out as much air as possible. Seal the bag and freeze for at least 3 hours.

Make the soup. Add the stock, beets, onion, and carrot to a medium pot and bring to a boil over medium heat. Reduce to a simmer and cook until the veggies are tender, about 30 minutes.

Carefully transfer the soup to a blender, add the salt, and blend, increasing the speed, until very smooth. Transfer to a covered container and chill in the refrigerator.

Make the cream. Combine the cream, turmeric, and salt in a small pot over low heat. Simmer for 10 minutes, or until yellow. If using fresh turmeric, strain the mixture through a strainer, discard the solids, and reserve the infused cream. Place the cream in a bowl, cover, and refrigerate.

HOLD IT? Store the soup components separately in the fridge for up to 3 days, or in the freezer for up to a month.

Assemble the soup. Thaw the watermelon in a colander or on a paper towel–lined plate so the excess juice doesn't dilute the soup. (By freezing the watermelon, we create a silkier texture, with a more concentrated flavor—see sidebar.) I don't mind having ice-cold bits of watermelon in my cold soup, but some folks have sensitive teeth.

Whip the cream. You can use a whisk, a hand mixer, or a stand mixer with a whisk attachment. Or use a cream whipper and charge with one cartridge of N_2O (see Tip at left).

Stir up the soup to make sure it has not separated.

PLATE IT! Serve the soup in individual bowls, and top with watermelon pieces, then the whipped cream. Or transfer the cold soup to a serving vessel. Divide the watermelon among the bowls, and add a healthy dollop of the turmeric whipped cream to the top. Serve the bowls and pour the soup around tableside.

BREAK IT: Just a tiny bit of vanilla bean seeds in the soup will make this round and rich, perfumed and earthy, all at once.

YIELD Makes a lot of soup; about 6 quarts

PREP TIME 15 minutes

COOK TIME 45 minutes

gear

large bowl

pressure cooker (at least 8-quart capacity; optional, see sidebar)

small bowl

ingredients

2 cups dried adzuki beans

2 cups dried pinto beans

¼ cup plus 2 tablespoons vegetable shortening (see Note)

1 large onion, diced

2 carrots, diced

2 celery ribs, sliced crosswise

3 quarts vegetable stock (or chicken stock or vegetable broth and cut the salt by half)

1 cup apple juice

2 dried bay leaves

1 garlic clove, minced

10 ounces kale, stems removed, chopped

2 tablespoons kosher salt

2 tablespoons plus 2 teaspoons whole wheat flour

adzuki bean and kale soup

(HOT SOUP)

When I was a captain at the Modern in NYC, a sous chef, Zisca Gardner, would source our produce at the famed Union Square Greenmarket. She'd roll up almost every day with something new and wild for us to try: crosnes, which look like larva but have a water chestnut–like crunch, or miner's lettuce, named because it looks like a pickax. Or nettles! Stinging freaking nettles! I digress. I enjoyed these experiences, but what I enjoyed most was what she managed to pull off in the dead of winter with "cellar vegetables," the far less glamorous roots, tubers, and beans. Let me tell you, modern art isn't really known for its warmth or hug-ability. Zisca's soups were the polar (get it?!!) opposite. I present the "Snuggie" of soups, which, thanks to the pressure cooker, can be made from dry beans in just 45 minutes. Adzuki beans are special to me in that they have a remarkable ability to coax out sweetness from other ingredients—in this case, a cup of apple juice. The pinto beans work like a thicker, creamier counterpart. Together, they keep the slightly bitter kale in check, and the dish balanced as a whole.

Rinse the beans. Rinse the beans in a large bowl of cold water and discard any that float to the top; they have been compromised. Rinse the beans until the water runs clear, then drain.

Cook the beans. Put the pressure cooker over low heat, add the ¼ cup shortening, and allow it to melt. Add the onion, carrots, and celery (called the *mirepoix*) and the beans and sauté until the vegetables have softened, about 5 minutes. Add the stock, apple juice, bay leaves, and garlic. Increase the heat to medium-high and bring to a boil. Reduce the heat to low, cover with the lid and lock, and cook under high pressure for 30 minutes.

After 30 minutes, release the pressure and remove the lid. Check the beans for doneness. If your beans are not yet tender, simmer, uncovered, until they're cooked through.

Finish the soup. When the beans are cooked through, add the kale and salt and cook until the kale is tender, about 10 minutes.

In a small bowl, mash together the remaining 2 tablespoons vegetable shortening and the flour to make an uncooked roux. Add it to the soup, stir until dissolved, and allow the soup to boil for a couple minutes. (Adding the roux makes for a nice silky texture.)

HOLD IT! Now that you've made a ton of soup, let it cool in the pot, then transfer to containers and refrigerate for up to 3 days, or freeze for up to 2 months.

PLATE IT! This is the kind of soup that should be plated with a rainy day, cats, blankets, and fireplaces.

BREAK IT: A few crumbles of grassy, floral goat cheese will also add some richness.

But I don't have a pressure cooker yet!

I built this recipe around the use of the pressure cooker because I rarely have the patience for bean-soaking. That said, you could soak the beans overnight and cook them in a heavy-bottomed pot with the liquid and *mirepoix,* cooking them longer until tender (the package will give you a good idea of the time). Then add the kale.

☞ Note

Animal-free: I'm using vegetable shortening because I like the idea of keeping this soup animal-free. If you want to amp it up, use the same amount of butter.

Gluten-free: If you can't consume gluten, don't fret; just leave out the flour. The soup won't be as thick, but the flavor will be there.

Bay Leaf Luck

Maybe she was pulling my chain, but my mother told me that getting the dried bay leaf in my soup was good luck, as opposed to a choking hazard. I leave them (and cinnamon sticks) in all of my recipes, and tell my guests the same story.

gear

small pan

blender

very large colander

pressure cooker (at least 8-quart capacity)

ingredients

SAUCE

1 teaspoon whole coriander seeds

½ teaspoon crushed red pepper flakes

3 cups arugula, loosely packed

Juice of 2 limes (about ¼ cup)

½ cup avocado oil

1 teaspoon kosher salt

OCTOPUS

One 3-pound octopus, eyes, beak, and brain removed (ask your fishmonger)

2 to 3 cups kosher salt

2 garlic cloves, smashed

GARNISH

Fleur de sel

Extra-virgin olive oil

octopus tiradito

(COLD FISH)

In Peru, raw fish is often consumed with chile flakes, herbs, and citrus juice, a cousin to ceviche known as *tiradito*. I wanted to combine the flavors of tiradito with the sweetness and tender texture of a *sunomono* (octopus with citrusy soy sauce and cucumbers) salad. Here, the bitterness of the arugula is evened out by the voluptuous richness of the avocado oil.

Make the sauce. In a small pan over low heat, toast the coriander seeds and red pepper flakes until fragrant, about 3 minutes. Transfer to blender.

Coarsely chop the arugula. Add the arugula and lime juice to a blender and pulse to combine.

With the blender on low, slowly stream in the avocado oil. Add the salt and blend until smooth and incorporated. Set aside.

Make the octopus. In the corner of a sanitized sink (or using a very large colander, if you have one big enough), cover the entire octopus extremely generously with salt; about 2 cups. Rub the octopus with the salt for about 10 minutes, adding salt to replenish what drains off. This will tenderize the octopus, begin to pull out some excess moisture, and remove any sliminess. Rinse the octopus with cool water.

Place the octopus in the pressure cooker. Cover with water and add the garlic and 1 additional tablespoon of salt.

Over high heat, bring the pot, uncovered, to a boil and boil for 10 minutes. Then lock on the lid, set on high pressure, and set a timer for 20 minutes. Cook over high heat until steam begins to come out, then turn the burner down to medium heat. After the 20 minutes, release the pressure and set aside to let the octopus cool in the braising liquid until the lid can be removed. Remove the lid and allow to cool further.

Once cool enough to handle, remove the octopus from the pot. Cut off the tentacles as close to the head as possible. Reserve the head for another meal—it can be chopped up and eaten in a salad (try it in the Greek Salad with Feta Dressing on page 196). Carefully remove and discard any stringy membrane from the tentacles, including most of the membrane from the top of the tentacles (opposite side of the suckers). Refrigerate the octopus until cold, about 2 hours.

HOLD IT? The sauce and the octopus will keep in the fridge, covered, until ready to use; up to 24 hours.

Slice the octopus tentacles thinly on a bias.

PLATE IT! In a bowl, toss the octopus and the sauce. Add a drizzle of olive oil and a few grains of fleur de sel. Or arrange the slices in a spiral, starting from the center of the plate with the smallest slices and ending on the outside with the largest. Carefully spoon the sauce on the inside to mimic the spiral. Add a drizzle of olive oil and a few grains of fleur de sel.

BREAK IT: Cook the octopus in Earl Grey tea. This will up the bitter notes, but also bring with it some citrus.

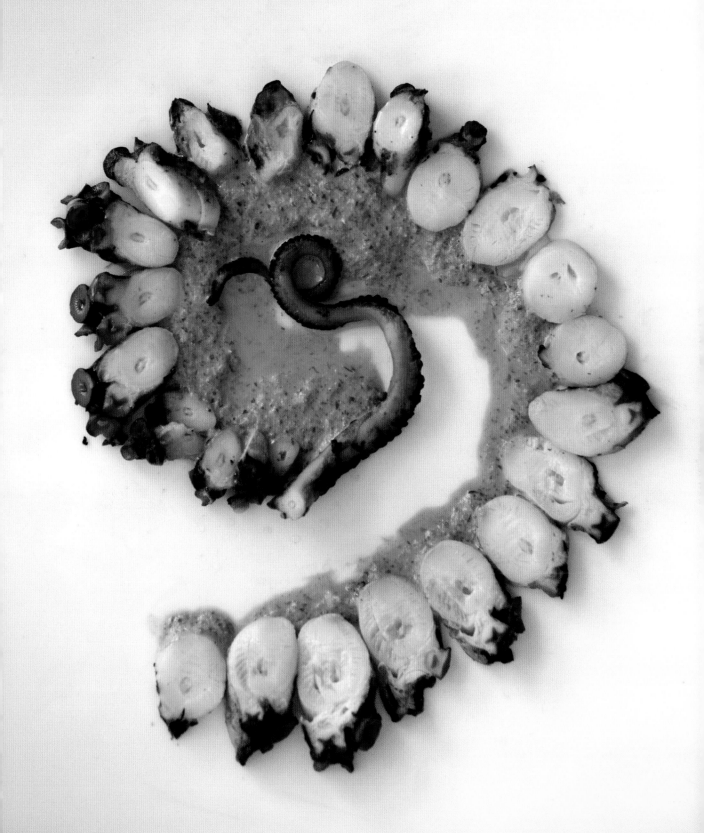

gear

cherry pitter (see sidebar below)

strainer

3 bowls

large cast-iron skillet

tongs

whisk

ingredients

SAUCE

½ pound sweet Bing cherries

1 tablespoon unsalted butter

Pinch of kosher salt

SCALLOPS

2 tablespoons black sesame seeds

2 tablespoons water

1 tablespoon cornstarch

1 teaspoon kosher salt

1 pound large (U/10) sea scallops

1 tablespoon vegetable oil

2 tablespoons unsalted butter

Finely grated zest of 1 lime, for garnish

This is the Pits!

If you don't have a cherry pitter, you can use a chopstick and your fingers, but it can get messy, so do it under water, or wear gloves and an apron. The pointy adapter tip from a pastry bag can also do this.

scallops with black sesame and cherry

(HOT FISH)

Scallops are pretty much the marshmallows of the sea. Sweet and pearly white, they are, in this recipe, the ivory to the black sesame seed's bitter ebony. A little butter adds a rich creaminess to the cherry juice, rounding off any tartness. As every dish needs a little acidity, lime zest finishes the dish like bright green confetti celebrating your cookery. The inspiration for these flavors comes from Sonic Drive-In. Next time you are there, grab a cherry limeade with a side of vanilla ice cream and watch the magic happen.

Prep the cherry sauce. Pit the cherries. (See sidebar.)

In a medium bowl, mash half of the cherries with a fork until thoroughly crushed, then push through a strainer to extract about 2 tablespoons cherry juice. Discard the pulp and reserve the juice. Slice the remaining cherries in half and set aside.

Prep the sesame seeds and scallops. Place the sesame seeds in a bowl. In a separate bowl, whisk together the water, cornstarch, and salt to make a slurry. Set aside.

Rinse the scallops and pat dry with paper towels. Dip the top of each scallop in the cornstarch slurry, then press the top into the sesame seeds to form a crust.

Cook the scallops. Put the oil in a cast-iron skillet and place the skillet under the broiler. Heat the broiler on high. (Be careful when cooking these scallops, as the pan throughout the cooking process is blazing hot and scallops are delicate.) Once your skillet is superhot (when the oil is shimmering), remove it from the broiler. Place the scallops, crust side up, in a single, evenly spaced layer in the skillet. Place the skillet back under the broiler, and set a timer for 4 minutes.

After 4 minutes, gently remove the scallops from the skillet and place on a cutting board. If they don't easily release from the skillet, place the skillet under the broiler for 1 minute more and then remove.

Place the hot skillet on the stovetop over medium heat. Add the halved cherries and the reserved juice and stir with a wooden spoon to dislodge any delicious scallop bits from the bottom of the skillet. Bring to a simmer, remove from the heat, then whisk in the butter and salt.

PLATE IT! Place the sauce down first, with a few cherries here and there. Don't be afraid to dribble it a little—it'll look cool. Divide the scallops equally among the plates, crust side up, on top of the sauce. Gently sprinkle a little lime zest on each plate and serve.

BREAK IT: Mix some Pernod or absinthe into the cherry sauce. This will bring a unique anisette quality to the sauce—both sweet and aromatic.

YIELD Makes 6 servings
PREP TIME 15 minutes
COOK TIME 35 minutes

gear

fine-mesh strainer

rice cooker (optional; see sidebar, opposite)

12-inch heavy-bottomed skillet

blender

cast-iron skillet

tongs

sheet pan

probe thermometer

ingredients

RICE

3 cups short-grain white rice

3½ cups water

1 tablespoon unsalted butter

2 pinches of kosher salt

SAUCE

¼ cup black sesame seeds

½ cinnamon stick

½ teaspoon whole coriander seeds

3 whole cloves

2 dried guajillo chiles, seeded, stems removed

1 dried ancho chile, seeded, stem removed

1 dried chipotle chile, seeded, stem removed

5 tablespoons (½ stick plus 1 tablespoon) unsalted butter

1 yellow onion, diced

2 garlic cloves, minced

12 pitted prunes

¼ cup raw pumpkin seeds

2 tablespoons slivered almonds

pork tenderloin molé donburi

(LIGHT MEAT)

While serving *donburi* (Japanese rice bowls of meat and sauce) in my early twenties to the raw-fish-phobics at Sushi JeJu in Fort Collins, Colorado, I met a young cook named German Ruiz, who introduced me to Mexican culture via the food he prepared as family meal for the Spanish-speaking staff (at this restaurant, every cultural group prepared and ate their own family meal—usually mine was beer). At that time, Chipotle burritos were authentic Mexican fare to me, so you can surely imagine how wide-eyed I was when I saw him saving the seeds from a soon-to-be-tempura-fried kabocha squash. Even more bizarre was the container of animal crackers that he added to the blender with the squash seeds, among other varied ingredients. Of course, I was dying to try this concoction, which he served with chicken. Molé, as he explained it, was kind of like the Mexican version of curry—a blend of many bitter, rich, and sweet components (often including seeds, nuts, dried fruit, and chiles) that when blended together create a concentrated, spicy, harmonious sauce. There are endless variations of molé. In my version, I've quickened the process and added some *gabacho* (i.e., *gringo,* but only gringos use that word) flavor in the form of vanilla wafers.

Make the rice. Put the rice into a fine-mesh strainer and rinse it under cold running water, rubbing it together with your fingers, until the water runs clear. (It's helpful to do this over a colored mixing bowl so you can see the water.) Allow the washed rice to drain in the strainer.

Place the washed rice, water, butter, and salt in the rice cooker and fire it up. When the rice is done cooking, fluff it up a bit with a fork or paddle, and utilize the "keep warm" setting until you are ready to eat. If you don't have a rice cooker (see sidebar), follow the directions on your rice package, adding butter and salt with the water.

Make the sauce. In a heavy-bottomed skillet, toast the sesame seeds over medium-high heat until fragrant, 1 to 2 minutes. Immediately put the sesame seeds in a blender.

Add the cinnamon, coriander, and cloves to the pan and toast until fragrant, about 2 minutes. Transfer to the blender.

Repeat the toasting process with the chiles, about 2 minutes, until fragrant. Transfer to the blender.

In the same skillet, melt 1 tablespoon of the butter over medium heat. Add the onion and garlic and cook until soft and translucent. Transfer the mixture to the blender.

In the same skillet, melt the remaining 4 tablespoons butter. Add the prunes, pumpkin seeds, and almonds and cook until the seeds are golden brown. Add the crushed vanilla wafers, and stir to soak up the butter. Transfer this mixture to the blender.

Add 2 cups of the stock and the salt to the blender. Blend the mixture until completely smooth, scraping down the sides as necessary.

8 vanilla wafer cookies (like Nabisco's Nilla brand), crushed

2 to 3 cups chicken or vegetable stock (or vegetable broth, and cut the salt by half)

2 teaspoons kosher salt

PORK TENDERLOIN

2 pork tenderloins (about 3 pounds total), trimmed and cut into 3 pieces each

Kosher salt

Freshly ground black pepper

2 tablespoons unsalted butter

GARNISHES (OPTIONAL, BUT FUN)

White sesame seeds

Sliced scallions

Lime wedges

Sour cream

Muy authentico!

In a Mexican household, the meat and rice are usually plated side by side, swimming in molé. Do that if you're looking for authenticity. Garnish away! This is largely a matter of personal preference.

Rice Cookers

Buy a rice cooker. Please buy a rice cooker. Because of my rice cooker, I've never had a complicated recipe or process for rice. No steaming or towels or hovering over it. Just wash it, cover it with water, and put it in the rice cooker. Then ignore it until you want to eat it. Many rice-consuming households have a rice cooker, and you should too. They are like twelve bucks. Just do it.

☞ Tip

Before you do anything with hot peppers, put your latex gloves on.

Return the mixture to the skillet. Simmer over low heat, stirring occasionally, until thick, about 10 minutes. If the sauce becomes too thick and scares you because it is belching hot blasts of brown at you, add more stock, but I like thick molé.

HOLD IT? The rice can be made up to 6 hours in advance using the "keep warm" setting on the rice cooker. The sauce can be refrigerated for 3 days, or frozen indefinitely, then reheated, adding chicken stock as needed for the desired consistency.

Make the pork tenderloin. Preheat the oven to 400°F.
Season the pork liberally with the salt and pepper.
In a large cast-iron skillet, heat the butter over medium heat until frothy. Add 3 pieces of the pork, increase the heat to medium-high, and sear the pieces on all sides, using the tongs to turn, about a minute per side. Transfer the seared pork to a sheet pan. Sear the remaining 3 pieces of pork and transfer to the sheet pan.

Place the sheet pan in the oven, and roast the tenderloins to your desired doneness. I like medium rare, 130°F in the center, about 10 minutes or so. (Bear in mind that the folks at the USDA specify 145°F.) Use a thermometer to check!

Transfer the pork to a cutting board and allow to rest for at least 6 to 8 minutes. Slice the pork into ¼-inch-thick medallions.

PLATE IT! In a big soup bowl, make a pile of rice, top the rice with meat, and then smother in sauce. This way the rice at the bottom catches all the good stuff and you can slurp it up like those college kids slurped up the donburi.

BREAK IT: Using jasmine rice is a pretty simple way to blow this one out. The fragrant rice plays off of all the components in the molé to make a mouth-kaleidoscope of flavors.

gear

small bowl

large cast-iron skillet

blender

microwave-safe bowl

sheet pan with rack

tongs

ingredients

RUB

4 tablespoons instant coffee granules

2 tablespoons kosher salt

½ teaspoon black pepper

CAULIFLOWER PURÉE

4 tablespoons (½ stick) unsalted butter

2 cups finely chopped cauliflower florets (about ½ head)

2 tablespoons maple syrup

½ cup plain Greek yogurt

1 teaspoon kosher salt

STEAK

2 pounds flank steak, cut into 4 even pieces, at room temperature

2 tablespoons unsalted butter

PAN SAUCE

1 tablespoon whole wheat flour

1 cup dark beer

2 tablespoons maple syrup

2 teaspoons kosher salt

coffee-rubbed flank steak with cauliflower purée

(DARK MEAT)

I like my coffee black, but I also love it with meat drippings. This flank steak combines a ton of roasted, toasted, bitter, bass-note, mega-"Maillardy," super-earthy flavors (whole wheat flour, instant coffee, dark beer, seared meat) and juxtaposes it against some sassy, high-hatted, creamy, fluffed-up cauliflower. Maple syrup works as the sweet-talking go-between. Flank steak is usually sliced and cooked through for stir-fries and fajitas, but I've fallen in love with its toothsome texture and meaty flavor, which can stand up to the most intense of seasonings. To intensify your enjoyment, start with room-temperature steak for maximum sear, don't overcook it, let it rest properly, and slice it thinly against the grain.

Make the rub. In a small bowl, combine the ingredients for the rub and reserve.

Make the cauliflower purée. Melt the butter in a large cast-iron skillet. Add the cauliflower and cook over medium heat until softened and beginning to change color, 6 to 7 minutes.

Transfer the cauliflower to a blender and add the maple syrup, yogurt, and salt. Blend until smooth.

Transfer the purée to a microwave-safe bowl. Save the skillet from the cauliflower to cook the steak.

Make the steak. Preheat the oven to 400°F. Place a sheet pan with a rack by the stove. Preheat the cauliflower skillet over high heat.

Season the steaks liberally on both sides with the rub. Melt 1 tablespoon of the butter in the preheated skillet. Sear 2 of the steaks, cooking for 2 minutes per side, and using tongs to flip. Transfer the seared steaks to the rack on the sheet pan. Sear the remaining 2 steaks with the remaining 1 tablespoon butter. Place the sheet pan with the steaks in the oven and cook until they are medium rare, 8 to 10 minutes, or until they register about 130°F on a thermometer. (Bear in mind that the folks at the USDA like 145°F.)

Transfer the cooked steaks to a cutting board and let them rest for at least 5 minutes. Reserve the skillet and drippings. Meanwhile, make the pan sauce.

Make the pan sauce. Put the reserved skillet over low heat. Make a quick roux by adding the flour to the drippings in the skillet, and whisk until it smells toasty, about 1 minute. Add the beer to the roux and bring to a boil. Cook, stirring, until thickened, about 3 minutes. Stir in the maple syrup and salt.

Reheat the cauliflower purée: Microwave on high, uncovered, stopping to stir halfway through, until hot, about 2 minutes.

PLATE IT! Divide the cauliflower purée among four plates, and serve the steaks whole, letting your guests do the work of cutting the steak, and top with the pan sauce.

BREAK IT: Smoke that cauliflower! The purée won't be as pristine and white, but the dish will be dazzlingly complex—sweet, bitter, rich, and smoky all at once.

STEP YOUR GAME UP

For a fancier presentation, you can divide the cauliflower among the four plates, then, using a large spoon, make a canyon in the cauliflower and drag the spoon to one side of the plate; it will look like a comet of cauliflower purée with a nice little crater to catch that pan sauce. Slice the rested steaks across the grain (see below), fan out the slices next to the purée, and top with the pan sauce.

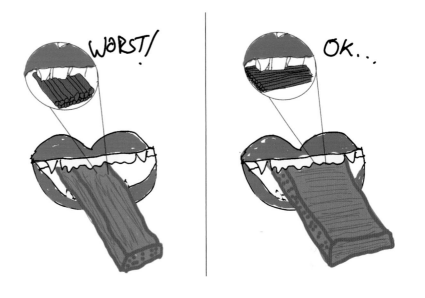

YIELD Makes 6 servings

PREP TIME 15 minutes

COOK TIME 2 hours

INACTIVE TIME 1 hour

gear

sheet pan with a nonstick silicone baking mat or parchment paper

stand mixer with whisk and paddle attachments

small bowl

rubber spatula

offset spatula (optional)

ingredients

DARK CHOCOLATE MERINGUE

3 egg whites (see sidebar page 78)

¼ cup sugar

1 teaspoon instant coffee granules

1 teaspoon room-temperature water

3 tablespoons unsweetened cocoa powder

MILK CHOCOLATE BUTTERCREAM

½ cup (1 stick) unsalted butter, at room temperature

¼ cup confectioners' sugar

½ cup milk chocolate chips

1 tablespoon unsweetened cocoa powder

¼ teaspoon kosher salt

GARNISH

¼ cup chopped, roasted, salted hazelnuts

milk and dark chocolate dacquoise

(Dessert)

Aside from my grandmother's orange freeze pie and my grandmother, I've never been especially enamored with desserts or those who craft them. I do respect what the confectioners of the world do: they make lights at the end of the tunnel, they specialize in rewards. It's just not my bag. That is, until I met Marc Aumont, the former pastry chef of the Modern. During my career there, we had a remarkable love-hate relationship. He would kick my ass, sometimes literally, for requesting asinine things from the kitchen, like "no ice-cream, whipped cream, or custard for the lactose-intolerant guest's coffee sundae" or "just a bowl of chocolate sorbet for the nearly dead lady at table two." At the same time, I was one of about three waiters who could remember the 10 flavors in his 10-Flavor Sorbet, so he thought I was pretty OK. I think he thinks more highly of me now, and I have now concluded that Marc is the most gifted pastry chef I've ever met. He can make things that are so dementedly delicious and visually striking that I actually get a little welled up thinking about them. This dish is an ode to him, combining the flavor profile of his Milk Chocolate Dacquoise with the presentation of his Concord Grape Vacherin; essentially a vertically oriented mash up of milk chocolate buttercream, dark chocolate meringue shards, and crunchy salty hazelnuts.

Make the dark chocolate meringue. Preheat the oven to 200°F. Line a sheet pan with a silicone baking mat or parchment paper.

Add the egg whites to the bowl of a stand mixer fitted with the whisk attachment and start the mixer at medium speed. Once the whites are very frothy, very slowly add the sugar, increase the speed to the highest setting, and beat just until stiff shiny peaks have formed, 7 to 8 minutes.

Meanwhile, combine the instant coffee and water in a small bowl and stir until dissolved. When the whites are at stiff peaks, and with the mixer still running, slowly add the coffee mixture to the egg whites.

Remove the bowl from the stand mixer. Using a rubber spatula, gently fold the cocoa powder into the egg whites just until no streaks remain; the egg whites will deflate a bit, but that's OK. Gently pour the mixture onto the lined sheet pan, then use an offset or rubber spatula to smooth the meringue mixture into a very thin, even sheet, less than ¼ inch thick and covering most of the pan.

Bake in the low oven until the entire sheet looks dry, dull, and crisp (like soil in a plant that needs to be watered), about 1 hour; don't touch it or open the oven door. Turn the oven off and leave the pan in the oven for an additional hour.

Make the milk chocolate buttercream. Cream the butter and confectioners' sugar in a stand mixer fitted with a paddle attachment until the mixture lightens, about 5 minutes.

Put the chocolate chips in a small bowl and melt in the microwave on the lowest setting for about 2 minutes, stopping to stir every 30 seconds, until it's smooth and just melted; do not overheat.

Meringues and Egg Whites

When you are making meringues, you cannot have even a speck of egg yolk in your whipped egg whites or they will not whip up properly. So I suggest separating the egg white from yolk over a small bowl, letting the white fall into the bowl and saving the yolk for another use. Then transfer the white to the very clean bowl of the stand mixer. Separating into the bowl first makes sure that NO YOLK gets into the stand mixer.

Add the chocolate to the butter and sugar mixture, a couple tablespoons at a time, then mix it through on high speed, turning off the mixer to add more chocolate, until all of the chocolate is incorporated.

Add the cocoa powder and salt, scrape down the sides of the bowl with a rubber spatula, and mix until smooth.

HOLD IT? The meringues do best living in the oven, where it is nice and dry, for up to 4 hours. If you are lucky enough to have silica beads for dessicating (see sidebar below), they can be stored up to 24 hours in a container with those. Store the buttercream in a covered container in the refrigerator for up to a week, and bring the buttercream back to room temperature, which may take up to an hour, before proceeding.

Assemble the dacquoise. Place the meringue, face down, on a clean, dry work surface, baking mat side up. Carefully peel the mat from the meringue.

PLATE IT! Place a dollop of buttercream on each plate. Break the meringue into shards and anchor them vertically in the buttercream, distributing them equally on each plate. Sprinkle chopped hazelnuts over each plate.

BREAK IT: Fruit, of any kind, would be fun in this. Personally, I love raspberries, cut in half, and distributed on the plate.

STEP YOUR GAME UP

Ever look inside a leather jacket and find a silica "Do Not Eat" packet? It keeps the leather from getting damp. It will also do the same for meringues. Silica beads for food preparation are available online, and generally they are blue because no food is blue, and they are not good to eat.

LAW
OF BAGEL
AND LOX

smoked meets acid and fat

'll never forget the day I learned about lox. In 1989, a joint called Bagel-Lisious opened in a shopping center in my hometown. My mother took me in, with the intent of teaching me all about lox and cream cheese, capers, and the like. The budding bagelry, to the chagrin of my mother, did not yet carry lox. She let loose on the fellow behind the counter, practically accusing him of heresy and treason. Within a week they were carrying lox. My mother still goes there, and still tells the story about how she brought lox to Washington County, Maryland. Great job, Mom. I've been a fan ever since, and even went on to work in a bagel shop for a few years. Don't get it twisted, I didn't write the law because I'm in love with bagels and lox. But with the loaded bagel as proof, smoked foods do play nice with fats (cream cheese!), acids (capers!), sweetness (tomato!), and sharp (onion!) flavors. Indeed, smoke is a flavor-butterfly. But aside from purchasing something presmoked, how does one get the flavor of combusted hardwood into food? I'm glad you asked, because there are ten smoked-out recipes ahead. I've put special emphasis on dishes where smoke meets fat and acid—but also included other combos.

smoked meets acid and fat

SMOKED FISH	EVERYTHING BAGEL NIGIRI	CAPER BRINE	WASABI CREAM CHEESE
SMOKED OYSTERS	SMOKED OYSTER CAESAR	LEMON JUICE	PECORINO
			EGG YOLKS
LIQUID SMOKE	STEAK TARTARE CROQUETTES WITH SMOKY MAYO	CAPERS	STEAK
MEZCAL	SALTY MEZCAL AND CHEESE	LIME	PEPPER JACK CHEESE
SMOKED GOUDA	SMOKED GOUDA AND RAUCHBIER SOUP	CAPER BRINE	CREAM
RAUCHBIER			
LOX	LOX, A BOX, AND A SMOKING MATTRESS PUMP	CAPERS	CREAM CHEESE
PAPRIKA	GRILLED SWORDFISH WITH DILL PICKLE EMULSION AND ONION "CHAW"	DILL PICKLES	SWORDFISH
PAPRIKA	POOR MAN'S SOUS-VIDE TURKEY PAPRIKASH	JALAPEÑO BRINE	BUTTER
SMOKER	F-YEAH BARBECUE	VINEGAR	BRISKET
LIQUID SMOKE	SMOKED CANNOLI	RICOTTA	

YIELD Makes 32 pieces

PREP TIME 15 minutes

COOK TIME about 1 hour

gear

fine-mesh strainer

rice cooker (optional; see sidebar page 73)

small pot

large mixing bowl (see sidebar page 86)

electric fan, or a human with a magazine (see sidebar page 86)

bamboo paddle or rubber spatula

clean 6-pack cooler (larger is fine), or wooden bowl

small bowl

rubber spatula

small pan

ingredients

RICE

2 cups sushi rice

¼ cup caper brine (see sidebar page 35)

¼ cup sugar

2 tablespoons unseasoned rice wine vinegar

WASABI CREAM CHEESE

2 tablespoons wasabi powder

2 tablespoons water

4 ounces cream cheese, at room temperature

EVERYTHING BAGEL MIX

2 tablespoons poppy seeds

1 tablespoon pretzel salt

1 tablespoon white sesame seeds

2 teaspoons dried minced onion

1 teaspoon dried garlic flakes

everything bagel nigiri

(CANAPÉ/SNACK)

When I was learning about sushi, I wanted everything to be correct and proper. I wouldn't be caught dead with a California roll between my chopsticks—not only because it's proper to eat sushi with your hands, but also because I thought the California roll was some sort of Americanized bastard product created for wusses and rookies. I also turned my nose up to its cream cheese–laden cousin, the Philadelphia roll. Frat boys would do sake bombs and cheer at how delicious these zany rolls were, while I quietly pondered the subtlety of a chewy piece of highly prized flounder fin. While my desire to eat with the utmost of authenticity was a great way to learn, it wasn't always very fun. Somewhere along the way, I realized that "fun" is just as important as "fine" when it comes to eating and even more so in cooking. With this in mind, I present the highly sacrilegious snack below, a tricked-out sushi bar version of a bagel and lox.

Make the rice. Put the rice in a fine-mesh strainer and rinse it under cold running water, rubbing it together with your fingers, until the water runs clear. (It's helpful to do this over a colored mixing bowl so you can see the water.) Allow the washed rice to drain in the strainer.

Cook the washed rice in a rice cooker with the amount of water specified by your rice cooker. (I used 3 cups of water for this amount.) I've never ever screwed up rice in a rice cooker so long as I cover the rice with water by about an inch. If you don't have a rice cooker (see the sidebar page 73), follow the directions on your rice package.

In a small pot over low heat, combine the caper brine, sugar, and vinegar and simmer, stirring occasionally, until the sugar is dissolved, about 3 minutes. Set aside to cool.

Set a large mixing bowl next to an electric fan or a friend—turn on the fan to low or have your friend wave a magazine over the rice. When the rice is done, use a bamboo paddle or spatula to gently remove portions of it from the cooker and spread them out around the inside of the large bowl. Removing it in portions exposes more surface area and allows for more rapid cooling. Once all of the rice is in the bowl, dribble the vinegar mixture onto the paddle while moving it back and forth a few inches above the rice, so as to thinly and evenly distribute all of the seasoned vinegar over all of the rice. Use the paddle to gently break up any chunks of rice in "slicing" motions. When the clumps are broken and cease to re-form, you can be sure that all of the rice has been seasoned. When ready, the rice should glisten and feel warm, but not hot, to the touch. Turn off the fan or dismiss your friend.

Wet your hands with water (the rice is very sticky) and, using your hands, gently transfer the rice to a cooler (which keeps it from getting too cold) or to a wooden bowl (see sidebar page 86). Run a clean, lint-free hand towel under warm water until entirely moistened and cover the rice until ready to use, or for up to 2 hours. If you use a cooler, close the lid. If using a wooden bowl, cover with plastic wrap.

FISH

1 pound assorted smoked fish, cut into ½-ounce slices (you could use the smoked salmon on page 93)

GARNISHES (OPTIONAL)

Very thinly sliced red onion

Very thinly sliced cherry tomatoes

Very thinly sliced caperberries

Very thin bâtons of cucumber

Non-Japanese Concessions

You'll see I've made some concessions to accommodate a non-Japanese kitchen. A *hangiri* is the traditional raw cypress bowl used to cool sushi rice. The raw wood of the bowl absorbs the excess moisture. Plus, it is never washed, so the seasoning of it affects the seasoning of the rice. If you want to be authentic, I'd highly recommend buying one of these from any number of sources you can find online. Also, electric fans are used these days to cool the rice. You can instead go the old-fashioned route and convince a friend to fan the rice by hand, ideally with the November 2012 edition of *Food Network Magazine*.

Make the wasabi cream cheese. Mix the wasabi powder and 2 tablespoons water in a small bowl until dissolved. Add the cream cheese to the bowl and use a rubber spatula to fully incorporate the wasabi.

Make the everything bagel mix. Combine all the ingredients for the everything bagel mix in a small pan. Toast until fragrant. Transfer to a small plate to cool.

Assemble the nigiri. Place the warm rice, wasabi cream cheese, seasoning mix, and sliced fish in close proximity.

Wet your hands with water. With your dominant hand, grab less than a Ping Pong ball's but a little more than a shooter marble's worth of rice. *Gently* squeeze it so it's about the length and diameter of a fat wine bottle cork. Too much squeezing makes the rice like clay, too little and it falls apart. (Luckily the recipe above makes enough rice for you and your guests to practice.)

Once the rice ball is formed, slide it a bit lower in your palm and hold onto it. Pick up a slice of fish with your nondominant hand. With your dominant pointer finger (rice ball still clutched) swipe a little wasabi cream cheese onto the fish. Gently press the rice ball onto the cream cheese–smeared fish in your nondominant hand. Flip the nigiri fish-side up in your nondominant hand, and gently apply pressure with two fingers of your dominant hand and a cupping motion from your nondominant hand.

Rotate the fish and rice ball 180 degrees and repeat, so as to round off the corners and strongly adhere the fish to the rice ball. See the diagram below.

Gently press the top of the fish into the everything bagel mix; it should stick to the surface of the fish.

PLATE IT! Place the nigiri on a plate, top with as few or as many garnishes as you like, and serve. Have your guests eat these quickly, as the rice will dry out if left unconsumed.

Continue forming nigiri, rewetting your hands as needed to keep the rice from sticking to your hands.

BREAK IT: Mince some fresh dill and cook it with your sushi rice. It will perfume it with its sweet, almost minty flavor. This will freshen up the oily fish nicely.

YIELD Makes 8 individual salads, plus enough extra dressing for 1 to 2 more salads

PREP TIME 5 minutes

COOK TIME 10 minutes

gear

food processor with blade attachment or blender

small bowl

medium skillet

ingredients

DRESSING

2 egg yolks

¼ cup fresh lemon juice

1 tablespoon Dijon mustard

2 teaspoons minced garlic

2 teaspoons kosher salt

1 teaspoon Worcestershire sauce

¾ cup vegetable oil

One 3.7-ounce can smoked oysters packed in oil

CRACKER CROUTONS

2 cups oyster crackers

1 tablespoon extra-virgin olive oil

1 teaspoon kosher salt

1 teaspoon freshly ground black pepper

SALADS

4 romaine hearts

Cracked black pepper, for finishing

¼ cup freshly grated pecorino Romano cheese

smoked oyster caesar

(COLD APP)

I get a lot of inspiration from staring at the supermarket shelves, and seeing what items are grouped together. I made this recipe because I found the smoked oysters next to the anchovies in the canned fish section and decided to try them out instead in my Caesar dressing. Once I did that, I decided to riff on the croutons a bit too. In this recipe, the smoky oysters complement the rich egg yolks, which in turn get cut by a healthy dose of lemon juice. Do you like other canned fishies? All are good Caesar salad material, providing they are packed in oil, which amps up their flavor almost to a condiment level of oomph. If you want to get real crazy, find the canned seafood section in an ethnic market.

Make the dressing. In a food processor fitted with the blade attachment, or in a blender, pulse the egg yolks, lemon juice, Dijon, garlic, salt, and Worcestershire until thoroughly combined. With the machine running, add the oil very slowly to make an emulsified dressing.

Drain the oysters from their oil, reserving 1 tablespoon of the oil for the croutons. Add the drained oysters to the dressing and pulse until smooth.

Make the cracker croutons. Combine all the cracker crouton ingredients with the reserved tablespoon of oyster oil in a medium skillet over medium-high heat. Cook, tossing often, until the crackers are toasty. Set aside to cool.

HOLD IT? The dressing will hold in the fridge, covered, for a week, and the crackers will store in an airtight container for 3 days.

PLATE IT! Lop off the base of each romaine heart, then split each heart from top to bottom. Put a spoonful of the dressing directly onto each plate. (This will sauce the underside of the salad and also keep it from sliding around.) Place a romaine heart half, face up, on the dressing, and drizzle with additional dressing. Top with the croutons, cracked black pepper, and cheese.

BREAK IT: Use this dressing in potato salad. The potato will mellow the smoke and mustard in the dressing. If you are feeling especially rebellious, add some celery and red onion for crunch.

gear

sheet pan

wax paper

2 medium mixing bowls

3 shallow bowls

sheet pan

Dutch oven or heavy-bottomed pot, for frying

candy thermometer

sheet pan with rack

spider or tongs

ingredients

STEAK TARTARE

12 ounces beef tenderloin, trimmed (see Note) (see instructions on page 307)

3 tablespoons whole-grain mustard

3 tablespoons capers, rinsed

3 tablespoons finely diced shallots (about 1 shallot)

1 tablespoon Worcestershire sauce

1 tablespoon sriracha sauce

2 large egg yolks

3 whole anchovy fillets, minced

½ teaspoon kosher salt

½ teaspoon freshly ground black pepper

SMOKY MAYO

½ cup mayonnaise

A few drops liquid smoke

steak tartare croquettes with smoky mayo

(HOT APP)

The first time I saw carpaccio being made, I was fascinated. The cook was slicing a seared and frozen beef tenderloin on a deli slicer. The almost completely raw slices would touch her hand for a half second, and then be placed right on the plate. By the time the meat got to the guest, it was still cool but not frozen. When I thought about creating a carpaccio for this book, I realized that would require you owning a deli slicer, so I decided against it. Still intrigued by the idea of freezing raw meat and having it thaw by the time it hits your mouth, I decided to dice and season the beef tartare-style with capers and anchovies, and form it into a quick-fried croquette. The capers and anchovies act as seasoning agents, while the liquid smoke mayo provides smoky richness.

Make the steak tartare. Line a sheet pan with wax paper.

Using a chef's knife, trim off any visible fat from the tenderloin, then cut the meat into a fine dice; slightly larger than peppercorns. (Do not use a food processor; it will turn the beef into a paste—a rookie mistake I made the first time I made tartare.)

Combine all the tartare ingredients in a medium bowl and mix together. With two serving spoons, form the mixture into quenelles (see graphic!) and place them on the prepared sheet pan. (Want to use a small ice cream scoop instead? Be my guest.) Cover the pan with plastic wrap. Freeze the quenelles for at least 1 hour and up to 3 hours.

Make the smoky mayo. Combine the mayo and liquid smoke. (Want more smoke? Add more.) Cover and refrigerate.

Make the croquettes. Place the cornstarch and ½ teaspoon of the salt in a shallow bowl and mix to combine. Whisk together the eggs in a second shallow bowl. Place the panko and remaining ½ teaspoon salt in the third shallow bowl and mix to combine. Place a clean sheet pan after the third bowl, to land the dredged croquettes.

Working in the order of dry-wet-dry-wet-dry, dredge each of your frozen croquettes in the cornstarch mixture, the egg, the panko mixture, the egg, and the panko mixture again, then land on a sheet pan.

HOLD IT? After dredging, you can store the croquettes in the freezer for up to a week before frying.

Fill a Dutch oven with ¼ inch of oil, clip on a candy thermometer, and heat over high heat until the oil reaches 350°F. Set up a sheet pan fitted with a rack, or line a plate with paper towels.

½ cup cornstarch

1 teaspoon kosher salt, divided

2 large eggs

2 cups panko bread crumbs

Vegetable oil, for frying

☞ **Note**

Only buy your beef from the best butcher you can find, and tell him/her that you will be eating it raw.

Using tongs or a spider, place some of the croquettes into the hot oil. You want the oil to come halfway up the sides of the croquettes. Fry the croquettes until golden brown, about 45 seconds on the first side, then flip them over and fry another 45 seconds or so. Throttle the heat as necessary to keep the oil at temperature. It's a fine line timing-wise: you're trying to crisp the outside but keep the inside raw. Using a spider, remove the croquettes from the oil and transfer to the lined plate to drain. Test one to make sure the inside is cool but not frozen. If they are frozen, allow them to sit a couple of minutes until cool and thawed. Fry the remaining croquettes in batches. As the inside is cool, it doesn't matter too much if these aren't served hot, but I think the hot exterior/cold interior is a fun experience.

PLATE IT! Line up all these croquettes and place a healthy dab of mayo right on top.

BREAK IT: Instead of mayo, roast a sweet potato and blend it up with some salt and liquid smoke. The sweetness will be a nice foil to the salty Worcestershire and sour capers.

Quenelles

YIELD 8 shots with cheese, plus more mezcal for another sitting

PREP TIME 5 minutes

INACTIVE TIME 2 to 3 hours

gear

Shot glasses

ingredients

LIQUOR

1 teaspoon kosher salt

One 750-ml bottle mezcal, stored in the freezer

CHEESE

1 lime, cut into wedges

One 8-ounce block Pepper Jack cheese

salty mezcal and cheese

(DRINK)

One of the oldest bars in New York is called McSorley's. In keeping with its nineteenth-century roots, it offers only two beers (light and dark) and a few interesting snacks. One such snack is the "cheese plate," which consists of slices of American or cheddar cheese, raw white onions, and Saltines. Mustard is optional. I once watched two old men sit together there, staring off in silence, slugging their beers, eating some cheese, and slugging some more beer, only really chatting when something caught their eye. I want to be like them someday, I thought. I've since been fascinated with the idea of growing old, and finding a buddy who I can drink and nibble with, not say much to, and be content. Ideally, we'd be doing this in a warm climate, not too far from Mexico, and we'd be drinking mezcal, the Scotch of the New World, the smoky cousin of tequila. If you add a little salt to the mezcal it gets supercold, and also primes the tongue for the creamy and spicy cheese I like to serve with it. Something perfect happens as the cheese is chewed and the memory of the salty/smoky shot dissipates. If only getting old were as simple.

Make the salty mezcal. Add the salt to the mezcal in the bottle, replace the cap or cork, and invert 10 to 15 times until the salt dissipates. Keep frozen until ready to consume. A good test of coldness is if the bottle develops frost upon removal from the freezer.

PLATE IT! If you are the kind of person who has a cheese board and knife, plate the cheese and lime wedges on there. If you are like me, and see the world and all its surfaces as a cheese board, plate there. It's best to keep the cheese uncut so it doesn't dry out.

To consume, cut a slice of cheese and squirt it with a little lime juice. Pour a small shot of mezcal and shoot it. Savor the mezcal's robustness for just a second before devouring the cheese slice. Note the way the cheese chases away the taste of the mezcal, and the way the smokiness develops.

BREAK IT: Infuse the mezcal with cilantro to bring a fresh and floral perfume to the smoky mezcal.

STEP YOUR GAME UP

Optional but ideal: find a leathery companion. Stare off into the abyss, and know that with a good buddy and some liquid courage, almost anything is possible. Just don't say it out loud.

YIELD Makes 4 to 6 servings

PREP TIME 15 minutes

COOK TIME 20 minutes

gear

heavy-bottomed stockpot

blender

small bowl

small skillet

ingredients

SOUP

2 tablespoons vegetable oil

1 medium onion, chopped

2 medium carrots, chopped

2 celery ribs, chopped

1 tablespoon loosely packed fresh thyme leaves

½ teaspoon freshly grated nutmeg

1 cup smoked beer, like Sam Adams Bonfire Rauchbier

8 ounces smoked Gouda, shredded

1 cup beef broth

½ cup heavy cream

½ cup whole milk

2 tablespoons caper brine

1 tablespoon soy sauce

1 tablespoon cornstarch

2 tablespoons water

FRIED CAPERS

1 tablespoon vegetable oil

2 tablespoons capers, patted dry

Crusty bread, for serving (optional)

smoked gouda and rauchbier soup

(HOT SOUP)

Somehow I managed to score tickets to the Great American Beer Festival in Denver, Colorado. If you ever want to discover what you didn't know about American beer, or you want to discover just how much beer you could possibly drink surrounded by people who want to discover the same, this is the party for you. Necklaces of pretzels are just the beginning. By the end of the night it descends into a series of OHHHH!!!!!s, as that is what is said when someone drops their plastic cup. Anyhow, before I lost all of my senses, I remember trying a Rauchbier, which is a smoked beer. It was like two of my favorite vices rolled up into one, and I was sold. Here is the kind-of-classic midwestern dish of cheddar beer soup, but smoked out, thanks to a smoked Gouda and a Rauchbier.

Make the soup. In a heavy-bottomed stockpot, heat the oil over medium-low heat. Add the onion, carrots, and celery and sauté until the onion is translucent, about 8 minutes. Add the thyme and nutmeg and cook, stirring, until fragrant, about 2 minutes. Add the beer and increase the heat to high to cook out the booze, about 5 minutes. Turn the heat back down to low, add the cheese, broth, cream, milk, caper brine, and soy sauce, and simmer until the cheese is smooth and melted.

Working in batches, transfer the soup to a blender, and carefully blend, starting slow and increasing the speed, until the soup is smooth. Transfer the blended soup back to the stockpot.

Using a fork, mix the cornstarch and 2 tablespoons water in a small bowl until dissolved. Add the cornstarch slurry to the soup. Bring the soup to a boil, stirring, then reduce to a simmer and cook until thickened, about 5 minutes.

Make the fried capers. Meanwhile, put the oil and capers in a small skillet over medium-high heat. They will start spitting; once they stop popping, they are done, 4 to 5 minutes. Transfer the fried capers to a paper towel–lined plate. *These are not optional.*

HOLD IT? You can refrigerate the soup in a covered container for up to 3 days. Hold the capers, covered and wrapped in paper towels, at room temperature for a few days.

PLATE IT! Ladle the hot soup into bowls, sprinkle with capers, and serve with crusty bread, if you like. Or bread bowl it and sprinkle with the capers.

BREAK IT: Add ground beef and mustard to this, and substitute chopped pickles for the fried capers and this becomes smoked cheeseburger soup. Smoked. Cheese-burger. Soup.

YIELD Makes just under 2
pounds smoked salmon (lox or
gravlax)

PREP TIME 10 minutes

COOK TIME 3 hours for lox

INACTIVE TIME 72 hours for lox;
48 for gravlax

gear

plastic wrap

small bowl

quarter-sheet pan

cast-iron skillet or heavy pot

Justin's Cold Smoker (see page
96 for diagram)

2 wire cooling racks

zip ties

zip-top bags

wood chips

culinary torch or propane torch

slicing knife (optional)

ingredients

LOX

2 pounds wild or responsibly
farmed Atlantic salmon fillet,
preferably a belly cut, pinbones
and skin removed

1 cup kosher salt

¼ cup packed brown sugar

Ice

GRAVLAX

2 pounds wild or responsibly
farmed Atlantic salmon fillet,
pinbones and skin removed

1 cup kosher salt

⅓ cup sugar

2 bunches fresh dill

10 black Twizzlers (my superfun
take, optional)

lox, a box, and a smoking mattress pump

(COLD FISH)

Smoked salmon isn't cheap, let alone lox, which is the fatty belly cut of a smoked salmon. The belly has more richness and flavor, and commands a higher price. If you are a smoked salmon junkie like I am, a one-time investment of about fifty dollars to make your own homemade cold smoker will save you hundreds of dollars over the course of a few years. More importantly, it puts the creativity into your hands. The recipe below is for a very traditional take, which needs to be smoked outside. The woods you choose for smoking are up to you. Most people enjoy hardwoods like hickory or oak, but lately I've fallen in love with smoking with pecan wood.

If smoking isn't your jam, or you don't have the time or outdoor space, consider the Nordic cousin of smoked salmon, gravlax, which I've given instructions for as well. Gravlax puts a ton of flavor in the cure, and bypasses the smoking altogether—so you can go from raw to finished in just two days. Both of these would go great on a bagel with all the fixings, of course, but I also like it as a nibble on a cracker with sour cream and pickled onions.

Make the lox. Eyeball the salmon and lay out enough plastic wrap on a clean work surface to envelop the salmon.

Combine the salt and brown sugar in a small bowl. Distribute half of this mixture on the plastic in the size and shape of the fillet, then place the salmon on top. Top the salmon with the remaining salt-sugar mixture, packing it firmly. Wrap the salmon tightly in the plastic wrap, and place in the refrigerator on a sheet pan to catch any liquid. Place a cast-iron skillet or pot on top to weigh down the fillet. Leave it in the fridge for 3 days, turning once a day.

FIXINGS (OPTIONAL)

Cream cheese and whipped ricotta

Capers or caperberries (feel free to fry them too; see page 92)

Sliced red onion or shallots

Sliced tomatoes

Sliced cucumbers

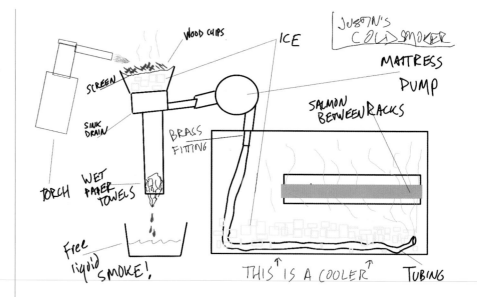

Assemble Justin's Cold Smoker in your backyard (hopefully away from your neighbors or fish-loving dogs), if you haven't already. If you have a smoker capable of cold smoking, go on and use that. Cold smoking leaves the fish uncooked. If you use a hot smoker, you will have cooked fish. It'll still be delicious, but it won't be lox.

After day 3 of curing, remove the salmon from the plastic wrap and wash off the salt and sugar thoroughly. Pat the fillet dry with paper towels. Place the salmon on an inverted cooling rack. Place another cooling rack on top, to make a cage. Zip-tie the racks together to secure the salmon.

Fill a cooler with ice, making sure not to crimp the smoking tube. Wedge the salmon between the walls of the cooler, above but not touching the ice. If you can't get it to wedge, get out some duct tape and make it work. Close the cooler, and fill the drain with ice. Dampen some paper towels and insert into the liquid catcher. Add some ice to the drain-chillum, followed by the screen. Add some wood chips, and turn on the pump. Use a culinary torch to set the wood chips ablaze. The goal is to provide gentle smoke, not a ton of fire. The smoke that escapes from the box should look cool, thin, and bluish.

When the wood is extinguished, turn off the pump and allow the salmon to rest in the smoke chamber. Don't forget to replace the ice in the chillum. Repeat this process every 30 minutes for 3 hours. This is a nice medium smoke, which can be adjusted as you see fit.

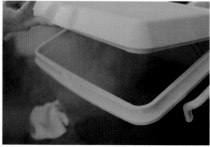

Or make the gravlax. Eyeball the salmon and lay out enough plastic wrap on a clean work surface to eventually fully envelop the salmon.

Combine the salt and sugar in a small bowl. Layer half of the dill, then half of the Twizzlers, then half of the salt-sugar mixture on the plastic wrap in the size and shape of the fillet. Lay the salmon on top, then repeat with rest of the salt-sugar mixture and the remaining ingredients. Wrap the salmon tightly in the plastic wrap, and place in the refrigerator on a sheet pan to catch any liquid. Place a cast-iron skillet or pot on top to weigh down the fillet. Leave this in the fridge for 2 days, turning once a day.

After day 2, remove the salmon from the plastic, discard the dill and Twizzlers, and wash off the salt and sugar thoroughly. Pat the fillet dry with paper towels.

HOLD IT? There's already a lot of hold it in here, but these whole prepped fillets will be good for up to a week, stored in a cold refrigerator.

Salmon should be sliced as thinly and flatly as possible. But don't kill yourself, either. Some people use a slicing knife for ultimate thinness. Lay the salmon, skin side down, on a cutting board and press the knife against the flesh at a very acute angle. Gently slice away.

PLATE IT! This would make a bonanza of a brunch bagel bar. Set up the salmon, half sliced, on a pan or plank. Place all the fixings in ramekins around it, and allow guests to make their own bagel sandwiches.

Alternatively, smoked salmon is great with pasta. Try it with the ramen on page 120, or in the mac and cheese on page 182. It also works nicely with eggs, like the omelet hand rolls on page 124 or in lieu of the bacalao in the Scotch egg on page 116.

BREAK IT: This recipe uses a pretty classic dill and anisette flavor profile. However, you could take it in many different directions, depending on your mood and the occasion, by replacing those flavorings with the following:
- Southwest: Tequila, cumin, red onion, cilantro
- Maryland: Cut the salt with Old Bay
- French: Some of the herbes de Provence (see recipe on page 243)
- Italian: Basil, fennel seeds, tomato paste
- Chinese: Soy sauce, five-spice powder, ground ginger
- Japanese: Shiso and ume paste (like the "sashimi" on page 176)
- Thai: Thai basil, Thai chiles, fish sauce

YIELD Makes 2 servings
PREP TIME 10 minutes
COOK TIME 10 minutes

gear

blender

mixing bowl

grill, grill pan, or skillet (a skillet won't give you grill marks)

cast-iron skillet

fish spatula (optional; see sidebar opposite)

slotted spoon or spider

ingredients

PICKLE EMULSION

2 whole (or 8 spears) dill pickles, chopped

½ teaspoon kosher salt

¼ cup extra-virgin olive oil

ONION "CHAW"

½ white onion (cut from root to stem), peeled

1 quart cold water

¼ cup all-purpose flour

1 teaspoon smoked paprika

½ teaspoon kosher salt

Vegetable oil, for frying

SWORDFISH

Olive oil

Two ½-pound swordfish steaks

Kosher salt

Freshly ground black pepper

GARNISH (OPTIONAL)

Citrus wedges, whatever you have on hand

Parsley sprigs

Dill sprigs

Cucumber blossoms

grilled swordfish with dill pickle emulsion and onion "chaw"

(HOT FISH)

When you own a restaurant, your fridge at home is generally empty, except for things that don't go bad. In my fridge, it's mostly booze, pickled things, and condiments. Often, I bring some naked proteins home from the restaurant, and see which of these random items I can MacGuyver into a sauce or accompaniment. In this recipe, swordfish steaks get all of the seasoning power of your favorite pickle—dill, coriander, pepper, vinegar—in a format that even my very astute girlfriend couldn't identify. The crispy fried onions, or "chaw" as I like to call them, provide a nice textural counterweight and a smoky component from the paprika. The first time I made this, my GF also thought the onions had come from a can, which is a ringing endorsement in my book.

Prep the swordfish. Don't touch the swordfish. You heard me. Don't touch it until you are ready to cook. Let it rest at room temperature.

Make the pickle emulsion. Place the pickles and salt in a blender and blend on high for 30 seconds. With the blender still running, slowly add the oil to emulsify. Set aside.

Prep the onions. Slice the onion as thinly as possible. Soak the slices in cold water until it's time to fry. Combine the flour, smoked paprika, and salt in a mixing bowl and set aside.

HOLD IT? You can leave the sauce at room temperature and the sliced onions in the water for up to 6 hours. If the sauce separates, shake or stir it up.

With olive oil, grease and preheat an outdoor grill, or grease and preheat a grill pan or skillet over medium-high heat.

Dredge the onions. Drain the sliced onions and shake off any excess water. Add them to the flour-paprika-salt mixture and, using your hands, toss them until they are thoroughly coated.

Meanwhile, heat ¼ inch of vegetable oil in a cast-iron or heavy-bottomed skillet over medium heat. If the oil begins to smoke, turn the heat down to low.

Make the swordfish. Liberally season the swordfish steaks with salt and pepper on both sides. Place the swordfish on the grill and cook for 4 to 5 minutes. Then, using a fish spatula, flip the swordfish and cook for 4 to 5 minutes on the opposite side, until both sides have nice grill marks. Remove the swordfish steaks from the pan and allow them to rest on a plate or platter for 5 minutes.

Right after you flip the swordfish steaks, carefully sprinkle the onions into the oil and fry until dark brown and crispy, like cut tobacco, about 4 minutes, stirring occasionally to circulate. Using a slotted spoon or spider, transfer the onions to a plate lined with paper towels to drain.

Notes on Fish Spatulas

Fish spatulas are thin, with a slight bend in them that makes them perfect for sliding under delicate pieces of anything, not just fish. They also have large holes in them, which reduce the surface area contacting whatever it is you are flipping. They are priceless in a kitchen, and practically the only spatula I use for anything other than eggs. I don't use them on eggs because I cook eggs in a nonstick pan, and most fish spatulas are metal, which will scratch the surface.

PLATE IT! You could serve the steaks on a plate with the sauce on top and the onion "chaw" on the side.

You could transfer the sauce to a squirt bottle and give the plate a neat zigzag. From there, you could put the swordfish down, with the onions "haystacked" on the side.

You could place the sauce down in a pool in the center of the plate, and smear it outward until half of the plate is covered, then place the swordfish in the center and the onions on top.

All of these methods would be nicely dressed up with some of the optional garnishes listed.

BREAK IT: This recipe could be made with pickled anything. You could use the spicy pickled carrots from page 264, which would add some extra heat and sweetness to the equation.

YIELD Makes 1 roast; 4 to 6 servings

PREP TIME 10 minutes

COOK TIME 4 hours 15 minutes

gear

2 very large stockpots

small bowl

gallon-size zip-top bag

48-quart cooler

probe thermometer

medium skillet

whisk

ingredients

SOUS-VIDE TURKEY

4 tablespoons (½ stick) unsalted butter, at room temperature

3 tablespoons pickled jalapeño brine

2 tablespoons sweet smoked paprika

3 garlic cloves, smashed

One 2½-pound brined turkey breast "roast," with netting (it's advertised as something you would roast, and is formed into a roast-like log)

1 tablespoon olive oil

PAPRIKASH SAUCE

½ cup heavy cream

Pasta or homemade noodles (page 122), for serving (optional)

poor man's sous-vide turkey paprikash

(Light meat)

Sous-vide ("under-vacuum") cooking is one of the defining methods of modern cooking. The idea is that by placing food in a vacuum-sealed pouch and cooking in a temperature-controlled water bath, it will cook more evenly, with minimal loss of flavor-packed juices. The biggest downside to sous-vide cooking for the home cook is cost—this gear can get very expensive very quickly. Thankfully, my pal the Internet came up with this clever hack using zip-top bags, a probe thermometer, and a picnic cooler. Here, I use the smoky flavors of paprikash—a Hungarian dish laden with paprika—to liven up an otherwise boring turkey breast. If you've ever had turkey breast and wondered why we bother eating this bland meat, this recipe will change your mind. If you already love turkey, this will make you love it more. Sous-vide cooking unlocks the delicious in almost everything. That said, if you want to cheat, I offer a slow-cooker version below as well.

Make the sous-vide turkey. Over high heat, bring two very large stockpots filled with water to 175°F.

In a small bowl, mix together the butter, brine, paprika, and garlic. Unwrap the turkey breast from its netting and place it in a gallon-size zip-top bag. Add the butter mixture to the bag, seal, and smoosh it around to coat the breast. Fill a sink with cold water, unzip the bag by about an inch, and slowly submerge the bottom of the bag in the water. As the water presses on the bag, it will push the air out to the top. Seal the bag once all the air is pressed out. Set aside until the water in the stockpots on the stovetop reaches 175°F.

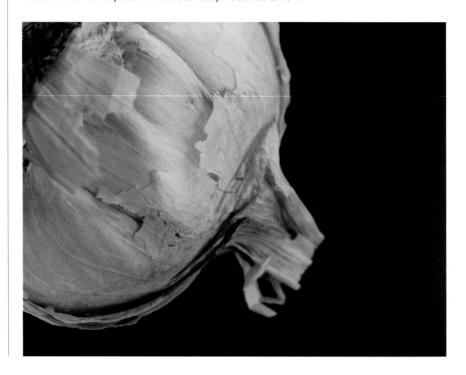

When the water reaches temperature, place the thermometer into the cooler, then carefully pour the water into the cooler and note the temperature of the water. The temperature of the water will drop considerably. Add the turkey bag to the water, and again, note the temperature. Our goal is to get the water to hover between 150° and 160°F. If needed, add more hot water. Submerge the thermometer into the water, with the display outside of the cooler. Shut the cooler for 4 hours. If the temperature drops below 150°F, add a little more hot water to bring it back up. Otherwise, don't open the cooler or all the heat will rush out. When the turkey is done, its internal temperature will be between 150° and 160°F. (Bear in mind that the folks at the USDA specify 165°F.)

HOLD IT? After the 4 hours, you can transfer the bag to an ice bath to rapidly cool it down, then transfer to the fridge to hold for up to 4 days.

After the 4 hours, remove the bag from the cooler; discard the cooler water. Carefully remove the breast from the bag, reserving the cooking liquid, and set the breast on a cutting board.

Heat the oil in a skillet over medium-high heat. When the oil is shimmering, add the turkey, and sear for 1 to 2 minutes on all sides to brown. Once seared, set the breast aside on the cutting board to rest.

Make the paprikash sauce. Add the cooking liquid from the bag to the skillet and scrape the bottom of the skillet with a wooden spoon to release any flavorful bits. Whisk in the cream, bring to a simmer, and remove from the heat.

PLATE IT! Slice or shred the turkey on a platter. Pour the pan sauce over, while telling your friends all about cooking sous vide. They will marvel at your resourcefulness. This would be really delicious with a side of pasta, and if you are feeling really ambitious, you could make your own noodles such as on page 122.

CHEAT IT! If you don't have enough time or energy for the sous-vide process, you can make a similarly flavored Cheater's Turkey Paprikash using turkey breast, which will not be quite as tender and flavor packed, but will be tasty nonetheless.
In a small bowl, combine the cream, butter, brine, paprika, garlic, and olive oil.
Remove the netting from the turkey and slather with the cream mixture. Add the turkey to a slow cooker and set to high. Cook until the internal temperature reaches 155°F (see above for note on temperature), about 4 hours. Remove the meat from the cooker and shred, then add it back to the sauce and serve.

BREAK IT: Get a fresh turkey breast (not brined). Brine it yourself in a mixture of orange juice, salt, and musky marjoram. Let it soak in this mixture for up to a day. This will flavor and tenderize the meat internally before getting even more tender from the sous-vide process. The orange juice will also provide a refreshing sweet-and-sour component to the otherwise rich paprikash.

YIELD Makes enough brisket to feed at least 10 hungry people

PREP TIME 10 minutes

COOK TIME 12 to 14 hours

INACTIVE TIME 1 hour

gear

blender, spice grinder, or mortar and pestle

smoker of some sort (bought, built, or borrowed)

hardwood (I like unsoaked pecan wood chips, or whole logs, but use your preference)

BBQ thermometer (see sidebar page 104)

notepad

ingredients

SPICE RUB

¼ cup whole black peppercorns

2 tablespoons allspice berries

3 tablespoons whole cumin seeds

1 cup kosher salt

½ cup packed light brown sugar

2 tablespoons ground ginger

1 tablespoon mustard powder

1 tablespoon garlic powder

BRISKET

One 13- to 15-pound packer cut brisket

At least 1 cup apple cider vinegar

1 loaf sliced bread (I like Martin's Potato Bread)

Two 24-ounce jars dill pickle spears

f-yeah barbecue

(Dark meat)

If you ever want to get very lost in one very small spectrum of food, I recommend barbecue. Barbecue is not grilling. Grilling is heating food over high heat with minimal smoking. Barbecue takes hours, it takes smoke, and it takes thought and practice. That said, my rub is nontraditional, and my methods are probably deplorable, but I'm not here to win a barbecue competition. I'm here to pull a piece of meat out of a smoker after twelve hours of staring at it while the onlookers say F-YEAH! The best thing about brisket is its generous fat layer—it's like a smoked meat with cream cheese (fat) built in. When served with white bread, vinegar, and pickles, you get the southern version of the classic Jewish bagel.

Barbecue also takes some gear. Namely, a smoker. For this recipe, I used a Masterbuilt Digital Electric Smoker. It works great for me, but talking about smokers is a huge can of worms among barbecue people. The reason I opted for an electric smoker is because I can't find propane anywhere in Brooklyn. Really, the borough is so densely populated, they don't want us to have it and risk setting places ablaze. Chances are, you don't live in New York, so you can combust the hell out of whatever you want. Either way, choose an option large enough to handle a whole brisket, which is enough to feed ten, at least.

Make the spice rub. Grind the peppercorns, allspice berries, and cumin seeds in a blender, spice grinder, or with a mortar and pestle. Add the salt, brown sugar, ginger, mustard powder, and garlic powder and pulse to mix through.

Make the brisket. I don't trim the fat off my brisket, which is sacrilegious in some circles.

Evenly coat the brisket with the rub and let sit at room temperature for an hour.

Smoke the brisket. If your smoker has a water pan, fill it. Preheat the smoker with heat only. No sense in adding wood until the meat's in. Once it has reached 225°F, insert the brisket into the smoker and probes into the brisket. From here, DO NOT OPEN THAT SMOKER. I REPEAT, DO NOT. OPEN. THE SMOKER. Every time you do this you might as well add another 30 minutes of cook time. The thermometers are your eyes and hands. Trust them.

Add the manufacturer's recommended amount of wood in the intervals that the manufacturer suggests, in whichever form the manufacturer recommends. The smoke will take some time to get going, but once it does, you will know you are doing the right thing by the color of the smoke. It will be bluish gray, thin, and not too harsh if it gets around your face or eyes. Remember, "billowing white smoke, your 'cue's a joke; thin and blue, that'll do." If you get billowing white smoke, chances are there's some fat burning somewhere, or you've added wood that's too wet. Do your best to resist opening the smoker to figure it out.

Take notes of everything you do: the time, the temperature, and your observations. When you don't see any smoke, add more wood. Note the time. You can bugger off for about that amount of time before you need to add more wood; for me, that's about every 45 minutes to an hour.

Is a barbecue thermometer different from other thermometers?

Is a barbecue thermometer different from other thermometers?

Yes. It's essentially two probe thermometers, one telling you the internal temperature of the meat, and the other telling you the temperature of the box. If you are barbecuing, it's a must.

———

Hey Squirt!

It may sound silly, but putting your vinegar in a squirt bottle really improves the eating experience as you can add just a dot of vinegar to an especially fatty piece.

The temperature will steadily climb within the brisket until it reaches what is called "the stall." It will not budge, sometimes for hours. Leave it alone, don't freak out, keep feeding it wood, and keep cruising until the internal temperature of the meat reaches 190°F. It will likely take about 12 hours to get here. This is my sweet spot to pull the cue. Remove the cue, and let it rest, untouched and uncovered, for at least 20 minutes.

HOLD IT? The brisket will keep for up to 4 days in the fridge, covered. I like to slice off what I want, and either warm it up in a dry pan or eat it cold. This will make some of the best sandwiches you've ever eaten.

Carve the brisket. Using a sharp knife, start carving the meat on the thin end, cutting at an angle against the grain to make very long ¼-inch-thick strips. Eventually you'll get to a point where the grain gets wonky, right as you start to go up the hill toward the fatty side of the brisket. There should be a thin layer of fat that I say "separates the mountain from the plains" (see diagram opposite)— i.e., separates the point from the flat. That "mountain" is called the point, and the "plains" is called the flat. Turn your knife sideways, and slice into that fat line horizontally to remove the "mountain" from the "plains." Continue carving your two newly separated pieces, cutting the strips against the grain. The parts from the point are my absolute favorite.

PLATE IT! Dribble vinegar on those really fatty pieces, if you want. Serve with bread and pickles.

BREAK IT: Brine your meat before you smoke it! It takes an additional couple of days, depending on the cut and size, but the brine will help the smoke permeate the meat. What you use to brine is up to you. I've seen brines that include juices, sodas, even milk (like on page 228). Think about where you want to go with the dish, and what sort of liquid can add to the equation.

POINT (THE MOUNTAIN)

FAT LINE

FLAT (THE PLAINS)

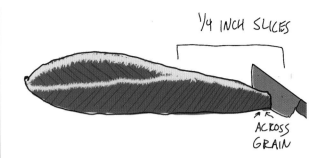

¼ INCH SLICES

ACROSS GRAIN

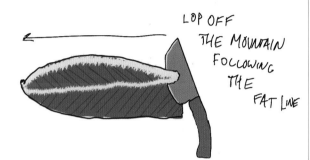

LOP OFF THE MOUNTAIN FOLLOWING THE FAT LINE

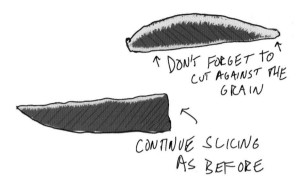

DON'T FORGET TO CUT AGAINST THE GRAIN

CONTINUE SLICING AS BEFORE

YIELD Makes 8 cannoli

PREP TIME 15 minutes

COOK TIME 10 minutes

gear

3 medium bowls

whisk

pastry bag or gallon-size zip-top bag

Dutch oven or heavy-bottomed pot

Candy thermometer

rolling pin

ring cutter or drinking glass

cannoli rollers (optional; see Tip)

tongs

ingredients

FILLING

2 cups whole-milk ricotta

½ cup confectioners' sugar

¼ teaspoon kosher salt

½ teaspoon liquid smoke

DOUGH

1½ cups all-purpose flour, plus more for the work surface

1 teaspoon kosher salt

4 tablespoons (½ stick) unsalted butter, cut into ¼-inch cubes, at room temperature

¼ cup Disaronno or other almond liqueur

1 tablespoon water

Vegetable oil, for frying

Mini chocolate chips (optional)

smoked cannoli

(DESSERT)

Ricotta, the cottage cheese of Italy, is generally not my jam. I even prefer cottage cheese's vinegary bite to ricotta's flat creaminess. But my problem is more an issue of how ricotta is used than of how it tastes. Ricotta is usually used as a paint rather than a canvas in cooking—and since it tends to be bland, it cannot add much color to a dish. However, ricotta readily adopts whatever flavors you throw at it, and that's where it shines. Here, a quick addition of liquid smoke turns a homemade cannoli into a heady, addictive, and mysteriously savory/sweet sort of treat.

Make the filling. In a medium bowl, whisk the ricotta to make it smooth, then add the confectioners' sugar, salt, and liquid smoke and whisk again until combined. Transfer to a pastry bag or zip-top bag and refrigerate.

Make the dough. In a medium bowl, combine the flour and salt and whisk until incorporated.

In another medium bowl, combine the butter and Disaronno and whisk gently until combined. Add the butter-Disaronno mixture to the flour and salt and mix with your hands until uniform and doughy.

HOLD IT? The filling can be kept in the fridge, covered, for up to 3 days. The unrolled dough can be kept in the fridge, tightly sealed with plastic wrap, for up to a day; remove it from the fridge at least 30 minutes in advance and let it return to room temperature before proceeding with the recipe.

Fill a Dutch oven halfway with oil, clip on a candy thermometer, and bring the oil to 375°F over medium heat.

Flour your work surface, turn out the dough, and roll it out with your rolling pin very thinly, to a thickness of less than ⅛ inch. Using a ring cutter or upside-down glass, cut out circles of the dough. You can reroll the scraps one time, if you'd like to squeeze out another.

Roll the dough circles around the cannoli rollers and press the two overlapping edges together tightly, sealing them together with a little water, then press with your fingers to securely seal. Working in batches, gently place the wrapped cannoli rollers into the oil and fry until bubbly and golden brown, 2 to 3 minutes. Carefully remove the cannoli from the oil with tongs, tipping each vertically so the oil from the interior can drain back into the pot, and allow to cool completely before removing the roller.

PLATE IT! If using a zip-top bag for the filling, snip the corner of the bag to make an opening. Then, using the pastry bag or snipped zip-top, fill each cooled shell with the ricotta mixture. (If the shells are not completely cooled, the ricotta will melt out.) Press each filled end of the cannoli into the mini chocolate chips if you'd like. Serve in cute little pairs.

BREAK IT: If you replaced the Disaronno with Tia Maria or Kahlúa and then used cinnamon chips on the outside and a little cumin powder in the cheese, you would have a smoked Mexican cannoli.

☞ **Tip**

If you don't have cannoli rollers, use a can opener to open up a clean small can of tomato paste, but rotate the can opener 90 degrees to cut into the side of the can. This will feel a little weird but it will keep the lip of the can from tearing the shells. It's also going to be sharp, so be careful. You will have to change the size of the circle you cut from the dough as well.

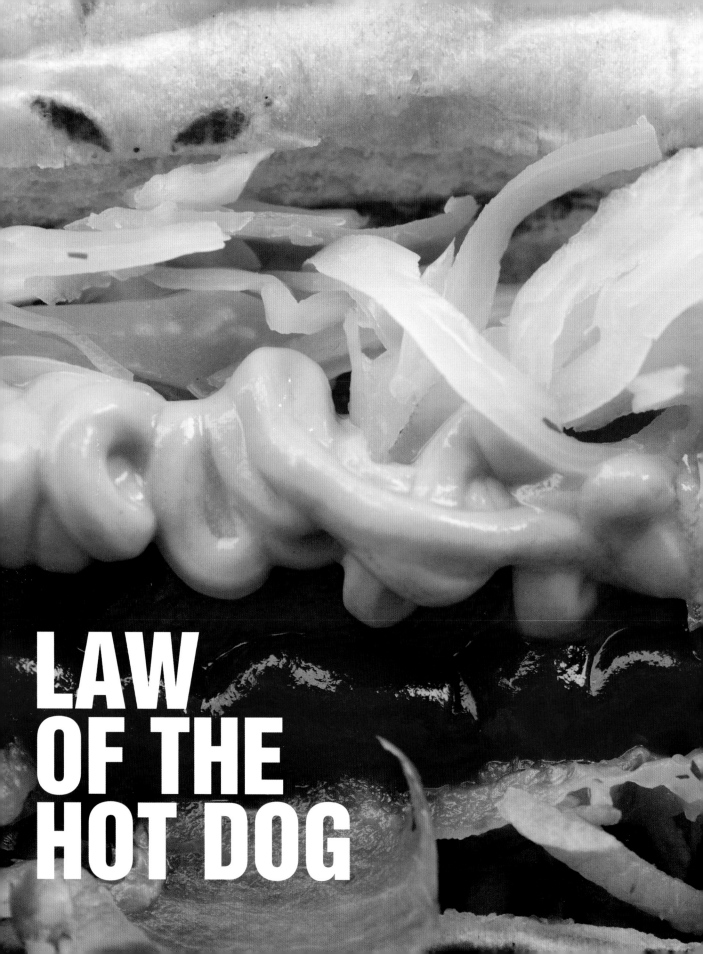

LAW
OF THE
HOT DOG

Aside from an extra-terrestrial visit, there isn't much that could change humankind more than salt has. Salt allows us to preserve food, which has allowed us to preserve ourselves when foraged or cultivated food was scarce. This is why we call awesome people "the salt of the earth." In the case of cured meat (that was a sausage joke), the distillate for me is the hot dog. The hot dog, which would be my vote if we need a new flag, appears to be a condiment covered in condiments. This might present the hot dog as a culinary strumpet. This is far from the truth. Look at beans and wieners. Who's got the upper hand there? By the time a Chicago dog is assembled, the hot dog is the minority shareholder. Do you ever see a pepperoni pizza made entirely of pepperoni? Or an Italian sub with bread between loaves of cured meat? The hot dog makes the bun delicious, and the law of the hot dog allows us to see salty/cured foods as discreet culinary enablers, bringing out the best in the ingredients with which they are paired.

salt meets world

PASTRAMI	MINI REUBEN WELLINGTONS	ENGLAND
CURED MEATS	CHEATER'S CHARCUTERIE BOARD	BROOKLYN
SALT COD	SALT COD SCOTCH DEVILED EGGS	GREAT BRITAIN
BOLOGNA	CHILLED WATERCRESS SOUP WITH FRIED BOLOGNA	CHICAGO
RAMEN	NOT-COLLEGE RAMEN	JAPAN
NORI	HAND ROLL PARTY	JAPAN
PEPPERONI	PEPPERONI-CRUSTED COD WITH PINEAPPLE	SPAIN
LARDONS	CORNISH HEN MEETS FRISÉE AUX LARDONS	FRANCE
VACA FRITA	CUBAN² CHIMICHANGAS	CUBA
PAPRIKA/SALT	BANANA SPLIT FOR SOPHISTICATES	USA

YIELD Makes about 36 bites

PREP TIME 25 minutes

COOK TIME 20 minutes

gear

small saucepan

mixing bowl

rolling pin

sheet pan

pastry brush

ingredients

SAUCE

½ cup water

1 tablespoon balsamic vinegar

1 tablespoon sugar

4 ounces fresh shiitake mushrooms, stems removed, finely diced

¼ cup ketchup

¼ cup mayonnaise

FILLING

½ pound corned beef, sliced thinly then diced

8 ounces sauerkraut, drained

½ pound Swiss cheese, sliced thinly then diced

PUFF PASTRY

All-purpose flour, for coating the work surface

4 sheets puff pastry, thawed in the fridge overnight

Nonstick cooking spray

2 egg whites, lightly beaten

1 tablespoon whole caraway seeds

mini reuben wellingtons

(CANAPÉ/SNACK)

When I was on *Food Network Star,* I was cohabitating with total strangers. I quickly befriended the funniest and smartest of them all: Martie Duncan. Martie and I were in the absolute trenches of culinary warfare together. When I was about to crack, she'd calm me down. And when she needed a hand, I was her octopus. During one of the challenges, Martie made a nifty party snack— Pastrami in Puff Pastry. She taught me how easy it is to use puff pastry in savory applications, much like the beef Wellington of yore, where an entire beef tenderloin is covered in mushroom pâté and wrapped in puff before baking.

As an ode to Ms. Duncan, I've created a Reuben version of her mini pastries, swapping the pastrami for corned beef and adding Swiss, sauerkraut, and even a Wellington-influenced (i.e., shiitake-mushroomed) Thousand Island. With the corned beef acting as a hot dog, this is the delicatessen version of a pig in a blanket.

Make the sauce. Combine ½ cup water, the vinegar, sugar, and mushrooms in a small saucepan. Bring the mixture to a boil over medium heat. Remove the saucepan from the heat and allow the mixture to cool to room temperature.

Once cool, drain and discard the liquid from the mushrooms. Combine the mushrooms with the ketchup and mayonnaise. Refrigerate until you are ready to make the filling.

Make the filling. In a mixing bowl, combine the corned beef, sauerkraut, and cheese. Add the sauce and mix with a wooden spoon until evenly dispersed.

Make the the Wellingtons. Preheat the oven to 350°F.

Flour a work surface and a rolling pin. Lightly spray a sheet pan with cooking spray.

Place one of the puff pastry sheets on the work surface, keeping the remaining sheets covered and cold. Roll out the pastry sheet into a 10-inch square. Using a sharp knife, cut the square into thirds longitudinally and latitudinally to make 9 smaller squares.

Place a tablespoon of the filling just above the bottom edge of each square.

Gently roll up each square like a little burrito, starting to roll from the bottom of the square, then folding both sides over the filling, finishing the roll. Make sure that none of the mixture is exposed, and that the dough is tightly crimped. If you've never rolled a burrito, check the method below.

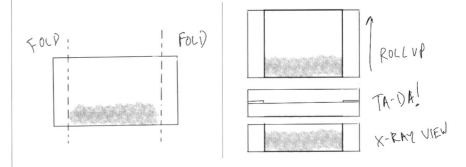

Place the assembled pastries on the prepared sheet pan, not touching. Roll, cut, and fill the remaining puff pastry sheets. Using a pastry brush, gently brush the tops of each assembled pastry with the beaten egg whites. Sprinkle caraway seeds over the egg white.

HOLD IT? If you want, you can keep the sheet pan with the assembled pastries covered with plastic wrap in the fridge for a whole day. These can also be wrapped tightly and frozen indefinitely—cook them directly from the freezer, though they'll likely take a few minutes longer.

Place the sheet pan in the middle of the oven and bake the Wellingtons until golden brown, 15 to 20 minutes, rotating the pan halfway through.

PLATE IT! This is the kind of thing that should be piled high on a platter in the middle of the room, or served as passed hors d'oeuvre. Serve hot.

BREAK IT: Mushrooms instead of meat makes for a heck of a vegetarian version, especially if you add some crushed black olives to the kraut.

gear

medium pot

bowl, quart-size deli container, or jar

small pot

microwave-safe bowl

blender

whisk

ingredients

PICKLED GRAPES

2 cups apple cider vinegar

1 cinnamon stick

¼ cup packed brown sugar

2 tablespoons kosher salt

6 cups water

1 intact bunch red seedless grapes (about 11 ounces)

TOMATILLO CHUTNEY

1 pound tomatillos (about 8), husked, rinsed, cored, and chopped

¼ cup agave syrup

1 tablespoon whole fennel seeds

2 teaspoons kosher salt

2 tablespoons water

cheater's charcuterie board

(COLD APP)

Fancy charcuterie boards often include artisanal meats and cheese, fancy jams and chutneys, and tiny pickles. For those of us who don't want to pay eight dollars for pickles, or don't have a spare coat closet for curing meats, we must CHEAT! Fooling our guests into thinking that we've procured only the finest cuts of what have you from a fellow in Brooklyn with a twirled mustache in a bespoke jacket is a matter of disguising store-bought meats with DIY accouterments. Homemade condiments step your game up with hardly any work, turning a cold cut platter (even with megamart salami and generic Swiss) into a charcuterie board. Sharp pine nut mustard, sour pickled grapes, and sweet tomatillo chutney enliven cured meats, and benefit from their rich salty flavor. With the simple recipes below, your megamart deli meats will be auditioning for a Wes Anderson movie in no time.

Make the pickled grapes. Combine the vinegar, cinnamon, brown sugar, and salt along with 6 cups water in a medium pot and bring to a boil. Remove from the heat.

Put the grapes in bowl, a quart-size deli container, or a large jar and pour the hot pickling liquid on top so the grapes are fully submerged. Cool to room temperature, then refrigerate at least overnight before serving.

Make the tomatillo chutney. Add all the ingredients for the chutney and 2 tablespoons water to a small pot, stir to combine, and cook over medium heat until the tomatillos are tender and the sauce is glossy, about 25 minutes. Transfer the finished chutney to a container and chill.

Make the pine nut mustard. Whisk together the vinegar, 2 tablespoons water, the mustard powder, salt, and turmeric in a microwave-safe bowl until dissolved. Fold in the mustard seeds and pine nuts. Microwave the mixture on high for 2 minutes. Transfer the mixture to a blender, pulse to break up the pine nuts, and chill until cool (about 2 hours), at which time it will be thick and spreadable.

HOLD IT? The best thing about condiments is that they have a long shelf life! All three of these will hold in the refrigerator in airtight containers for up to 2 weeks.

Remove the condiments from the fridge about an hour before serving to bring to room temperature. Drain the pickled grapes.

PLATE IT! Charcuterie looks best on wood or stone, served family style. Spoon swoosh (drop a spoonful and swoosh it with the back of a spoon) out the mustard. Transfer the chutney to a ramekin or bowl. Keep the grapes on the stem, but divide the bunch to maximize aesthetic appeal if necessary. Shingle or roll the thin slices of meat, keeping each type together. Pile your accompaniments all around.

BREAK IT: Cook the chestnuts minus the peppers and onions from page 184, allow them to cool, and then slice them like little pieces of charcuterie. They will delight carnivores and vegetarians alike!

PINE NUT MUSTARD

½ cup red wine vinegar

2 tablespoons water

2 tablespoons mustard powder

1 teaspoon kosher salt

1 teaspoon ground turmeric

2 tablespoons whole mustard seeds

¼ cup toasted pine nuts

CHARCUTERIE PLATE

Thinly sliced cured meats (3 ounces per person—it seems like a lot, but people scarf this stuff down without knowing what they've done), at room temperature

Thinly sliced or soft scoopable cheeses (2 ounces per person), at room temperature

Crackers or wafers

Olives

Get Creative!

The hot vinegar-sugar-spice-salt-water combo from the pickled grapes is pretty magical for keeping things edible, and imbuing them with fun flavors. Try swapping out the components or the main ingredient and coming up with something new, entirely of your own imagination.

YIELD Makes 6 servings

PREP TIME 20 minutes

COOK TIME 10 minutes

INACTIVE TIME 24 hours

gear

large bowl

pot

food processor

shallow bowl

Dutch oven or heavy-bottomed pot

candy thermometer

small bowl

slotted spoon or spider

serrated knife

sheet pan

ingredients

SCOTCH EGGS

About ½ pound dried salt cod (see Note)

8 large eggs

½ teaspoon smoked paprika

¼ cup rice flour, for dusting

Vegetable oil, for frying

FILLING

2 tablespoons chopped dill pickles

2 tablespoons mayonnaise

2 teaspoons sriracha sauce

1 teaspoon Dijon mustard

GARNISH

Sriracha sauce

salt cod scotch deviled eggs

(HOT APP)

When I first moved to Bed-Stuy, in Brooklyn, I was living off of Fulton Street and Nostrand Avenue. All around that neighborhood are Caribbean joints pushing out roti, doubles, and salt cod bakes. It took me some time to muster up the courage to go into A&A Bake and Doubles. I leaned over the counter and asked a smiling man (who I now know as Noel, the owner) for "One, please." "Which one?" "Just one. One of something." "We have two things. A bake and a doubles." "How can something called doubles be one thing?" "Do you like fish?" "Yes." "Salt cod bake, with pepper." He handed me a fried bread (oddly called a bake) stuffed with salt cod, onions, and spicy peppers. It was the most wondrous mid-morning snack I've ever had, and it serves as the inspiration for this dish. This paprika-spiced, salt cod–crusted, hard-boiled egg works like a hot dog of the sea, its spicy, deviled filling a combination of relish and mustard.

Soak the cod. Soak the cod in water in a bowl in the fridge for 24 hours, changing the water 4 times, every 6 hours or so.

Prep the eggs. Place only 6 of the eggs in a pot and cover with water. Bring the water to a boil over high heat, then remove from the heat and allow the eggs to cook for an additional 5 minutes in the hot water. Carefully drain the water off, and run cold water briefly over the eggs just to cool them down enough to handle. Peel the eggs, then soak them in cold water to cool them off completely.

Drain the fish from the water and press dry. In a food processor fitted with the steel blade, process the fish until finely chopped. Add the 2 remaining raw eggs and the paprika to the processor and process until thoroughly mixed and pasty. Divide the paste into 6 equal portions, about ¼ cup each.

Put the rice flour in a shallow bowl. Roll the hard-boiled eggs in the rice flour and shake off any excess. Gently wrap each egg in the fish mixture until completely covered, transfer to a plate, and put them in the freezer to chill for 5 to 10 minutes.

HOLD IT? The coated eggs can be stored in the fridge, covered, for up to 24 hours. Just freeze for 10 minutes before frying.

Finish the eggs. Preheat the oven to 200°F. Place the Dutch oven with the clip-on candy thermometer over medium heat, fill halfway with oil, and bring the oil to 375°F.

In a small bowl, mix together the ingredients for the filling.

Using a slotted spoon or spider, carefully lower the coated eggs into the oil, adjusting the heat as necessary to keep the temperature consistent. Fry the eggs until golden brown, 2 to 3 minutes.

Transfer the fried eggs to a cutting board and, using a serrated knife, slice the eggs in half lengthwise. Scoop out the yolk and add it to the filling mixture. Place the yolk-less eggs on a sheet pan in the oven to keep warm.

Mash up the yolks and filling mix with a fork until smooth. Remove the warm eggs from the oven and spoon the filling into the cavity of each egg. Garnish each egg with one dot of sriracha sauce.

☞ **Note**

I buy salt cod from Latin and Caribbean markets. I look for fully dried cod, sold open-air. The stuff in bags is generally an inferior fish, and because it isn't fully desiccated, it has a shorter shelf life.

PLATE IT! I like to serve these guys in clean egg cartons as an appetizer. If you are scared of salmonella, don't do that, as there is a small risk associated. They also make for a nice little brunch side dish, or an out-of-the-ordinary snack.

BREAK IT: That salt cod mix is just dying to be wrapped around an avocado. Treat the avocado like a hard-cooked egg, removing the skin, then applying the cod mix. Cook it, slice it open, remove the pit, and add some cooked, crumbled Spanish chorizo to the well in the center.

gear

large pot

blender

small bowls

sauté pan

ingredients

SOUP

2 tablespoons vegetable oil

1 tablespoon whole coriander seeds

chilled watercress soup with fried bologna

(COLD SOUP)

Sometimes a vegetable needs to be told to shut up—in a loving way, of course. Strong, slightly metallic-tasting watercress is one of those vegetables that could easily rage out of control and take over a dish. Here, a bit of sugar is that sweet slap it needs to back off. The result of this culinary altercation is a refreshing but hearty soup, the type I want for dinner on a muggy summer night in an apartment in a city. With its pickled cucumber cubes, poppy seeds, spice-infused broth, and crisped-up bologna strips, it is loosely based on the flavors of the Chicago Dog, which I find to be one of the most complex and gratifying "peasant foods" that America has produced. If you live in Maryland or Pennsylvania, use Lebanon bologna for maximum flavor overload; otherwise I'd recommend getting whatever kind you like sliced fresh from the deli.

1 teaspoon whole mustard seeds

4 cups vegetable stock (or vegetable broth, and cut the salt by half)

4 bunches watercress, stems removed (about 8 cups loosely packed/10 ounces)

1 tablespoon fresh lemon juice

1 tablespoon kosher salt

2 teaspoons brown sugar

CUCUMBER GARNISH

1 tablespoon poppy seeds

3 tablespoons apple cider vinegar

½ teaspoon kosher salt

1 cucumber (I prefer hothouse)

6 slices bologna

¼ cup golden raisins

1 tablespoon celery seeds

Make the soup. In a large pot over medium heat, heat the oil with the coriander and mustard seeds until aromatic, about 2 minutes. Add 2 cups of the stock and bring to a boil. Reduce the heat to low, add the watercress. and let it wilt into the stock; work in batches as necessary. Add the remaining 2 cups stock.

Transfer the soup to a blender and blend, starting slow and increasing the speed, until very smooth. Add the lemon juice, salt, and brown sugar and blend to incorporate. Transfer to a container and chill in the fridge for at least 4 hours.

Make the cucumber garnish. In a small pan over low heat, toast the poppy seeds, swirling the pan, until fragrant. Transfer to a small bowl. In another small bowl, combine the vinegar and salt.

Cut the cucumber with the skin on into 18 cubes. Put 6 in the vinegar mixture to quick-pickle. Give them a stir to coat. Put the remaining 12 in the poppy seed mixture, and roll them around to coat. Place all of the cucumbers, covered, in the refrigerator, for at least an hour.

HOLD IT? Keep the soup and cucumber cubes in the fridge until ready to use, or for up to 3 days.

Cook the bologna. In a small pan over medium heat, fry the bologna slices in batches to get color and crisp up a bit, about 2 minutes on each side. Slice into bite-size strips.

PLATE IT! Drain the pickled cucumbers, and put one in each bowl; put two poppy seed–coated cucumber pieces in each as well. Evenly divide the crisped bologna, golden raisins, and celery seeds among the bowls, then pour the soup around.

BREAK IT: A tiny scoop of simple pasta salad laced with sweet pineapple would make this very similar in flavor to a Hawaiian plate lunch.

STEP YOUR GAME UP

Instead of cutting the cucumber into cubes, you could use a set of "parisienne scoops," which is a fancy term for "melon ballers that are smaller than a normal melon baller." You can find them at specialty kitchen stores or online.

gear

butcher's twine

slow cooker (at least 8-quart capacity)

small bowl

pressure cooker (at least 8-quart capacity)

grill pan or heavy skillet

colander

large stockpot

stand mixer with dough hook

extruder attachment for the stand mixer or rolling pin or pasta machine

small bowl

whisk

immersion blender

medium pot

large bowl

large pot

sheet pan

small bowl

ladles

spaghetti fork, strainer insert, or pasta basket

culinary torch

ingredients

PORK BELLY

4 pounds pork belly, skin on

Zest of ½ lemon

6 scallions, roots still attached

½ cup Worcestershire sauce

½ cup soy sauce

(continued on page 122)

not-college ramen

(HOT SOUP)

Say ramen to most anyone, and the first thing that comes to mind is packets of dried noodles and a hot plate. This is good stuff for snacks, or when hot water is the only thing you can cook. Real ramen is anything but "instant," and its flavoring components can hardly be reduced into a powder. I had my first "real" ramen in New York, and I was blown away. The broth was rich and salty, to the point that it almost felt sticky—like a cured meat distillate. The noodles were zippy, they smacked my lips as I slurped them up. I became obsessed, and still am—now I make a ham hock–, kombu-, and shiitake-infused broth, which uses mustard and pork fat to emulsify some richness into the finished soup. Eventually, I found the movie *Tampopo*, which is a Japanese movie about some truckers who are obsessed with ramen. It's the best food-centric movie ever made. Like they say in *Tampopo*, "the soup animates the noodle." Here the noodles work like an animated hot dog bun. Do like they do, and take some time to make this real ramen, which, thanks to the pressure cooker, can be done in a day. Hardly instant, but worth the wait.

Make the pork belly. Place the pork belly on a work surface, skin side down, with the long side facing you. Distribute the lemon zest evenly over the pork belly. Lay the scallions horizontally in the center of the pork, and roll the pork belly around them. Tie the pork with twine to form one roll of pork belly. Place the rolled and tied pork in a slow cooker. In a small bowl, mix the Worcestershire, soy sauce, halved garlic, brown sugar, and beer. Add the mixture to the slow cooker. Turn the slow cooker on to low heat and cover. Cook the pork for 5 hours, rotating occasionally.

Remove the pork belly from the liquid, allow it to cool, and refrigerate until it's time to plate.

Start the broth. Put the trotters and ham hock in a pressure cooker and cover with water. Set the pressure cooker over high heat, uncovered, until it comes to a boil.

Meanwhile, on a grill pan over high heat (a heavy skillet will work if you do not have a grill pan), place the onions, ginger, and garlic, cut side down. Add the serrano. Char the vegetables on one side, about 10 minutes, then remove from the grill.

When the water comes to a boil, drain the trotters and ham hock in a colander; discard the water. Rinse the cooker, the trotters, and the ham hock under cool water to remove any remaining scum or brown bits. Return the trotters and ham hock to the pressure cooker and add the charred vegetables and dried mushrooms. Fill the pot with water up to the max fill line, lock the lid, and set to the highest pressure over high heat. Once it starts releasing steam, set the timer for 1 hour and 30 minutes and turn the heat to low.

After an hour and a half, transfer the pressure cooker to the sink and release the pressure. Run cold water over the whole kit to cool it down. Release the lid and, using a colander, strain the broth from the pressure cooker into a stockpot; discard the trotters and ham hock. Place the stockpot of broth in a sink filled with ice to rapidly cool, and refrigerate for at least 3 hours.

1 head garlic, cut in half horizontally

½ cup packed light brown sugar

1 quart light-colored beer (I use a pilsner or a lager)

BROTH

4½ pounds or 4 pig trotters, split lengthwise (ask your butcher to split them)

1 smoked ham hock (about 11 ounces)

2 large yellow onions, halved lengthwise

One 2-inch piece fresh ginger, halved lengthwise

1 head garlic, halved horizontally

1 serrano pepper

1 ounce dried shiitake mushrooms

1 tablespoon Dijon mustard

4 cups water

½ cup bonito flakes

One 4 x 4-inch piece kombu

Kosher salt

FOR THE RAMEN NOODLES

1 cup all-purpose flour, plus more for dusting

1 cup bread flour

1 tablespoon wheat gluten

1 teaspoon kosher salt

2 whole large eggs

2 large egg yolks

1 teaspoon Kansui solution (see sidebar opposite) (optional, but awesome)

¼ cup water

1 tablespoon sesame oil

1 tablespoon vegetable oil

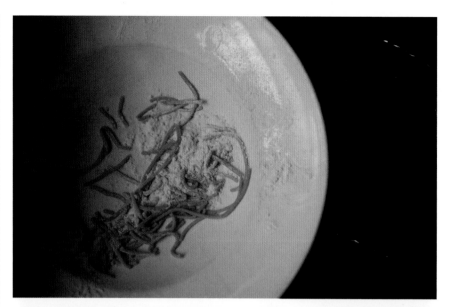

Make the noodles. Combine both flours, the wheat gluten, and the salt in the bowl of a stand mixer fitted with the dough hook attachment. Add the eggs, egg yolks, Kansui solution, ¼ cup water, and both oils to the dry ingredients and knead with the dough hook until it comes together and has some elasticity, about 10 minutes. Remove the dough from the mixer and place it on a work surface. Continue kneading the dough by hand for another 10 minutes. Shape the dough into a disk, wrap it in plastic wrap, and chill in the fridge for at least 20 minutes.

To extrude the noodles (I prefer extruding on a spaghetti setting, because I like round noodles), feed the dough into the extruder according to the manufacturer's instructions.

Or you can roll out the noodles with a manual pasta roller or rolling pin until just thinner than spaghetti. Flour the sheets of pasta and fold over each other 4 times. Flour a knife, and then cut the pasta sheets thinner than spaghetti.

Sliced scallions

Fish cakes

Nori strips

Poached eggs

Corn kernels

Sautéed mushrooms

Bamboo shoots

Whatever sounds delicious

What is kansui solution?

Kansui solution is a mix of sodium bicarbonate and potassium carbonate. What this does is make the noodles alkaline. Alkaline noodles turn slightly yellow, and make for a chewier, springier texture, with a distinctive sheen on the outside surface of the noodle.

☞ **Tip**

Before you do anything with hot peppers, put your latex gloves on.

Dust the noodles with flour to keep them from sticking to each other. Divide the noodles into 6 portions.

HOLD IT? You can gently wrap the portioned noodles in plastic wrap. The wrapped noodles can be frozen for up to 2 weeks. The broth and pork belly can be kept in the fridge for up to 3 days.

Finish the soup. Using a big wooden spoon, scrape all of the white fat from the top of the chilled broth and transfer it to a small mixing bowl. Add the Dijon and whisk together vigorously.

Bring the skimmed broth back up to a rolling boil. Carefully use an immersion blender to slowly reincorporate the whipped Dijon-fat mix, bit by bit, back into the broth. Blend each bit until it is thoroughly emulsified. Keep the broth on low heat. Now season the broth with salt to taste.

In a medium pot over high heat, bring 4 cups water, the bonito flakes, and kombu to a boil. Strain into a large bowl; discard the solids and keep the stock in a pot over low heat.

Fill a large pot two-thirds of the way with water, and salt heavily. Bring it to a boil over medium heat. Simultaneously, bring both the pork broth and seaweed stock to just under a boil.

Slice the cooled pork belly and set the slices out on a sheet pan.

The noodles cook very quickly (in less than a minute), and they will continue to cook in the soup, so be sure not to overcook them. If you need to prepare any garnishes, do it now, before you cook the noodles.

Add one portion of noodles at a time to the salted boiling water, using a spaghetti fork, strainer insert, or pasta basket to remove them when just al dente, 30 seconds to 1 minute.

PLATE IT! Transfer the noodles to individual bowls. Quickly torch the pork belly on the sheet pan until warm and slightly dried and add on top of the noodles. Divide the pork broth evenly among the bowls. Add ¼ cup seaweed stock to each bowl and give it a stir, then taste. If the broth is too rich, add more seaweed stock one tablespoon at a time until the ratio is to your liking. Add the same amount of seaweed stock to the remaining bowls. Top the ramen with your garnishes. Devour immediately.

CHEAT IT! If this is too much of a project for you, you can always just make your own broth and use store-bought noodles, or make the noodles and use the broth from packaged ramen. Either way, don't skimp on the garnishes.

BREAK IT: Now that you know how to coax all the flavors out of bones and hocks and bits, make a vegan version. Use the same mustard emulsifying technique to suspend a rich nut oil in a vegetable broth for maximum effectiveness.

---

gear

Dutch oven or heavy-bottomed pot

candy thermometer

small bowls

whisk

chopsticks

small fine-mesh strainer

small pot

2 medium bowls

nonstick pan

rubber spatula

rice cooker (optional; see sidebar page 73)

small saucepan

mixing bowl

bamboo paddle or rubber spatula

electric fan, or a human with a magazine (see sidebar page 86)

ingredients

CRISPY TEMPURA BITS

Vegetable oil, for frying

2 tablespoons all-purpose flour

1 tablespoon rice flour

¼ cup soda water

JAPANESE OMELET

¼ cup water

One 2 x 2-inch piece kombu

2 tablespoons lightly packed bonito flakes

1 tablespoon sugar

1 teaspoon soy sauce

4 large eggs

hand roll party

(COLD FISH)

Hand rolls are the most underrated way to get "sushified," and I don't really understand why. They have much more texture and flavor than the average cut roll, and the filling to vessel ratio is very high. They are like the hot dog of Japan. The key to success is to enjoy a hand roll right after it's made to experience the crunch of the nori, which gets soggy quickly. Here you have some recipes for hand-roll staples—spicy tuna, a Japanese omelet, crispy tempura bits, and, of course, rice—but I wouldn't be upset if you added your own fillings and condiments. It might be sacrilegious, but there isn't much I wouldn't consider putting in a hand roll, as almost anything in this format is good: SPAM, macaroni salad, Cheetos, Twix bars. Of course, the recipe here is entirely flexible. You can cook only the omelet, or skip it entirely; tempura bits are nice to have but not necessary; you can even buy sushi rice from your local spot and go from there.

Make the crispy tempura bits. Fill a Dutch oven with 1 inch of vegetable oil, clip on a candy thermometer, and bring the oil to 350°F over medium heat. Line a plate with paper towels.

Whisk together the flours in a small bowl. Add the soda water and whisk with chopsticks.

Using chopsticks or your fingers, flick bits of the batter into the hot oil and fry until golden brown, 30 seconds to a minute. Remove the bits with a strainer and land on the paper towel–lined plate.

Make the Japanese omelet. To make dashi, combine ¼ cup water, the kombu, bonito flakes, sugar, and soy sauce together in a small pot and bring to a simmer over medium heat, then let simmer about 5 minutes. Strain the dashi over a bowl, pressing against the solids to extract the liquid; discard the solids. Chill the dashi in the freezer to bring it to room temperature, at least 10 minutes.

Using a whisk, beat the eggs in a bowl until very thoroughly combined. Push the eggs through a clean fine-mesh strainer. This makes sure that the egg is totally broken down and smooth. Discard whatever matter does not easily press through.

Gently whisk the cooled dashi into the egg and mix until combined. In a nonstick pan over medium heat, add the dashi and egg mixture. When the edges become opaque, use a rubber spatula to stir once. Let cook through completely and transfer to a plate to cool.

Carefully wrap the omelet in paper towels and then plastic wrap, and refrigerate until cold.

Make the spicy tuna. Finely chop the tuna with a very sharp knife, remembering your goal is to cut rather than mash the tuna. If there is any sinew—thick white membrane sometimes found in fish—gently scrape the tuna meat from it using the back of your knife, and discard the sinew.

Put the tuna and the remaining spicy tuna ingredients in a medium bowl and gently fold them together using a rubber spatula. Cover and refrigerate.

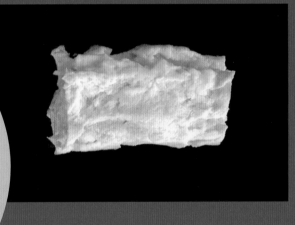

SPICY TUNA

12 ounces (¾ pound)
sushi-grade tuna

1 tablespoon sriracha sauce

1 tablespoon mayonnaise

½ teaspoon chile sesame oil

½ teaspoon kosher salt

Zest of ½ lemon

RICE

2 cups sushi rice

¼ cup unseasoned rice wine
vinegar

¼ cup sugar

1 tablespoon mirin

2 teaspoons kosher salt

GARNISHES

7 to 10 sheets of nori, cut in
half

2 thinly sliced cucumbers
(optional)

1 avocado, peeled, pitted, and
thinly sliced (optional)

Additional raw fish (optional)

Make the rice. Put the rice in a fine-mesh strainer and rinse it under cold running water, rubbing it together with your fingers, until the water runs clear. (It's helpful to do this over a colored mixing bowl so you can see the water.) Allow the washed rice to drain in the strainer.

Cook the washed rice in a rice cooker with the amount of water specified by your rice cooker. (I used 3 cups of water for this amount.) I've never, ever screwed up rice in a rice cooker so long as I cover the rice with water by about an inch. If you don't have a rice cooker (see sidebar page 73), follow the directions on the rice package.

In a small pot over low heat, combine the rice vinegar, sugar, mirin, and salt, and simmer, stirring occasionally, until dissolved, about 3 minutes. Set aside to cool.

Set a large mixing bowl next to a fan or friend—turn on the fan to low or have your friend wave a magazine at the rice. When the rice is done, use a bamboo paddle or spatula to gently remove portions of it from the cooker and spread them out around the inside of the mixing bowl. Removing it in portions exposes more surface area and allows for more rapid cooling. Once all of it is in the bowl, dribble the vinegar onto the paddle or spatula while moving it back and forth a few inches above the rice, so as to thinly and evenly distribute all of the seasoned vinegar over all of the rice. Use the paddle or spatula to gently break up any chunks of rice in "slicing" motions. When the clumps are broken and cease to re-form, you can be sure that all of the rice has been seasoned. The rice should glisten and feel warm, but not hot, to the touch, about 10 minutes. Turn off the fan or dismiss your friend.

Wet your hands with water (the rice is very sticky) and, using your hands, gently transfer the rice to a cooler (which keeps it from getting too cold) or a wooden bowl. Run a clean hand towel under warm water until entirely moistened and cover the rice with it until ready to use, up to 2 hours. If you use a cooler, make sure the lid is closed. If using a wooden bowl, cover with plastic wrap.

Toast the nori. Hold all the sheets of nori in one hand like a fan. Fan the nori over direct heat or flame to toast it until just aromatic. (If the nori changes color dramatically or begins to curl up, it's overtoasted.) Change your grip to the other side of the nori and repeat.

PLATE IT! Slice the omelet into strips.

Lay out platters of the spicy tuna mixture, additional raw fish, cucumbers, avocado, the omelet, the tempura bits, and rice. Lay the nori away from everything else to keep it from getting accidentally moistened. Include a bowl of water for moistening hands, and show your guests how to assemble.

In your nondominant hand, place a sheet of nori with a corner pointed down and a corner between your thumb and pointer finger. Dip your dominant hand in the water, then grab a shooter marble–size to Ping Pong–size ball of rice and spread it from the corner of the nori between your thumb and pointer, down to your palm's corner. This is the landing pad for the ingredients. Working quickly, layer the rest of your desired ingredients in that corner, moving down to the palm. Gently roll the nori around itself like a cone, and use a grain of rice to affix the nori to itself. Devour.

BREAK IT: Grains like quinoa and farro can work in lieu of rice if you are looking to make toastier, more hearty sushi.

STEP YOUR GAME UP

 If you want to do as the Japanese do, make your omelet in an official tamago pan. You can find one in a specialty Japanese store or online. Here's the technique: Use a paper towel and some vegetable oil to grease the tamago pan. Set the pan over the lowest heat and add a very thin layer of egg, just enough to cover the bottom of the pan. Cook until just set on the bottom, about 1 minute. Using a thin spatula and chopsticks, gently lift up the egg at one end of the pan and roll it onto itself, leaving the rolled-up egg at the other end of the pan. Remove the pan from the heat, grease the exposed part of the pan, and add another thin layer of egg to the pan. Put the pan back on low heat, cook the egg until just set, and roll up the egg toward the opposite end, starting with the already rolled-up egg so that it is covered with the newest omelet. Repeat until you run out of egg and are left with a thick log of omelet. Allow to cool.

YIELD Makes 4 servings

PREP TIME 5 minutes

COOK TIME 20 minutes

gear

sheet pan

basting brush

fish spatula (see sidebar page 99)

ingredients

One 20-ounce can pineapple slices in pineapple juice

4 thick cod fillets, about 1¾ pounds total

1 large egg, beaten

Kosher salt

2 ounces pepperoni (I use large charcuterie-style pepperoni, but pizza-size will work)

☞ **Tip**

You might notice throughout this book that I do not always season with both salt and pepper. This is because although we think them siblings or opposites, they do entirely different things. Black pepper has heat, hence the name. In this dish, I don't use pepper because I think the pepperoni does a fine job. In the steak au poivre recipe on page 158, the steak gets a healthy dose. In both cases, "liberal" means that roughly every square centimeter has at least 1 grain of salt or pepper in it. You could get out your jewelers' monocle and check your work, or you could just season knowing that the goal is to get a little salt all over the entire fillet. If you season from higher up, you have a better chance of seasoning evenly.

pepperoni-crusted cod with pineapple

(HOT FISH)

I feel badly for pepperoni. Pepperoni doesn't make it onto fancy charcuterie boards or into uppity dishes at high-end restaurants. It's cured and spiced just like salami and special hams, but is somehow in a different class of meats, often relegated to the sad super-processed section of the supermarket with American cheese. Let's be honest: when we think of pepperoni, we see it in its pizza dungarees. But that's negligent. Pizza is wonderful, but it's not the only way to showcase pepperoni's meaty, salty flavor. This dish was inspired by a legendary dish by Gabriel Kreuther, formerly of the Modern: Chorizo-Crusted Cod with White Bean Purée. The chorizo was bound to the cod with egg, and it looked like little fish scales. Just as Chef Kreuther knew that cod would make for a great canvas to showcase the intensely flavored Spanish chorizo, I also knew pepperoni could shine given a similar setting. Thanks to the insulating power of the pepperoni shingles, the cod stays moist and flaky, and is punched up with a bright ring of nature's ketchup, better known as pineapple.

Preheat the oven to 350°F.

On a sheet pan, assemble 4 stacks of 2 pineapple rings each. Brush the fillets liberally with the beaten egg, and salt liberally. Shingle the pepperoni onto each fillet, overlapping the pepperoni slightly, and pressing down firmly around the fillet to set; each fillet will use 6 to 8 slices. Brush the pepperoni liberally with the remaining egg wash and press firmly again. Place a pepperoni-wrapped fillet on each stack of pineapple. Bake until the fish is flaky and the pepperoni is crisp, about 20 minutes.

PLATE IT! Use a fish spatula to lift the pineapple and cod off the pan together and place directly onto a serving plate.

BREAK IT: Chef Kreuther used to serve his dish with adzuki and cannellini beans. This dish would be bonkers with some of the beans from the bean and kale soup on page 66. Use a slotted spoon to transfer the cooked beans to a small pot, warm them up over low heat, and spoon around the pineapple.

gear

cast-iron skillet

slotted spoon

boning or chef's knife (optional; see sidebar)

mixing bowl

whisk

trivet (see sidebar, page 62)

ingredients

4 ounces slab bacon, cubed

1½- to 2-pound large Cornish hen

Kosher salt

Cracked black pepper

1 tablespoon apple cider vinegar

2 heads frisée, woody ends trimmed, split

Boning vs. fillet knives

A boning knife is a knife that is skinnier than your average kitchen knife, designed to get into the crevices between flesh and bones. The best boning knives also have a thicker side at the hilt, used for cutting through bones. I have a boning knife for chickens and anything larger. For smaller creatures, I use a fillet knife, which is thinner than a boning knife, and is generally flexible to some extent.

cornish hen meets frisée aux lardons

(LIGHT MEAT)

Not many cooks can claim Alton Brown as their mentor. As a matter of fact, I think I'm the only one, and that feels pretty darn good to type. Alton has an encyclopedic knowledge of food and cooking. He can call an *Iron Chef* battle as though it were football. He's creative—he's made multitiered wing steamers, dehydrators from box fans, and condiment caddies from egg cartons. Here, his favorite weeknight protein, the Cornish hen, is amalgamated with one of my favorite salads, frisée aux lardons, to make a skillet-dish for two, which I would be proud to share with him and I believe Alton might like to eat. The Cornish hen serves as a vessel for the cured salty bacon and its fat, with its richness cut by fruity apple cider vinegar and the crunch of frisée.

Preheat the oven to 500°F.

Place the bacon in a cast-iron skillet over medium heat. Rotate the bacon to crisp evenly on all sides and render out lots of fat, turning it about every 2 minutes. Using a slotted spoon, transfer the bacon to paper towels to drain. Take the skillet off the heat, but do not clean it.

Meanwhile, spatchcock the Cornish hen with a boning or chef's knife, removing the wing tips, spine, ribs, and breastbone of the bird while leaving the leg, thigh, and wing bones attached. (You can also ask your butcher to do this for you.)

Liberally season both sides of the bird with salt and cracked pepper.

Heat the skillet over medium-high heat. Place the spatchcocked bird, skin side down, in the rendered bacon fat in the skillet and cook until the skin is browned, 4 to 5 minutes.

Flip the hen in the cast-iron skillet, tranfer to the oven, and roast, uncovered, until a thermometer in the thigh reads 155°F, 10 to 12 minutes. (Bear in mind that the folks at the USDA think 165°F is best.)

While the bird is cooking, measure out the vinegar and ½ teaspoon salt into a mixing bowl.

Remove the bird from the skillet and set aside to rest. Slowly whisk the bacon fat remaining in the skillet into the apple cider vinegar to make a vinaigrette.

Place the frisée in the pan with the bacon, top with the bird, and drizzle with the vinaigrette.

PLATE IT! Serve this right in the cast-iron skillet, on a trivet, and enjoy with Alton Brown (optional).

BREAK IT: Try using an alternative vinegar for a fruitier flavor profile. Lychee vinegar would be crazy!

YIELD Makes 6 chimichangas

PREP TIME 20 minutes

COOK TIME 1 hour 10 minutes

INACTIVE TIME 2 hours to overnight

gear

gallon-size zip-top bag

Dutch oven or heavy-bottomed pot

candy thermometer

colander, plus bowl to fit underneath

tongs

cast-iron skillet

candy thermometer

sheet pan with rack

small bowl

ingredients

VACA FRITA

1 pound flank steak, cut into 2 x 2-inch pieces

4 garlic cloves, crushed

¼ cup fresh lemon juice

3 tablespoons fresh lime juice

1 tablespoon ground cumin

1 tablespoon dried oregano

2 teaspoons chili powder

2 teaspoons kosher salt plus 1 tablespoon

5 tablespoons vegetable oil

12 ounces (about 2) green bell peppers, seeds and ribs removed, cut into ½-inch strips

8 ounces (about ½) large yellow onion, halved and cut into ½-inch slices

2 cups dry red wine

¼ cup torn fresh cilantro leaves

½ cup sour cream

cuban² chimichangas

(Dark meat)

Roast pork, ham, Swiss, and pickles—when it comes to Cuban food, the Cuban sandwich gets all the fame and glory, and rightfully so. It's their own version of the chili-cheese dog, flattened into a crispy brick of delicious.

Vaca frita, "fried cow!"—one of *my* favorite Cuban dishes—is a bit like marinated, pulled pork that has been crisped up in a hot pan, except that it's beef, of course. Replacing the roast pork in a Cuban sandwich with vaca frita didn't seem like such a stretch, so I took it one step further by wrapping up all of these Cuban flavors and ingredients—pickles, mustard, Swiss, ham—into a tortilla and frying it, making a Cuban² chimichanga. "Chimichanga" has become a verb in my life. Look at the world around you, and ask, "Can I chimichanga that?" Generally, the answer is a mouthwatering yes.

Make the vaca frita. Combine the flank steak, garlic cloves, lemon juice, lime juice, cumin, oregano, chili powder, and the 2 teaspoons salt in a zip-top bag. Seal the bag and refrigerate for at least 1 hour, or up to overnight.

Preheat the oven to 350°F.

In a Dutch oven over medium-high heat, heat 2 tablespoons of the oil. Remove the pieces of flank steak from the marinade and pat dry with paper towels; discard the marinade. Sear the pieces of flank steak about 1 minute per side in the hot oil and remove from the pan. Add the bell peppers and onion and cook until most of the moisture has evaporated, 4 to 5 minutes. Add the wine, cilantro, remaining 1 tablespoon salt, and the seared meat back to the pan. Cook with the lid on until the meat is fork-tender, about 45 minutes.

Pour the entire braise through a colander with a bowl underneath to catch the braising liquid. Use the tongs to separate the meat from the veggies and set aside to cool. Once the meat is cool enough to handle, shred it with two forks. Reserve 4 tablespoons of the braising liquid and mix with the sour cream to make the crema. Discard the rest of the braising liquid.

HOLD IT? Keep the meat, veggies, and braising liquid–sour cream mixture in separate containers in the fridge for up to 3 days.

Heat the remaining 3 tablespoons oil in a cast-iron skillet over medium-high heat. Add half of the shredded meat and cook, turning occasionally, until it is crispy and seared, about 5 minutes. Transfer to a plate. Repeat with the remainder of the meat.

Add all your vegetables to the same skillet and cook until hot.

Make the chimichangas. Fill a Dutch oven with an inch of oil, clip on a candy thermometer, and heat over high heat until the oil reaches 375°F. Preheat the oven to 200°F.

CHIMICHANGAS

Vegetable oil, for frying

Six 10-inch flour tortillas

6 tablespoons whole-grain mustard

8 ounces thinly sliced Swiss cheese (about 18 slices)

8 ounces thinly sliced deli ham (about 18 slices)

6 ounces dill pickles, thinly sliced

¼ cup fresh cilantro leaves (optional)

Gather all of the chimichanga components. Lay a tortilla on your cutting board and build the chimichanga: first spread on 1 tablespoon of the mustard, then evenly layer 3 slices cheese, 3 slices ham, a few pickle slices, and some of the crispy meat and veggies. Roll the tortilla into a burrito (see below) and, using water and your fingers, wet the edge of the tortilla and press like an envelope to help it seal. Using tongs, place a chimichanga, seam side down, in the hot oil and fry until golden brown, flipping once, about 1 minute on each side. Transfer the fried chimichanga to a rack on a sheet pan and place in the oven to keep warm. Continue assembling and frying the chimichangas.

PLATE IT! Cut the hot chimichangas on the bias, stack 'em up, drizzle with crema, and sprinkle with fresh cilantro.

CHEAT IT! Use shredded leftover pot roast or grilled steak instead of the finished vaca frita.

BREAK IT: To max out the "Cubanness" of this dish, do not fold the braising liquid into the sour cream. Instead make 1 mojito (see page 222, minus the ice and soda water), cook it in a small pot for a few minutes to burn off the alcohol, cool it, and fold that liquid into the sour cream instead.

SAUCE ZONE WHEN APPLICABLE

TOPSIDE

UNDERSIDE

YIELD Makes 1 giant banana split (traditionally serves 2, but might serve 4 with less indulgence) with plenty of ice cream and sorbet left to do it again

PREP TIME 30 minutes

COOK TIME 20 minutes

INACTIVE TIME 24 hours plus, depending on your ice cream machine

gear

ice cream machine, insert bowl frozen ahead of time as per manufacturer's instructions

small saucepan

whisk

sealable containers or bowls

food processor

large bowl

medium pot

small pot

strainer or fine-mesh sieve

medium bowl

whisk, egg beater, hand mixer, or cream whipper with N_2O cartridge

small bowl

sheet pan

sifter

culinary torch (optional)

ingredients

VANILLA BEAN SORBET

2 cups water

1½ cups sugar

1 vanilla bean, split lengthwise

½ cup fresh Meyer lemon juice (about 2 Meyer lemons); you can substitute regular lemons

1 ounce vodka

½ teaspoon kosher salt

banana split for sophisticates

(DESSERT)

Visually, the banana is the hot dog of fruits (even great with mustard, as in the amba on page 207), so in this recipe I give it a hot dog treatment with salt, sugar, and some sweet paprika. Like a hot dog, the saltiness of the banana would enhance the ingredients around it, making it ideal for a tricked-out banana split. On top I put spicy chocolate ice cream, fruity strawberry ice cream, sorbet that's practically throwing a vanilla temper tantrum, and then crunchy and bitter cocoa nibs, whipped cream with a hot ginger bite, and toasted coconut. Lastly, I remedy a fault of the split—that when you get somewhere near halfway into it, you are left with a Chiquita raft in a pond of melted ice cream—so I thought to put the whole thing in a sponge in the form of a croissant.

Make the vanilla bean sorbet. Combine 2 cups water, the sugar, and vanilla bean in a small saucepan over low heat. Bring to a simmer and whisk to dissolve the sugar and release the vanilla aroma. When the sugar has completely dissolved, remove the pan from the heat and allow the mixture to cool. Add the lemon juice, vodka, and salt. Scrape the seeds from the bean into the mix; discard the vanilla pod. Transfer the mixture to a sealable container or bowl. Chill the mixture in the freezer until cold, about 1 hour.

Process the cooled mixture into sorbet in the ice cream maker according to the manufacturer's instructions. Transfer the finished sorbet to a container and place in the freezer until ready to serve.

Make the strawberry ice cream. Combine the thawed strawberries and sugar in the food processor. Blend until smooth and the sugar has dissolved. Add the cream, milk, and salt and pulse to combine. Transfer the mixture to a sealable container or bowl. Chill the mixture in the freezer until cold, about 1 hour.

Process the cooled mixture into ice cream in the ice cream maker according to the manufacturer's instructions. Transfer the finished ice cream to a container and place in the freezer until firm and ready to serve.

Make the chipotle chocolate ice cream. In a large bowl, whisk together the egg yolks, then, still whisking, gradually add the sugar to the yolks and whisk until the sugar has dissolved. Set aside.

In a medium pot over low heat, whisk together the cream, milk, cocoa powder, adobo liquid, and salt. Bring to a simmer, then remove from the heat. While whisking, slowly add small amounts of the cream mixture to the egg-sugar mixture to slowly heat up the eggs; otherwise we will have chocolate egg-drop soup. (Note to self: make that for next cookbook!) Once half of the warm cream mixture has been incorporated, add the rest of the warm mixture while still whisking. Transfer the mixture back to the pot and cook over low heat about 3 minutes, until just warm, stirring constantly. Transfer the mixture to a sealable container or bowl. Put the mixture in the fridge to cool, uncovered, for about 1 hour, then chill in the freezer until cold, about 1 hour.

Process the cooled mixture into ice cream in the ice cream maker according to the manufacturer's instructions. Transfer the finished ice cream to a container and place in the freezer until firm and ready to serve.

STRAWBERRY ICE CREAM

10 ounces frozen strawberries, thawed and drained

¾ cup sugar

1½ cups heavy cream

½ cup whole milk

1 teaspoon kosher salt

CHIPOTLE CHOCOLATE ICE CREAM

8 large egg yolks

1 cup sugar

2 cups heavy cream

2 cups whole milk

½ cup unsweetened cocoa powder

2 tablespoons liquid from a can of chipotles in adobo

1 teaspoon kosher salt

GINGER WHIPPED CREAM

1 cup heavy cream

One 1-inch knob fresh ginger, peeled and then grated on a microplane

1 tablespoon confectioners' sugar

TORCHED BANANAS

1 tablespoon sugar

1 teaspoon kosher salt

1 teaspoon paprika

1 almond croissant

4 Luxardo cherries (see sidebar page 136)

1 tablespoon cocoa nibs

1 tablespoon unsweetened toasted coconut flakes

Make the ginger whipped cream. Combine the cream and ginger in a small pot and bring to a simmer over medium heat. Remove from the heat and strain through a fine-mesh strainer into a medium bowl; discard the ginger. Chill in the refrigerator at least 2 hours.

Whisk in the confectioners' sugar. Whip the mixture with a whisk, an egg beater, using a stand or hand mixer, or using a cream whipper with one N_2O cartridge.

HOLD IT? Keep the ice cream and sorbet in the freezer. Specially designed ice cream containers (or even reused old ice cream cartons) prevent freezer burn. The whipped cream can be made a day in advance and stored in the fridge. I like to torch the banana within 10 minutes of serving to keep the sugar warm and crackly, but if necessary you can do it up to an hour in advance.

Torch the bananas. Combine the sugar, salt, and paprika in a small bowl. On a sheet pan, split the bananas lengthwise and, using a fine sifter, dust the cut side liberally with the sugar mixture. Torch the sugar mixture with a culinary torch or under the broiler until it is bubbling and brown.

PLATE IT! Split the croissant, leaving the two halves attached. Place it in a long bowl or even a plate. Place a scoop of the vanilla into the center, followed by the strawberry on one side and the chocolate on the other. Slide the banana along each side of the scoops. Top with whipped cream in large peaks. Add a cherry to every pile of whipped cream, then sprinkle the whole thing with cocoa nibs and coconut flakes until you feel unworthy. Devour with a sophisticated date.

CHEAT IT! You can use whatever store-bought ice cream you like instead of making your own. You can also not make homemade ginger whipped cream and instead use store-bought plain whipped cream and top the sundae with a little chopped candied ginger.

BREAK IT: You could add the wasabi marshmallows from page 210 to deliver some mustardy bite to this confectionary hot dog.

STEP YOUR GAME UP

Make sparkling ginger whipped cream by charging your cream whipper with both a N_2O cartridge and a CO_2 cartridge.

What are Luxardo Cherries?
Luxardo cherries are what those neon "maraschino" cherries are supposed to be. Luxardo makes actual maraschino liqueur from actual Marasca cherries from Croatia. They are very sophisticated, and are used in fancy cocktail bars these days. Don't get me wrong though, I think there's a time and place for those neon-colored cherries, mostly in Shirley Temples or when you want to feel like a kid again. For most Americans that weren't born before Prohibition, those neon bombs are synesthetically synonymous with happiness and good times. That's convenient, because the FDA doesn't consider them to be an actual "food"— they are considered a garnish, like a plastic sword or a tiki umbrella. Don't try eating those, though.

LAW
OF THE
WEDGE
SALAD

funky meets fresh

t's like flowahs and gahbudge." The wedge salad is like Jennifer Lawrence's nail polish in *American Hustle*—something lovely, but something off as well. It's an addictive olfactory game of cat and mouse in your mouth. In the instance of the wedge salad, iceberg lettuce and tomatoes duke it out with blue cheese and bacon. Eating it is like having *My Fair Lady* performed on your tongue. That crisp, fresh lettuce and bright acidic tomato want nothing more than to give that homely blue cheese a scrub and that bawdy bacon a bath. Fowl, aged beef, porky pork, stinky cheese, gamey game, fishy fish, and musky melons—these flavors are the George Clinton of the flavor spectrum: they are funky, and that's not a bad thing. The law of the wedge salad and the subsequent recipes prove that with some fresh, bright counterbalance, "funky" is the key to fun.

funky meets fresh

SEA URCHIN	MINTED SAKE SEA SHOOTERS	MINT / LIME
DUCK	OPEN-FACED DUCK SALAD SANDWICHES ON A GIANT SESAME PANCAKE	CILANTRO
LAMB BREAST	LAMB BREAST WITH CORIANDER, CUMIN, AND LIME	CILANTRO / LIME
CANTALOUPE	COLD CANTALOUPE SOUP WITH PEAS AND MINT	YOGURT / MINT
CLAMS	CLAM CHOWDER WITH CELERIAC AND PARSNIP	CELERIAC / PARSNIP
SARDINES	SARDINES, THEIR SKELETONS, AND SUMAC	CUCUMBER / SUMAC
MACKEREL	MACKEREL WITH SWEET POTATO AND CHIMICHURRI	CHIMICHURRI
SQUAB	SQUAB WITH CUTE VEGETABLES AND GINGER	GINGER
DRY-AGED RIB EYE	DRY-AGED RIB EYE AU POIVRE	GREEN PEPPERCORNS
BLUE CHEESE	BLUE CHEESECAKE WITH FRANK'S REDHOT CARAMEL	LIME ZEST

YIELD Makes 8 big gulps

PREP TIME 15 minutes

gear

blender

fine-mesh strainer or chinois
(see sidebar page 37)

oyster shucking knife with oyster
box (see sidebar opposite)

ingredients

MINTED SAKE

One 300-ml bottle ice-cold
junmai sake

½ cup loosely packed fresh mint
leaves (about 30 mint leaves)

1½ teaspoons fresh lime juice

SHOOTERS

8 cold raw oysters

1¾ ounces cold salmon roe

8 "tongues" cold sea urchin

Sake-to-Me

Sake is essentially a flat rice beer, not
a rice wine. Wine comes from grapes,
which means it comes from fruits.
Beer comes from grain, of which rice
is. It gets put into the wine category
because of its potency, which generally
hovers around 15 to 20 percent. There
are many styles of sake from different
places in Japan and the world. Mostly,
it comes down to the kind of rice
used, and how much of the rice husk
is polished away to make the sake. The
more the rice is polished, (generally)
the better the flavor, but the more
rice is needed to produce a bottle.
The best sakes polish away more
than half of the rice. These are called
Junmai Daiginjo. Most sake should be
consumed cold or cool. Warming sake
is generally reserved for the winter, or
when the sake is so poorly made that
its off-flavors are masked by the heat. I
still drink it, though.

minted sake sea shooters

(Canapé/snack)

Sea urchin is very high up on my list of "polarizing" ingredients. What, the
idea of consuming the possibly hermaphroditic gonads of what looks like a
living medieval torture device isn't appealing to you? Listen, I feel you, but if
you go into it knowing what you are going to get, you won't be *surprised* by the
unusual texture and flavor, you'll be amazed by it. The Japanese classify foods
like sea urchin as *chinmi,* which means "rare taste," much more appropriate
than our calling it a mere delicacy. Sea urchin tastes like low tide smells, with a
trace of honeysuckle and nickel. If you are looking for a funky taste, sea urchin
fits the bill nicely. Paired in a shot glass with the almost cheeselike taste of
salmon roe, these bits from the sea benefit from a little freshening up before its
romp with an oyster in your mouth. Don't get me wrong, I've eaten sea urchin
straight from the ocean, but the cold, cold sake and refreshing mint make this
amuse-bouche shot suitable for anyone who enjoys seafood.

Make the minted sake. In a blender, add the sake, mint, and lime juice and
process on high for about 1 minute, until supersmooth. Strain and refrigerate
until ready to use.

PLATE IT! Clean, then open up your oysters (see sidebar opposite). Plunk each one with
their liquor (the flavorful liquid inside the shell) in a big shot glass and top with portions
of salmon roe and sea urchin. Divide all of the minted sake among the shot glasses.
Serve immediately, filling your mouth with the glass's contents in one fell swoop.

BREAK IT: Grating up some daikon radish to make a "snow" and then freezing it would
make for a nifty way to keep these cool, not to mention add a little zippy zap of sharpness to the mix.

Shuck U

Shucking oysters isn't very hard, it's just very dangerous. Slippery, easily chipped, and oddly shaped, oysters are practically designed to not just foil our attempts at obtaining their liquidy lucre lurking inside, but also to maim us for trying.

Most cooks show up to an oyster knife fight with a towel. They wrap the towel around their hand to help steady the oyster and provide a soft surface to grip. Still, if the knife slips or the shell shatters, a towel is only minimally more resistant to stabs and cuts than your bare hand. This I can forgive, but towels also absorb precious oyster liquor, and require constant changing during marathon shuck fests.

Enter the oyster shucking kit, made in France. It consists of a wooden box, with a little lip that will sit right on your cutting board or counter, which both holds the oyster, practically cementing it in place, and keeps your hands shielded from penetration. These little kits also include a special knife. They cost about fifteen bucks on the Internet. To use, place the flat side of the oyster face up in the box, with the hinge closest to you. Slowly and forcibly wiggle the flat side of the knife into the hinge of the oyster, then twist to pop open the shell. Scrape the knife under the top shell and along the bottom of the bottom shell to release the oyster. Remove from the box and discard the top shell.

YIELD Makes 32 servings

PREP TIME 35 minutes

COOK TIME 4 hours

gear

very sharp knife (see Tip on page 33)

baking dish

blender, spice grinder, or mortar and pestle

small bowl

basting brush

small pot

large mixing bowls

heating pad (optional)

rolling pin

10-inch stainless-steel skillet (or larger)

whisk

toothpick

wire cooling rack

serrated knife

ingredients

DUCK

1 whole Pekin duck, about 6 pounds

1 cinnamon stick

2 star anise pods

5 whole cloves

1 cup molasses

½ cup tamari

¼ cup water

PICKLED VEGGIES

½ cucumber, seeds removed, julienned

3 small carrots, peeled and julienned

¼ cup rice wine vinegar

½ cup water

1 teaspoon sugar

1 teaspoon kosher salt

open-faced duck salad sandwiches on a giant sesame pancake

(COLD APP)

My girlfriend turned me on to a joint called Vanessa's, a dumpling house with a few locations in NYC. Sometimes we'll hop on her metallic mint Vespa and grab some lunch before one of us heads to work. My favorite menu item is the sesame pancake sandwich with duck. Every time I eat one I can't help analyzing the flavor, trying to figure out what's going on in every miraculous bite. Simple pickled vegetables and a few leaves of cilantro are the bright and fresh counterweight to an intensely flavored, funky shredded duck, all packaged up in a crispy/crunchy/chewy thick scallion pancake. (If you are short on time, you can skip the pancake and serve this sandwich style between two slices of your favorite bread.) As opposed to the recipe on page 32, this recipe isn't about a perfectly crisped duck skin. Here, the skin and fat provide the silky texture of a dressed salad, without any dressing at all. One could easily slice the entire pancake in half and put the fillings inside like a giant Chinese panino, but I think they make an exceptionally noteworthy hors d'oeuvre, portioned into tiny triangles.

Make the duck. Preheat the oven to 300°F. Remove the giblets and trim off excess skin around the neck and rear cavity and discard. Rinse the duck under cool water and pat dry with paper towels. Carefully crosshatch the skin, avoiding cutting through to the meat. Place the duck, breast side up, in a baking dish and roast for 3½ hours.

Meanwhile, use a blender, spice grinder, or mortar and pestle to pulverize the cinnamon, star anise, and cloves. Make the glaze by combining the molasses, tamari, pulverized spice mix, and ¼ cup water in a small bowl.

Using a basting brush, coat the roasted duck with half the glaze. Return the duck to the oven and roast for an additional 30 minutes. Remove the duck from the oven and allow to cool.

Once cooled, pull the meat and skin off the bones and shred with two forks or your fingers; discard the bones.

Make the pickled veggies. Line up all the julienned vegetables on a cutting board and roughly chop into shorter pieces, about 2 inches long, and put them all in a medium bowl.

In a small pot over low heat, heat the vinegar, ½ cup water, the sugar, and salt until dissolved. Pour the hot brine over the vegetables to quick pickle them, and let them sit for at least 1 hour, transferring to the refrigerator once they are at room temperature.

Make the pancake. Combine 2 cups warm water with the sugar, yeast, and salt in a large bowl. Gradually add the flour to the middle of the bowl, and stir to combine.

Once the dough becomes a cohesive mass, flip it out onto a clean, lightly floured work surface and knead until firm and elastic. Dust a little flour in another clean bowl, add the dough, cover tightly with plastic wrap, and let rise in a

GIANT SESAME PANCAKE

2 cups warm water

2 tablespoons sugar

1 tablespoon active dry yeast

1 tablespoon kosher salt

4 cups bread flour, plus a little more for dusting

Olive oil nonstick cooking spray

3 scallions, thinly sliced

2 tablespoons olive oil

¼ cup black sesame seeds

Fresh cilantro leaves

warm place or on a heating pad set on the lowest setting (see doughnut recipe on page 48) until doubled in size, about 1 hour.

Flour the work surface once again and, working with well-floured hands, turn out the risen dough. Knead for a few turns. Then, using a rolling pin, roll the dough into a 10-inch round about ¾ inch thick. Lightly spray the top with the cooking spray and scatter the scallions on it, leaving a ½-inch border around the edge.

Grab the edge closest to you, and tightly roll up the dough (like cinnamon buns or a jelly roll), pinching the ends with each rotation to ensure it says together. Once it has been rolled up, coil the rolled up dough around itself into a circle. Roll out the circle again into a 10-inch disk (or the size of your biggest pan).

Preheat your largest pan over low heat with the oil until it shimmers.

Place the dough in the pan, generously brush the entire surface of the dough with the glaze, then sprinkle with half of the sesame seeds. Cook, undisturbed, until lightly toasted, about 5 minutes. Flip, then generously glaze the other side and sprinkle with the remaining sesame seeds. Now that both sides are seared, cover and continue cooking the pancake on the lowest heat, flipping and reglazing every 10 minutes, until an inserted toothpick comes out clean, about 40 minutes in total. Transfer the pancake to a wire rack to cool.

HOLD IT? The cooled duck meat will hold for up to 3 days, covered, in the refrigerator. The pickles will keep, refrigerated, for up to a month. The pancake can be kept in the fridge, wrapped tightly in plastic wrap, for up to 2 days. Before proceeding, set the duck and pancake out to return to room temperature.

Assemble the dish. Use a serrated knife to slice the pancake in half. Cut each half into 16 wedges. Top the glazed side of each pancake wedge with duck, cold pickles, and a few leaves of cilantro.

PLATE IT! These guys look real nice on long plates pointing in opposite directions. Pass them around!

BREAK IT: Try smearing a bit of the Jasmine Chicken Liver Pâté (page 290) on the scallion pancakes before topping with the duck and veggies to make a banh mi–inspired snack.

YIELD Makes 6 servings

PREP TIME 10 minutes

COOK TIME 6 hours 10 minutes

_____

gear

blender, spice grinder, or mortar and pestle

2 sheet pans (one with rack)

_____

ingredients

LAMB

2 tablespoons whole coriander seeds

¼ cup whole cumin seeds

¼ cup whole black peppercorns

¼ cup kosher salt

One 5-pound lamb breast (if your butcher doesn't carry it, ask! It's a great cheap cut, and you can start the trend!)

GARNISH

2 limes, cut into wedges

Chopped fresh culantro or cilantro

_____

☞ **Tip**

If you have the grill already going for other items, feel free to finish the lamb on the grill instead of in the hot oven—the hot grill grates will add some nice scorch.

lamb breast with coriander, cumin, and lime

(HOT APP)

My buddy George McNeese and I used to be roommates long before we opened Do or Dine. We were generally broke as a joke, preferring to spend our tip money on beer and video games. One day we were feeling fancy, so we went to the store and found these giant slabs of "lamb breast," a huge hunk of tough, fatty meat on a smattering of bones, for the waiter-friendly price of something like $2.00 a pound. We grabbed them up. We had a good idea of the flavors we wanted to use to counterbalance the gaminess of the lamb—coriander and earthy cumin, tangy lime and refreshing cilantro to finish—but because we were just waiters at the time, we had no idea how to cook it. We blasted it with heat and it turned out to be chewy and weird. Then, another day, we tried a low temp, played some Wii Golf, drank some beers, and forgot about the time. Six hours later the place was dripping with aromas, and the recipe below was born.

_____

Make the lamb. Preheat the oven to 250°F.

Combine the coriander seeds, cumin seeds, and peppercorns in a blender, spice grinder, or mortar and pestle and grind into medium-fine powder. Stir in the salt until incorporated.

Rub the entire lamb breast with the spice mix. If there is any left over after you've coated every crevice, save it for next time or try adding it to popcorn. Put the lamb, fat side up, on a sheet pan fitted with a rack and roast until the bones slide out easily and the meat is supertender, about 6 hours. Remove the lamb from the oven and remove and discard the rib bones while the meat is warm. Let rest for at least 15 minutes.

_____

HOLD IT? The lamb will keep in the fridge for up to 5 days.

_____

Increase the oven temperature to 450°F.

Portion cooled lamb into rectangular pieces. The thickness may vary, but that's okay. Place the lamb pieces in a single layer on a sheet pan and roast until browned and crisp, about 10 minutes.

_____

PLATE IT! I like to serve these guys in a big pile for people to grab. Garnish with the lime wedges and the culantro or cilantro.

_____

BREAK IT: If you can't find lamb breast, use this same rub and technique on lamb shanks, though they won't be as rich or fatty.

_____

YIELD Makes 4 servings

PREP TIME 10 minutes

COOK TIME 10 minutes

INACTIVE TIME 1 to 2 hours

gear

blender

2 bowls

ingredients

SOUP

2 cantaloupes (about 2½ pounds total)

2 teaspoons kosher salt

¼ cup loosely packed fresh mint leaves, roughly chopped

YOGURT-PEA PURÉE

1 cup plain Greek yogurt

1 cup frozen green peas, thawed

¼ teaspoon kosher salt

¼ cup olive oil, for serving

cold cantaloupe soup with peas and mint

(COLD SOUP)

Summers in Maryland, where I grew up, were marked by the arrival of corn and peaches, as they are up and down the Atlantic seaboard, but also by an onslaught of Eastern Shore cantaloupes. My grandparents taught me to sprinkle salt on the ridge of the giant orange smile-shaped wedges. The salt would make it taste sweeter, which really blew my mind. One time we got some cantaloupes from a family friend and forgot about them in the trunk of the car. The smell was so pungent and intoxicating when we opened the trunk later in the afternoon that I will have that olfactory memory in my melon forever. Cantaloupe's sweet muskiness is often paired with salty prosciutto, with its gentle echoing funk, but you can head in the other direction. In this cold soup, the fresh flavors of peas, yogurt, and mint add some elegance and brightness to the cantaloupe funk.

Make the soup. Cut the melons into wedges, and remove the rind and the seeds.

Put the wedges in a blender with the salt and blend until smooth. Add the mint and pulse just to break up the leaves. Refrigerate the mixture in a bowl until cold, at least 1 hour.

Make the yogurt-pea purée. Rinse out the blender and add the yogurt, peas, and salt. Blend until mostly puréed. Refrigerate in a bowl until cold.

HOLD IT? The cantaloupe and yogurt-pea mixtures will both keep, refrigerated, for up to 3 days.

In your blender, combine the oil and the chilled cantaloupe mixture and blend.

PLATE IT! Pour the cantaloupe soup into bowls and add a drizzle of the yogurt-pea purée.

PARTY ON! This would make a fun soup shooter in Dixie cups on a hot summer day. The recipe makes about twenty 2-ounce portions.

BREAK IT: This would also be fun garnished with a slaw of thinly sliced raw cabbage, just to add bite and texture.

YIELD Makes 6 servings

PREP TIME 15 minutes

COOK TIME 30 minutes

gear

sheet pan

deep heavy-bottomed pot

slotted spoon

immersion blender or blender

ladle

ingredients

6 parsnips (about ¾ pound), peeled and cut into ½-inch dice

½ celeriac (about ½ pound), peeled and cut into ½-inch dice

2 tablespoons olive oil

18 Littleneck clams (about 1½ pounds in shells), scrubbed

4 strips bacon, cut into ¼-inch strips

1 large yellow onion, cut into ½-inch dice

5 medium potatoes (about 1½ pounds), peeled and cut into ½-inch dice

2 cups whole milk

Four 6½-ounce cans chopped clams in clam juice

Kosher salt (see Note)

Fresh tarragon leaves, for garnish (optional)

☞ **Note**

Clams and bacon have a ton of salt in them already, and vary dramatically. Normally I'll tell you what I think is a good amount of salt; here, though, you should play it by mouth.

clam chowder with celeriac and parsnip

(Hot soup)

I used to eat clam chowder at Friendly's in the mall when I was still sitting in booster seats. I love clam chowder, and I think pretty much everyone else should as well. I use a mix of canned clams for a big boost of funky flavor and whole roasted clams for visual appeal and true sea brininess. For a fun trompe l'oeil effect, puréed potatoes and milk thicken the soup instead of cream, and cubes of super-fresh-tasting roasted celeriac and parsnip stand in for the standard potatoes. This recipe is also pretty quick, and freezes nicely for those "I-forgot-to-buy-groceries-before-the-blizzard" moments.

Preheat the oven to 400°F.

Toss the parsnips and celeriac with the oil and spread out in a single layer on a sheet pan. Add the fresh clams to the sheet pan. Roast until the clams have opened, 10 to 12 minutes.

Meanwhile, start the chowder base. Preheat a deep heavy-bottomed pot over medium-low heat. Add the bacon and cook until most of the fat has rendered, about 8 minutes. Using a slotted spoon, transfer the bacon to paper towels to drain; leave the bacon fat in the pot. Add the onion to the fat in the pot and cook, stirring occasionally, until translucent, about 8 minutes. Add the potatoes and milk to the pot and bring to a boil. Reduce the heat to a simmer and cook until the potatoes are fork-tender, about 10 minutes. Working carefully, use an immersion blender to blend the chowder base, or transfer it to a blender in batches and process until smooth, adding it back into the pot as you go.

Add the canned clams and juice, whole clams in their shells, and roasted parsnips and celeriac. Bring to a simmer and season with salt to taste.

HOLD IT? The finished soup will keep in the fridge for 3 days, but you shouldn't reheat it more than once, so I recommend trying to serve this in one go and freezing the leftovers for up to a month.

PLATE IT! Use a ladle to fish out a couple of the clams for each bowl, crumble the bacon, then top the chowder with the bacon crumbles and tarragon, if you desire.

BREAK IT: Ladle off some of the liquid from the finished chowder and mix it with wasabi powder. Drizzle this back over the chowder. The wasabi will put the clam flavors in check and bring out the sweetness of the parsnips and celeriac.

YIELD Makes 4 appetizer portions

PREP TIME 45 minutes

COOK TIME 20 minutes

INACTIVE TIME 1 hour

gear

grater

small bowl

paring knife or small offset spatula

medium bowl

sheet pan

large sauté pan

candy thermometer

spatula or fish spatula (see sidebar page 99)

baking dish

skillet

ingredients

YOGURT SAUCE

1 hothouse cucumber (about 14 ounces)

½ cup plain Greek yogurt

2 teaspoons sumac (see sidebar page 153)

¼ teaspoon kosher salt

SARDINES

8 fresh whole sardines, cleaned, gutted, and scaled (by the fishmonger, if you like)

2 to 3 cups olive oil

4 garlic cloves, smashed

Kosher salt, for seasoning the skeletons

Fleur de sel, for finishing

sardines, their skeletons, and sumac

(Cold fish)

As the food of cartoon cats, sardines get a bad rap. But they are good for humans to eat too. Fresh, oily sardines have a rich sea funk that I put in check with zippy Greek yogurt, cool cucumbers, and sour-tasting sumac. Plus, sardines are unique in that they have a potential textural element built in. Enter the "potato chips of the sea": fried sardine skeletons. Here, they provide salty crispiness and eye-popping visual appeal.

Make the yogurt sauce. Using the largest holes on a grater, grate approximately one-fourth of the cucumber into a small bowl. Mix in the yogurt, sumac, and salt and set aside. Reserve the remaining cucumber.

Prep the sardines and skeletons. With a paring knife, cut one slit along the belly all the way from behind the sardines' gill flaps to the tails. (There will already be a partial cut where your fishmonger cleaned them out.) Wash away any scales or blood line.

Using a paring knife, separate the skeleton from the fillet by placing the tip of the knife between the spine and the bottom fillet, carefully threading the dull side of the knife under the first few bones, and gently pulling upward to separate them from the fillet. Flip the sardine over and repeat on the other side. Carefully pinch the neck of the fish and run your fingers along the spine to release the rest of the fillet from the spine. Make a cut above the tail and behind the back of the head to release the spine, which will still have the head and tail attached to it. Repeat with the remaining sardines. Set the skeletons aside in a bowl, cover, and chill.

Trim away and clean up the dark area on the outside edge of the fillet. Fold the fillet lengthwise, and use the knife to cut out the tiny spines left from the dorsal fin. Lay the fillet flat, skin side up, on a sheet pan and refrigerate. Repeat this entire process with all the remaining sardines, carefully adding the fillets to the sheet pan, not touching, and collecting the skeletons in the bowl in the fridge.

Make the sardines. Fill a sauté pan with 1 inch of oil. Add the garlic to the oil. Clip a thermometer onto the side of the sauté pan. Over low heat, bring the oil to 160°F.

Working in batches, and using a fish spatula, carefully lower the sardine fillets into the oil, skin side up, making sure they do not touch or overlap. Cook until the flesh is opaque, carefully checking the underside of the fillets, and the edges are curved ever so slightly, 5 to 8 minutes. Transfer the fillets to a baking dish and refrigerate immediately. Cook and refrigerate the remaining fillets.

Allow the oil to cool to room temperature, discard the garlic, and cover the chilled fillets with the oil. Cover the oil-covered fish with plastic wrap and refrigerate. The oil keeps the fillets moist and preserves their integrity.

HOLD IT? Freeze the skeletons and hold the cooked fillets in the oil in the fridge until ready to serve; up to 4 days. The yogurt sauce will keep in the refrigerator, covered, for up to a week.

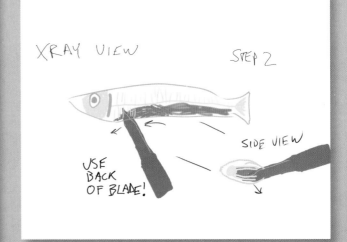

XRAY VIEW STEP 1

DON'T CUT THROUGH THE SPINE!

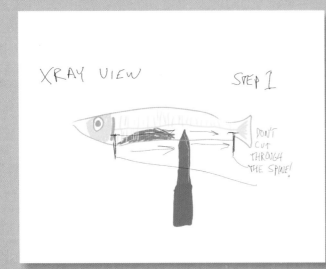

XRAY VIEW STEP 2

USE BACK OF BLADE!

SIDE VIEW

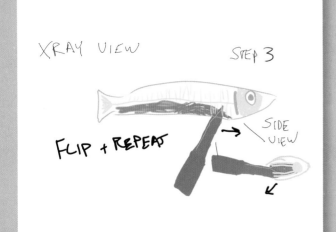

XRAY VIEW STEP 3

FLIP + REPEAT

SIDE VIEW

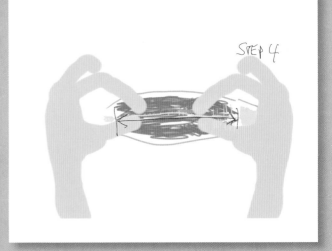

STEP 4

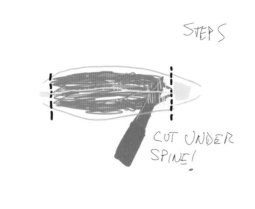

STEP 5

CUT UNDER SPINE!

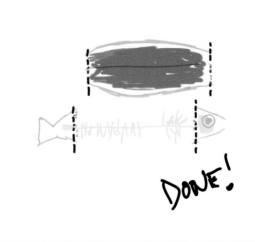

DONE!

Fry the skeletons. If needed, thaw the sardine skeletons. Bring the sardines to room temperature. Transfer the sardines to a plate, and return the oil to a skillet with the thermometer. Bring the oil to 350°F. Line a sheet pan with paper towels.

Very thinly slice the remaining cucumber and divide it into 8 portions.

Working in batches, carefully add the fish skeletons to the oil and fry until golden and crispy, about 3 minutes. Remove from the oil, transfer to the prepared sheet pan, and, while still hot, sprinkle with a little kosher salt.

PLATE IT! Place two spoon swooshes (drop a spoonful and swoosh it with the back of a spoon) of the yogurt sauce on the plate, like a bottom-heavy X. Lay down one portion of the cucumber slices, overlapping them slightly. Place 2 of the room-temperature fillets on top of the cucumbers and sauce, then sprinkle with a little fleur de sel. Top with the skeletons and serve.

BREAK IT: Some shaved raw turnips would add a spicy bite to kick around the rich yogurt and assertive sardines.

YIELD Makes 4 servings

PREP TIME 20 minutes

COOK TIME 15 minutes

gear

food processor

small saucepan

large bowl

grill pan

spatula or fish spatula (see
sidebar page 99)

ingredients

CHIMICHURRI

1½ cups loosely packed fresh
flat-leaf parsley leaves

½ cup loosely packed fresh
cilantro

1 garlic clove, minced

2 tablespoons rice wine
vinegar

1 teaspoon grated lemon zest

2 tablespoons fresh lemon
juice

1 teaspoon kosher salt

¼ teaspoon crushed red
pepper flakes

½ cup olive oil

SWEET POTATOES

1 tablespoon kosher salt

One 14-ounce sweet potato,
peeled and cut into ½-inch
slices

MACKEREL

4 mackerel fillets (about
1 pound total), pinbones
removed

Olive oil

mackerel with sweet potato and chimichurri

(Hot fish)

When I worked at Sushi JeJu in Fort Collins, Colorado, the boss, Brian Yoo, would often invite me to his house for a Korean feast prepared by his mother. Sometimes fifteen distinct dishes, or more, would be piled onto a table on the floor. She'd hand me a bowl of rice and crunch her fist at me to encourage me to eat it all. Grandma, as we called her, got a kick out of watching me eat specialties like mackerel and sweet potatoes smothered in gochujang, or perilla leaves soaked in sesame oil. Brian would brokenly translate what his mother said in Korean about me: that I didn't look Korean, but ate like a Korean. That was surely an endorsement. The dish below is an homage to Grandma, and rather than compounding the fishy, earthy flavors of the mackerel with chile paste, I've added the fresh flavors of chimichurri.

Make the chimichurri. Pulse together all the ingredients for the chimichurri, except for the oil, in a food processor until finely ground. With the machine still running, slowly stream in the oil until emulsified.

Cook the sweet potato. Bring a saucepan halfway full of water to a boil and add the salt. Add the sweet potato slices to the pan and simmer for 7 minutes, or until almost cooked through. Drain the potatoes, then immediately shock in a large bowl of cold water to keep them from overcooking. Drain again and put them on a paper towel–lined plate to dry.

HOLD IT? The chimichurri and parcooked sweet potatoes can be kept in the fridge for up to 3 days.

Make the mackerel. Preheat a grill pan or outdoor grill to high heat. Season both sides of each fillet very liberally with salt.

Oil the grill pan or grill. Sear the fish, skin side down, to get the skin crispy, about 4 minutes; do not move the fillets until then or they could break apart. Using a spatula or fish spatula, and moving it in the same direction as the grill grates so it doesn't break the fish, flip and grill the flesh side for an additional 3 minutes.

Simultaneously, grill the sweet potato just to finish the cooking and obtain some grill marks and scorch flavors, about 3 minutes on each side.

PLATE IT! On each of four plates, lay down 3 pieces of sweet potato, place the fish fillet atop, and drizzle with the chimichurri.

BREAK IT: I'd be utterly delighted to see you break the law of funky by blow-torching Wasabi Marshmallows (page 210) on top of this mackerel.

YIELD Makes 4 servings

PREP TIME 20 minutes

COOK TIME 25 minutes

gear

kitchen shears

paring knife

butcher's twine

large oven-proof skillet with oven-proof lid

probe thermometer

whisk

ingredients

SQUAB

2 squabs (about 1 pound each), backbone and ribs removed, all bones, heads, feet, and giblets reserved

Kosher salt

Freshly ground black pepper

1 tablespoon unsalted butter

VEGETABLES AND GINGER

¼ cup fresh ginger juice (see Tip)

¼ cup chicken stock or broth

3 ounces haricots verts, trimmed

5 ounces Brussels sprouts, trimmed and halved lengthwise

8 small whole Japanese eggplant, halved lengthwise

1 tablespoon unsalted butter, for finishing the sauce

☞ **Tip**

If you don't have a juicer or don't feel like breaking it out, go to any juice bar and ask them for some ginger, juiced. They'll do it. That's what I did.

squab with cute vegetables and ginger

(Light meat)

I normally think of ginger as spicy and slightly sweet, but when paired with the avian-gamey flavor of squab, ginger becomes bright and fresh, like a sip of cold water after exiting a summer subway station.

Prepare the squab. Season both sides of the squab halves liberally with salt and pepper. Lay the semiboned squab, skin side down, straighten out the leg, and use the leg as a guide (like rolling up a flag on a flag pole) to help roll up the boned meat of the bird in the skin, overlapping the skin back onto itself. Using butcher's twine, tightly tie at the top, middle, and bottom. It will look like a corn dog with one leg and a wing. This is kind of like a *jambonette*, which is French for "little ham."

HOLD IT? You can keep the rolled and tied squabs, covered and refrigerated, for up to 12 hours. Don't prep the vegetables ahead of time.

Cook the squab and vegetables. Preheat the oven to 400°F.

In a large oven-proof skillet over medium-high heat, melt the butter. Add the squab halves to the pan, breast side down, and sear for about 1 minute; turn 3 more times and cook until golden all around. Remove the squab from the skillet and set aside.

Add all the reserved giblets, the head, and the bones to the skillet and sear off in the drippings for about 5 minutes, turning occasionally. Once dark brown bits have accumulated, remove the giblets, head, and bones and discard. Turn the heat to low and add the ginger juice, scraping up the brown bits from the bottom of the skillet. Add the stock, squab, and vegetables.

Transfer the skillet to the oven for about 15 minutes. It's hard to tell when a squab is done because the flesh is reddish to begin with and its juices don't run clear. The main indicator to me is temperature, which should read about 155°F when checked with a probe thermometer (bear in mind that the folks at the USDA specify 165°F), or how firm it is on the breast. Give it a test: if the breast feels like your thumb at medium well (see diagram page 32), you are good to go.

Remove the vegetables and squab from the pan and finish the sauce by whisking in the butter over low heat until thickened and shiny, about 2 minutes. Snip the string on the squab and remove.

PLATE IT! Place some of the vegetables down on the plate. Place the squabs so the claws are nicely exposed, and add the remaining vegetables here and there. Spoon the sauce over the plate in a circular motion.

BREAK IT: Make corn squabs: Completely bone the squabs. Then, completely insert a clean dowel before tying and cooking the squabs according to the recipe. Blend all the pretty vegetables up with the sauce to make a ginger-veggie dipping sauce. Allow all of this to cool, then make the plantain batter from the recipe on page 173. Coat the squabs in this and fry until warmed through and golden. Reheat the sauce, and dip away. You just made corn dogs of squab, with a ginger-vegetable sauce.

Squab Butchery

I prefer to purchase squabs with their organs still inside them and to butcher them myself. So if you are not squeamish, or if your butcher is, do the following with head-on, whole squabs:

• Snip the extra skin around the tail to open up the cavity. Use your hands to remove the innards and reserve. Trim the wing tips by cutting them off at the "wrist" joint and reserve. Cut the head off at the shoulders and reserve.

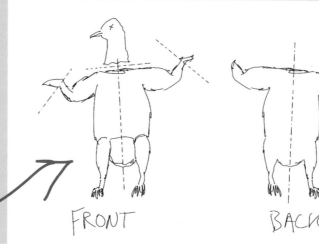

FRONT   BACK

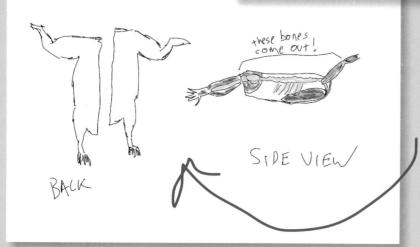

BACK   these bones come out!   SIDE VIEW

• Working with the bird facing breast side up, start at the bottom end and use the kitchen shears to cut between the breasts, and through the keel and wishbone. Turn over, and cut from bottom to top along one side of the backbone. Using a paring knife, carefully detach the skin from the backbone by cutting horizontally between the backbone and the skin/fat. (This ensures you have plenty of skin to later tie up the bird.) Carefully cut along the other side of the backbone to detach it (leaving the skin attached) and reserve it with the rest of the bones and innards.

• Separate the thighs from the thigh sockets by popping the joint out; move the leg so you can feel where it is attached to the pelvis. While bending the leg backwards, press your thumb on the joint to make it the fulcrum. Keep bending the leg back until it pops out. Using a paring knife, remove the thighbone by gently cutting through the meat to reveal the thighbone, and continue until it's released from the meat. Debone the wing using the same method. Remove the keel bone, which is what anchors the bottom of the breast to the rib cage. Reserve all the bones with the rest of the parts. Repeat the process with the remaining squab. I think leaving the claw of the squab attached is beautiful, maybe in a Tim Burton sort of way, but if it weirds you out, cut it off.

ROLL OVER AND TIE   USE LEG LIKE A SPOOL!   tied UP!   tied UP XRAY   COMPACTING MEAT LIKE CORNDOG!

dry-aged rib eye au poivre

(Dark meat)

YIELD Makes 1 massive steak; enough for 2 servings

PREP TIME 10 minutes

COOK TIME 10 minutes

gear

fire extinguisher, just in case

cast-iron skillet

tongs

grill lighter or long match

whisk

ingredients

STEAK

1¼ pounds (20 ounces) dry-aged, bone-in, rib-eye steak

Kosher salt

Cracked black pepper

2 tablespoons unsalted butter

SAUCE

1 shallot, finely minced

2 tablespoons green peppercorns in brine, crushed

2 ounces vodka

½ cup beef broth

½ cup heavy cream

Dry-aged meat is one of the best favors you could ever do for yourself. It can be a little hard to find, but a lot of specialty butchers now offer it for sale, frozen, online. Eat this before you die. Dry aging beef is costly business, because the beef has to be kept very cold and dry for days upon days. It also has to be done with the best cuts of meat, because the marbling (fat/meat ratio) has to be high. It tastes better than money. The process removes moisture from the meat, which amps up the beefy flavor. Think about the amount of water in a cup of coffee versus an espresso, and you'll understand what I'm saying. Next, enzymes in the meat start to break down connective tissue, which is the stuff that makes meat tough. Good mold—whose existence may not be the best selling point—is what helps this process along and, like the kind in awesome cheese, gives the meat a whisper of delicious funk. Normally a *steak au poivre* dabbles in a funky/fresh balance, with fresh meat and a ton of aged (black) peppercorns. But here the dish cannonballs into funky freshness by swapping the attributes of the core ingredients, so the aged black-peppered beef seesaws with the green peppercorn, the fresh peppercorn, which works like a peppery Binaca blast to the rich, funk-whispered beef. Most poivre sauces call for cognac, but I freshen mine up more with vodka. If you are nervous about flambéing, just don't use the vodka at all and instead add another 2 ounces beef broth; otherwise, read the directions carefully and keep a fire extinguisher handy. This is the best *á-la-minute* dish in the book.

Cook the steak. Put a cast-iron skillet in the oven and preheat the oven to 500°F.

Liberally season the steak with salt and black pepper. When the oven is fully heated, carefully remove the HOT cast-iron pan from the oven and place it over high heat. Add the butter, let it melt, then quickly add the steak. Don't touch it for the first 3 minutes: you're making a super-"Maillardy"-crusty caramelized outside (see sidebar opposite). After 3 minutes, flip and sear the second side for 1½ minutes. Then place the entire skillet in the oven for 4 minutes.

Transfer the steak to a cutting board and let it rest while you make the sauce, at least 7 minutes.

Make the sauce. In the same (unwashed) cast-iron skillet, now set over medium-high heat, add the shallot and green peppercorns and cook until the shallot is just beginning to color, about 2 minutes. Stand back and carefully pour in the vodka (all that vapor is flammable). Quickly position a grill lighter on the edge of the pan, turn your face away, and ignite. Just look at what you've done. Then gently swirl the pan and turn the heat to low, until the flames die out. Add the broth and cream and bring to a simmer, whisking, and cook the sauce until it thickens and coats the back of a spoon (a *nappé* consistency), about 5 minutes.

AT YOUR OWN RISK!

The Maillard Reaction

The Maillard reaction, or the browning of foods as they cook, is why I say "brown things taste like brown things." Think about it! Nuts, caramel, whiskey, oatmeal, coffee, and chocolate all sound pretty good together, and that's because of browning. When things roast or toast, sugars react, turn brown (caramelization), and create hundreds of desirable new flavors.

PLATE IT! On a nice, clean wooden cutting board, slice the rested steak off the bone in one whole piece, and set the bone aside. If it's too red for your liking, put it back in the oven for a few minutes. Slice the steak at angles, against the grain. Honestly, you can't mess this up too badly, because the steak will be so good and tender you'll be using all your restraint to not eat it with your fingers. Once sliced, reposition the slices against the bone, fanning them out a bit.

Pour the sauce over the meat and eat directly from the board. I rarely get this to a table to sit down and "enjoy it." Pour your wine in advance with your comrade in consumption at your side, and have no shame at eating it in the kitchen. If you are married or in love with a carnivore, this says, "I'm sorry," "I love you," and "I want to share the best things in life with you."

BREAK IT: Add some strong Dijon to the sauce to beat that meat even more into submission.

YIELD Makes one 9-inch cheesecake; serves about 12

PREP TIME 20 minutes

COOK TIME 2 hours 15 minutes

INACTIVE TIME 8 hours

gear

9-inch springform pan

medium bowl

stand mixer with paddle attachment

large pot or teakettle

large baking dish or roasting pan

medium, heavy, high-sided saucepan

candy thermometer

rubber spatula

whisk

small pan

fishing line or unflavored dental floss (optional)

ingredients

CRUST

1 sleeve of Ritz crackers (still in the sleeve)

2 tablespoons unsalted butter melted, plus more for greasing the pan

2 tablespoons sugar

FILLING

1½ pounds cream cheese, at room temperature

1 pound inexpensive blue cheese, at room temperature

1¼ cups sugar

2 teaspoons sherry

Finely grated zest of 1 lime

¼ cup all-purpose flour

2 large egg yolks

5 large whole eggs

blue cheesecake with frank's redhot caramel

(DESSERT)

This is essentially a wheel of blue cheese fluffed up in a crust. If that sounds good to you, you will dig the heck out of this recipe. If you are "just OK" with blue cheese, or are "experimenting with blue cheese" like you are a freshman in queso college, skip to the sidebar and I'll fix you up with something else. This recipe is for those whose wool is dyed blue. Those who bleed blue. Those who often choose the cheese course over the dessert course, but are torn. Those who know the "funkadelia" that results from a bite of blue cheese combined with a bite of something sweet. This blue cheesecake is the entire package, complete with a visit from blue's longtime boo, Frank, of RedHot fame, whose zippy cayenne and twangy vinegar are the backbone of the caramel sauce. (If you don't have access to Frank's, use your other favorite hot sauce.)

Make the crust. Preheat the oven to 375°F. Grease the bottom of a 9-inch springform pan.

With the Ritz crackers still in the sleeve, crunch them up into crumbs with your hands. In a medium bowl, combine the crumbs, butter, and sugar. Press the crumb mixture into the bottom of the prepared pan, distributing it evenly. Bake for about 10 minutes to set. Set aside to cool.

Make the filling. In a stand mixer fitted with the paddle attachment, beat together the cream cheese, blue cheese, sugar, sherry, and lime zest until smooth. Add the flour and mix on low just until incorporated. One by one, beat in the egg yolks and then the whole eggs, mixing on low between additions.

Bake the cake. Preheat the oven to 350°F. Bring a large pot or teakettle of water to a boil.

Pour the filling onto the cooled, parbaked crust in the springform pan. Set the springform pan in the baking dish or roasting pan, open the oven and pull the oven rack out, and set the baking dish on it. Carefully pour boiling water halfway up the side of the springform pan in the roasting pan. (I specify this order of operations so you aren't walking with boiling water and don't get your cake wet.)

Bake until the middle of the cheesecake is slightly jiggly and the top is light golden in color, 1½ to 2 hours. Jiggly is good. Turn the oven off, crack the oven door, and let the cheesecake slowly cool in the oven for an additional hour. After 1 hour, remove the cake from the oven and water bath and let cool completely on a rack. Cover the cooled cake in plastic wrap and refrigerate overnight.

Make the caramel. Make sure you have all your ingredients ready and measured out, as this goes very quickly.

Put the sugar in a medium, heavy, high-sided saucepan over medium heat and clip on a candy thermometer. Once you see the edges beginning to brown and caramelize, stir once with a rubber spatula. Let the sugar continue to melt until there are no lumps. When the sugar is coppery brown and no hotter than 345°F, carefully add the salt and hot sauce to the pan and stand back; it will bubble up vigorously. Let the bubbles subside for a minute, then whisk the two together.

CARAMEL

1 cup sugar

1 teaspoon kosher salt

½ cup Frank's RedHot hot sauce, or comparable hot sauce

4 tablespoons (½ stick) unsalted butter, at room temperature

But I Don't Like Blue Cheese

Replace the blue cheese with additional cream cheese, and replace the sherry with an equal amount of vanilla extract. You could swap the lime zest for lemon zest if you are a real traditionalist, but I don't think you would have read this far if you were.

☞ Tip

Nervous about your springform pan leaking? Fit a 9-inch silicone cake pan around the bottom of your springform pan before baking.

Whisk in the butter and remove from the heat. Let cool to room temperature.

HOLD IT? It's cheesecake! Keep it in the fridge for up to a week, covered with plastic wrap. The caramel will keep in the fridge for up to 2 weeks.

Cut the cheesecake. Slide a knife around the outside edge of the cake before releasing from the pan. Use the fishing line or dental floss to cut the cheesecake: Wrap a few inches of the end of the string around each of your pointer fingers and hold it taut. Slice down the center of the cake, carefully pulling one side of the line out through the cake after each cut; repeat to make slices.

PLATE IT! Place a slice on a plate and drizzle with the caramel.

CHEAT IT! You can always mix the hot sauce into your favorite store-bought caramel sauce.

BREAK IT: Toss finely chopped pork rinds in confectioners' sugar to make "crispies" that will provide a savory-sweet textural and flavor balance.

LAW OF
GUACAMOLE

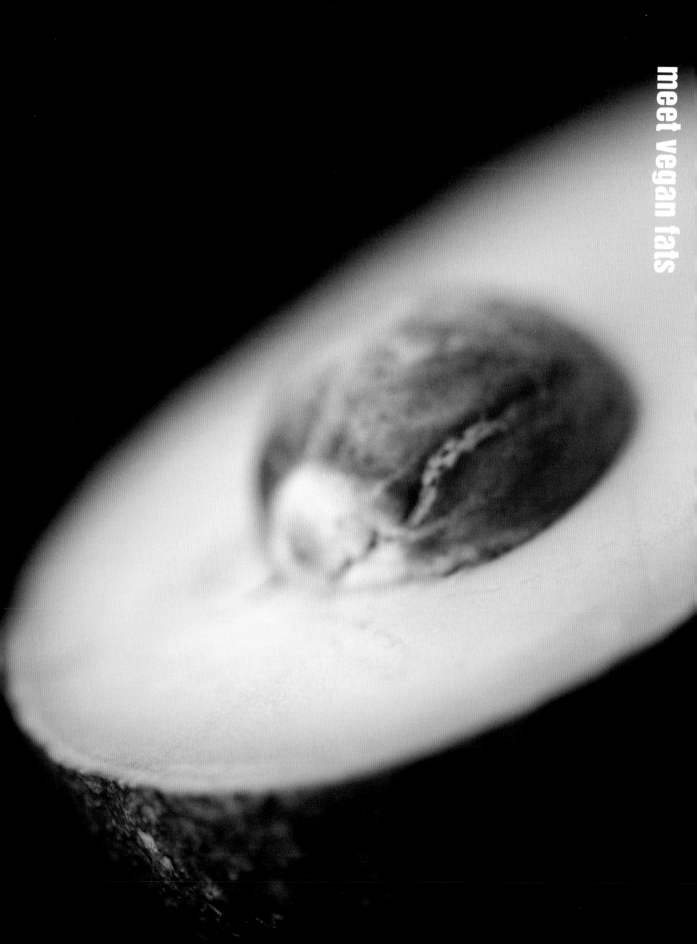

meet vegan fats

This law isn't about the components in guacamole and their analogs. This law is about the avocado, and its analogs. The avocado is a miracle, in that it is one of a few plants that can be described as "rich" or "creamy." Can you think of another plant that could be described as creamy? It's not so easy! The plants in this group are what I like to call the "fresh fats." The law of guacamole is about identifying these fresh fats and using them as the focus of a dish. Therefore, by nature, this chapter includes only dishes that are entirely vegan. I used to be a total meathead—it wasn't a meal if there wasn't meat on the plate. I've gradually transitioned out of that mentality, and prefer to eat animal products in moderation. One of the most influential meals I've ever eaten was vegan, at Michelin-rated Kajitsu, a Shojin Buddhist restaurant in New York. Course after course of delicious, artfully plated food was offered. By the third course the novelty of it being vegan wore off. It was just great food. I hope these recipes will have a similar effect on you and those for whom you cook.

meet vegan fats

GUAC CORNETS	AVOCADOS
YOUR VERY OWN HIYAYAKKO	SOYBEANS
CORN FRITTERS WITH CURRY	PLANTAINS
CHIA COSMOPOLITAN	CHIA SEEDS
BETTER TOMORROW VEGAN CHILI	PECANS
	KIDNEY BEANS
COCONUT "SASHIMI"	COCONUT
THE MOST DANGEROUS CATCH: VEGAN FISH STICKS AND VEGAN TARTAR SAUCE	COCONUT MILK
	OLIVES
VEGAN MAC AND CHEESE THAT IS ENTIRELY HOMEMADE	CASHEWS
CHESTNUT "PHILLY CHEESESTEAKS"	CHESTNUTS
	DURIAN
STRAWBERRY BELLINI AND DURIAN TERRINE	ALMOND MILK

YIELD Makes 30 to 40 filled cornets, plus a little extra batter for test runs/mistakes

PREP TIME 10 minutes

COOK TIME 40 minutes

gear

bowl

whisk

sheet pan with a nonstick silicone baking mat (I really don't recommend parchment for this, but if that's all you have, use it)

cornet molds (see Tip opposite)

offset spatula

tiny ice cream scoop, pastry bag, gallon-size zip-top bag, or spoon

ingredients

CORNETS

6 tablespoons room-temperature vegetable shortening

1 cup confectioners' sugar

2 teaspoons kosher salt

¾ cup all-purpose flour

1 tablespoon plus 1 teaspoon cornstarch

½ cup water

1 teaspoon tequila (if you don't have a bottle, buy a mini)

½ teaspoon onion powder

Olive oil nonstick cooking spray

GUACAMOLE

2 avocados, peeled and pitted

1 jalapeño pepper, seeds and ribs removed, finely diced

1 shallot, finely diced

1 garlic clove, finely diced

1 teaspoon kosher salt

Juice of 1 lime

2 tablespoons chopped fresh cilantro (optional)

guac cornets

(Canapé/snack)

Occasionally, I get a wild hair to write a rap song. It started in the tenth grade, when I wrote a rap about Julius Caesar for Mr. Malone's English class: "I'm trippin on the man who's controllin' the empire/got it goin' on you know we gonna conspire/my homie Casca gonna be the first assassin—Caesar will be screaming like young Michael Jackson." It was pretty good, to the tune of a Cypress Hill track. Later on in life, I met Belinda Chang, one of the greatest wine minds of our time. She tasked me with writing a ditty about Châteauneuf-du-Pape, which I did, over Snoop Dogg's "Drop It Like It's Hot."

So what does this have to do with Guac Cornets? As payment for that track, Belinda Chang took me to Per Se, easily one of the best restaurants in the world. Before the meal, a flurry of small bites and snacks are offered. What stood out most was a little pink, slightly sweet ice cream cone filled with salmon and red onion, studded with sesame seeds. It was adorable. It made me feel like a kid. And most of all, it was what everyone wants—a self-contained chip and dip. If ever you were to serve a fancy vegan meal, this would be the most ideal of starters.

Make the cornets. Preheat the oven to 425°F.

In a mixing bowl, whisk together the shortening, confectioners' sugar, and salt until smooth. Add the flour, cornstarch, ½ cup water, the tequila, and onion powder and whisk until smooth.

Spray a nonstick silicone baking mat with nonstick cooking spray. Spoon 2-teaspoon portions of the batter onto the mat, leaving 4 inches between them, and, with the back of the teaspoon or a wet finger, gently smooth each into a flat round circle about 3 inches in diameter.

Bake the cornets until a ¼-inch border of dark golden brown develops around the edge of each circle, 5 to 8 minutes. Let cool only a few seconds, just until barely cool enough to handle, then quickly, while they are still hot, roll the circles around the cornet molds to shape them. Let them cool with the seam side against a cool work surface, which will help them keep their shape. Now that you've seen how they behave, and what the window of shaping opportunity looks like, continue adding more spoonfuls of batter to the mat and repeat the process until you've used all of the batter. If a couple get burned or weird, don't get bummed out.

Make the guac. Guacamole is like pizza and Bloody Marys (see page 198) in that everyone has their own idea of what makes the best one. It's entirely an art of figuring what your personal preference is.

The Justin Method: Pile all of the ingredients into a bowl and use a fork to mix and mash, leaving some chunky bits among some mashed bits.

The Mom Method: Pile all of the ingredients in a bowl and use a whisk to mix and mash, leaving a silky, uniform sauce.

The Martha Stewart-ish Method: Dice the avocado and gently combine all ingredients with a spoon.

☞ **Tip**

No cornet molds? You can wrap these around a clean dowel or a thick marker to make pirouettes, then fill with a piping bag.

☞ **Tip**

Before you do anything with hot peppers, put your latex gloves on.

HOLD IT? Keep the cornets covered in a cool, dry place (not your fridge, it's hella damp in there), for up to 3 hours. If you have silica beads (see STEP YOUR GAME UP page 78), this would be a great time for them. Wrap the guacamole with plastic wrap, pressing the wrap directly on the surface of the guac, and refrigerate for up to 6 hours.

Assemble the cornets. Use a tiny ice cream scoop, a pastry bag, a cut zip-top bag, or a spoon to get some guac up into those cornets. Serve immediately.

PLATE IT! Make these in the moment and serve by hand.

BREAK IT: Instead of tequila, give these some smoky oomph with a few drops of liquid smoke!

YIELD Makes five to six 1-cup
servings, or twelve ½-cup
servings

PREP TIME 20 minutes

COOK TIME 45 minutes

INACTIVE TIME 8 hours

gear

blender

large stockpot with lid

nutmilk bag or tea towel

medium pot

large bowl

Twelve ½-cup ramekins

large steamer pot

tongs or heatproof mitts

ingredients

FRESH SOY MILK

10 ounces soybeans

4 cups water

TOFU

¼ cup liquid nigari (see Note)

TSUKUDANI SAUCE

¼ cup sake (regular, not the
cooking kind)

5 sheets nori

1 tablespoon apple cider vinegar

2 teaspoons soy sauce

GARNISHES (OPTIONAL)

Minced fresh ginger

Shredded scallions

Bonito flakes (if you don't eat
fish, don't put them on)

your very own hiyayakko

(COLD APP)

Like guacamole, most fresh fats are very appropriate for hot weather. *Hiyayakko* literally means "cold tofu." It is one of my favorite summer treats: it's rich and creamy without being cloying. Traditionally it's served with a soy-based sauce, some scallions, grated ginger, and bonito flakes. My GF and I are obsessed with the hiyayakko at a joint called Samurai Mama in Williamsburg, Brooklyn. They pour it into ramekins like it's a freaking panna cotta, and the texture is smoother than ice cream made of silk. They top it with ginger, a little avocado (more fresh fat!), and some sort of ground seaweed mix that I don't understand but never remember to ask about. Here I make a riff on *nori no tsukudani,* which is a seaweed condiment that works like a pasty version of American seasoning salt.

If you are a vegan, the soybean is probably on your speed dial, but I know very few people, vegan or not, who have actually made their own soy milk and then tofu. It's a shame, as it's not that difficult and the result is significantly better than anything you can buy. I made my first batch years ago with my buddy Anson Brown when we were comanaging Sushi Tora in Boulder, Colorado. We agitated the heck out of our soy milk and pressed the curds to make firm tofu, so when I set out to make a soft tofu, I figured I'd just do it the opposite way. The problem is, direct heat alone agitates the soy milk, which causes clumpy curds. So we set up a water bath, which had our tofu jiggly and silky soft with ease. I use a nutmilk bag (see page 311) to extract the soy milk, but you can use a clean tea towel if you'd like.

Make the fresh soy milk. Soak the soybeans in at least 3 cups water overnight in the fridge.

Drain the soaked soybeans and transfer them to a blender. Blend the soybeans and 4 cups water for about 3 minutes until super smooth. Pour into a heavy-bottomed, large stockpot. Add another 1¾ cups water to the blender, then blend to get the remaining soy mixture "rinsed" from the blender, and add to the pot.

Bring the soy mixture to a boil over medium heat, stirring the bottom often to prevent sticking. Reduce to a simmer, cover, and cook for 10 minutes more on the lowest heat, stirring occasionally. After 10 minutes, turn off the heat.

Arrange the nutmilk bag—or lay the dishtowel—in a pot. Pour the soy mixture into the nutmilk bag and allow to drain into the pot; alternatively put the mixture on top of the dishtowel, gather up the edges of the towel, and gently squeeze to extract the milk. Let the milk drain from the bag or towel. Once cool enough to handle, squeeze out any additional milk with your hands into the pot.

Once all of the milk has been pressed through and the solids left over in the bag/towel are mostly dry, discard the soybean solids. Pour all of the soy milk into a medium pot, set over the lowest heat, and cook again until the milk just begins to simmer and no longer tastes like raw soy, an additional 15 minutes more. Raw soy tastes like grass clippings or weeds; cooked soy tastes vaguely nutty, creamy, and pleasant. Remove the soy milk from the heat and refrigerate immediately until cold, about 2 hours.

What is nigari?

Nigari is magnesium chloride, which can be extracted from brine or seawater. Here it is used as a coagulant, much like rennet in cheese.

Make the tofu. Add cold water to the bottom of the steamer pot.

Divide the cold soy milk among the ramekins. Add ½ teaspoon nigari to each and stir once.

Place the ramekins in the flat bottom of the steamer pot's insert and set the pot over medium-high heat. Cover and steam for 12 to 15 minutes, or until tofu is jiggly.

Carefully remove the ramekins and allow to cool, then refrigerate until ready to use.

HOLD IT? Pat yourself on the back, because you just made a week's worth of fresh tofu. It will keep for about that time, covered, in the fridge.

Make the tsukudani sauce. Add the sake, nori, vinegar, and soy sauce to a blender. Blend until smooth, scraping down the sides or using the blender's plunger to help, if you have one. This is potent stuff, and a little goes a long way. This mix can get thick and dry out as the seaweed absorbs the moisture, so use it quickly.

PLATE IT! Evenly divide the tsukudani over the chilled tofu. This is enough to send me to tofu heaven. If you'd like to try to reach nirvana, consider adding ginger, scallion, or bonito flakes. I like to take small bites with tiny demitasse spoons, savoring every little bite.

BREAK IT: Once the soy milk is made, infuse it with flavor with dried spices, herbs, or teas (steeping your preferred flavorings in the hot milk, then straining out), then proceed. Now you can make Mexican hiyayakko (using chipotle powder and cumin), green tea hiyayakko, etc.

gear

2 large bowls

whisk

blender

Dutch oven or heavy-bottomed pot

candy thermometer

2 soup spoons

spider or tongs

ingredients

FRITTERS

2 very ripe plantains (9 ounces), peeled

One 11-ounce can sweet white corn, drained, or 2 ears of corn, kernels removed from the cob

Zest and juice of 1 lime

½ cup fine white cornmeal

½ cup all-purpose flour

1 tablespoon curry powder

2 teaspoons kosher salt

2 teaspoons baking powder

SAUCE

1 medium mango, peeled and roughly chopped

One 13.66-ounce can unsweetened coconut milk

Juice of ½ lime

1 teaspoon curry powder

1 teaspoon kosher salt

Vegetable oil, for deep-frying

kosher salt

corn fritters with curry

(HOT APP)

Plantains have just a little fat, but taste far richer due to their sweet and earthy flavor. In this recipe, the plantain does double duty, serving as a starchy binder, and adding some richness to highly snackable, curried corn fritters. While the plantain provides depth and intensity, the corn is bright and fresh. Amping up the Caribbean taste-vibes in this dish is a simple coconut sauce, with mango providing some acidity and sweetness to echo the fritters. Pair this dish with a rum-based beverage and some Desmond Dekker.

Make the fritter batter. In a bowl, mash the plantains with a wooden spoon until completely broken down. Using the wooden spoon, gently fold in the corn and lime juice and zest.

In separate large bowl, whisk together the cornmeal, flour, curry powder, salt, and baking powder.

Add the plantain and corn mixture to the dry ingredients and stir gently to create a thick batter, trying not to mash up the corn.

Make the sauce. Combine the mango, coconut milk, lime juice, curry powder, and salt in a blender and process until smooth.

HOLD IT? You can refrigerate the batter and sauce for up to 8 hours.

Fry the fritters. Fill a Dutch oven halfway with oil, clip on a candy thermometer, and bring the oil to 350°F over medium heat. (Do not heat any higher, or the corn will pop.) Line a plate with paper towels.

Working with two spoons, scoop a shooter marble–size bit of batter with one spoon and push it into the oil with the other. Fry 4 to 6 fritters at a time, throttling the heat as necessary to maintain the oil's temperature. Fry each batch, rotating the fritters a few times, until golden brown and crispy, about 4 minutes. Remove the fritters with tongs or a spider and land on the paper towel–lined plate to drain. Continue cooking the fritters in batches until all of the batter is gone.

PLATE IT! I'd love to see these fun nuggets served hot in a pile on a parchment paper–lined platter sprinkled with a little salt, with a little ramekin of sauce on the side. Serve whilst irie.

BREAK IT: Adding the plantains to the smoker for a bit would add some dimension and "backyard" flavor. You could also add some of the jerk flavors on page 279 instead of the curry in the sauce.

gear

jar with lid

jigger

cocktail shaker or pitcher

straws, cut to fit rocks glasses (optional)

ingredients

CHIA GEL

¾ cup cranberry juice cocktail

2 tablespoons chia seeds

CHIA COSMO

1½ fluid ounces vodka

2 tablespoons prepared chia gel (see above)

1 tablespoon Cointreau

1 tablespoon fresh lime juice

Ice

Lime wheels (optional)

chia cosmopolitan

(DRINK)

Known as the "runner's food," chia seeds are full of fiber and omega-3s, which do awesome things for your body. In addition to making terra-cotta busts of Obama grow an Afro, chia seeds absorb liquids and become a silky gel. So when most people consume chia seeds, they "drink" it, but really, they just let it slide down their throats. This decidedly special and certainly weird and healthy food, I determined, should be cloaked in a veil of normalcy to highlight how unusual it is. "If I were normal," I asked myself, "what would I order at a bar?" The answer is the cosmopolitan, so the Chia cosmo is the ultimate yin and yang of healthy cocktails, an odd-normal drink. This will yield a whole lot of gelled chia seeds: enough for eight cocktails, which, for four people, should be enough to warrant car service home. I make mine strong. Cut out ½ ounce of vodka for a more traditional and namby-pamby version. But still get car service, okay?

Make the chia gel. Combine the cranberry juice and chia seeds in a jar with a lid, shake well, and refrigerate for at least 3 hours to gel.

Make a drink. For each individual drink, put the vodka, 2 tablespoons or 1 ounce of the chia gel, the Cointreau, lime juice, and a scoop of ice in a cocktail shaker. Shake vigorously for 1 minute and strain into a glass.

PLATE IT! I like serving these neat (without ice) in a rocks glass, with a drinking straw that I've cut in half. Garnish with lime wheels if you wish.

BREAK IT: You can chia-gel almost any liquid, so why not? Lemon juice chia is a great way to get lemon onto a salad or protein. It would also provide yet another fun textural element to the burrata on page 225.

YIELD Makes 6 servings

PREP TIME 25 minutes

COOK TIME 45 minutes

INACTIVE TIME 8 hours or overnight

gear

large heavy-bottomed pot

ingredients

3 tablespoons vegetable oil

16 ounces button mushrooms, stems removed, wiped clean, and quartered

1 yellow onion, diced

1 large green bell pepper, seeds and ribs removed, diced

2 jalapeño peppers, seeds and ribs removed, finely minced

2 garlic cloves, finely minced

2 cups pecans (about 7 ounces), toasted, very finely chopped

1 tablespoon chili powder

1 tablespoon ground cumin

1 tablespoon dried oregano

1 cinnamon stick

Two 15-ounce cans kidney beans, drained and rinsed

One 28-ounce can diced tomatoes, with juice

2 cups vegetable stock (or vegetable broth, and cut the salt by half)

One 15-ounce can tomato sauce

One 1-ounce package dried mushrooms (whatever is cheapest), pulverized in a blender

1 tablespoon kosher salt

☞ **Tip**

Before you do anything with hot peppers, put your latex gloves on.

better tomorrow vegan chili

(Hot soup)

The story of chili always ends with the statement that it's better the second day. So why don't we just make it ahead of time and consider that first day as part of the cooking process? I do. My "vegan-ified" version uses pecans, which have a distinct richness and "meaty" mouthfeel, and play very nicely with the brown spices. The dried mushrooms are a nifty addition that I learned from *Cook's Illustrated*. Not only do the pulverized mushrooms thicken the chili, they also add that forest-floor bass note that we interpret as "hearty." I keep some dried mushroom powder in my spice rack at all times—whatever's cheapest—and you should too. A spoonful will add a layer of complexity to vegan dishes and omnivorous dishes alike.

In a large heavy-bottomed pot over medium-high heat, heat the oil and add the fresh mushrooms. Cook, stirring only once, until browned, about 6 minutes.

Add the rest of the ingredients to the pot. Scrape the bottom of the pot and stir to incorporate. Simmer until the vegetables and nuts are soft, about 30 minutes. Let cool. Refrigerate overnight.

HOLD IT? Keep the chili in the fridge for up to 4 days.

Reheat the chili in a pot over low heat, stirring often.

PLATE IT! My ideal chili-serving vessel would be the *dolsot,* which is an individual Korean earthenware bowl that retains tons of heat. You can find them online. Warm them up slowly in the oven, and then ladle in the chili. Or you can scoop the chili into a bowl. Garnish with whatever you like (see below).

BREAK IT: Chili is kind of an open-source recipe. Now that you've made it, customize it to your liking. Change the beans, add some greens, or even wrap it in a tortilla and fry it up like the chimichangas on page 132.

RAMEN OF THE SOUTHWEST

I like to think of chili as the ramen of the Southwest, so I arrange my garnishes on top, as opposed to just chucking them on. You can garnish it however you want. Here are some ideas:

- Cheese or vegan cheese sauce, like on page 182
- Sliced scallions
- Avocado slices
- Tortilla chips (tossed in ranch powder; see page 250)
- Pickled carrots (see recipe on page 264, or the reserved ones from the canned jalapeños on page 34)
- Sour cream or vegan substitute
- Scrambled eggs or vegan substitute
- A pat of pumpkin butter (from page 58)

gear

goggles

work gloves

high-speed hand drill with a
3-inch hole saw attachment (or a
coconut opening device like the
Coco Jack)

paring knife

bowl

ingredients

COCONUT "SASHIMI"

One 1- to 2-pound white young
coconut with green outer flesh
peeled off

One 4-inch piece daikon radish,
peeled

2 teaspoons ume paste

4 fresh shiso leaves

AT YOUR OWN RISK!

coconut "sashimi"

(COLD "FISH")

Remember when there wasn't coconut water? I do. Used to be if you wanted to hydrate yourself quickly you slugged Gatorade or Pedialyte. Right before the coconut water craze hit America, I took a trip to Rio de Janiero in Brazil. For about an American buck, a dude would lop the top off of a chilled big green coconut, shove a straw in it, and send you off. You'd return to him after drinking all the delicious water, and he'd bust it open so you could scoop out the meat. Maybe it was the cachaça, maybe it was the sun, maybe it was the *fio dental* (dental floss!) bikinis, or maybe it really was the best coconut ever generated by mother earth. Regardless, the sensation of scooping the silky, slightly chilled, rich coconut meat, another one of my favorite fresh fats, out of the shell was like eating sashimi from the hands of Gaia. Unfortunately, here in America, we don't experience young coconut meat very often. I think this is because the process of trying to access it is a bit intimidating. A young coconut is either green and shaped like an underinflated football, or, with the green exterior removed, matte white with a pointy end. I like the latter, but both will work using the slightly dangerous procedure below. The superfresh Japanese version of mint, shiso, along with Japanese pickled plum paste serve as the foils to the supple coconut meat.

Disassemble the coconut. Put on your gloves and goggles. This is dangerous. You've been warned. Don't do it like the dummy on page 177. If you have no experience with using a hole saw and drill, ask someone who does to do it for you.

Place the coconut in the corner of your sink and hold it there securely with your nondominant hand. With the drill set to maximum torq, position the saw attachment at the top of coconut. Apply very gentle pressure and slowly pull the trigger, being careful not to go too fast and spin the coconut out of your other hand. Drill until you have created a hole through to the interior, then reverse the drill to pull the "plug" back out. Empty the coconut water into a separate vessel and reserve for another purpose.

Use a soup spoon to gently scrape out strips of the coconut meat, starting from the bottom of the inside of the coconut and moving to the top. Place the strips on a cutting board.

Use a paring knife to remove any bits of brown skin from the strips. Using the same paring knife, shred the daikon by carefully cutting around and around, making long, thin, wide ribbons of daikon. It takes practice, but it's worth it for the long shreds. Once you've made as many long, thin, wide ribbons as you can, fold them over themselves. Slice the ribbons lengthwise as thinly as possible to make fine long shreds of daikon. Mix the shredded daikon with the ume paste until pinkish and evenly distributed.

HOLD IT? Hold the coconut meat in coconut water for up to 3 days, covered, in the refrigerator. The radish-ume mix can be held for up to 1 day, covered, in the refrigerator.

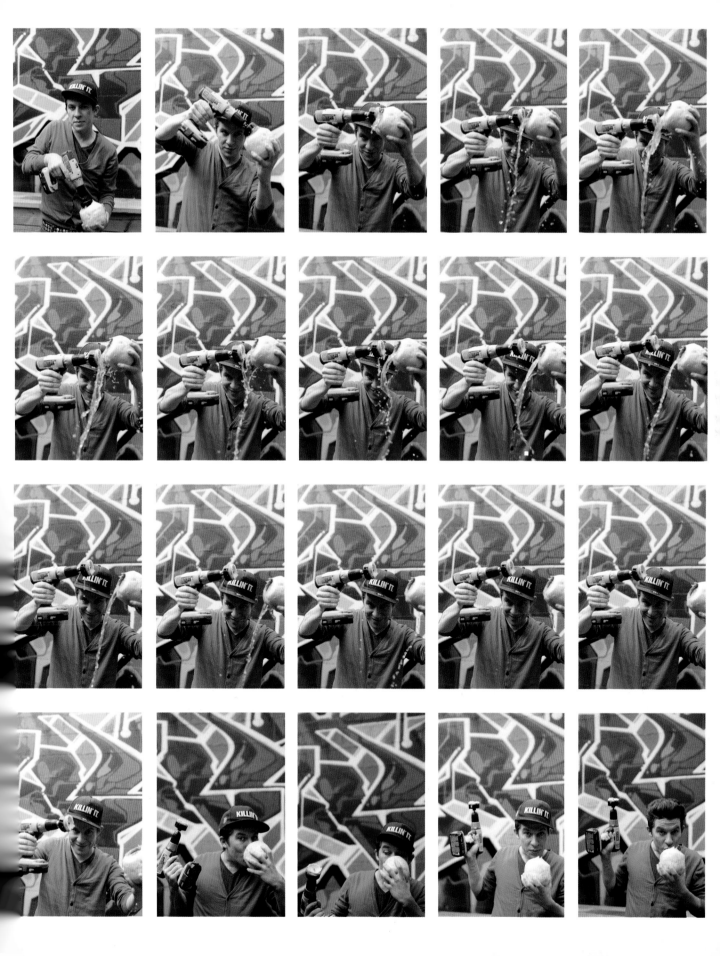

On a clean work surface, lay the trimmed coconut strips into 4 horizontal lines, overlapping end to end. Roll them up gently to make little rosettes!

PLATE IT! Place a little pile of the radish mix on the plate, like a little haystack. Then place the shiso leaf, pointy side up, against the stack. Set the rosette of coconut against the shiso, and serve to the unsuspecting.

I don't think this needs soy sauce or wasabi to be delicious, but if you want to really maximize the sashimi effect, go on ahead.

BREAK IT: Use coconut instead of the fish in the usuzukuri on page 202!

 STEP YOUR GAME UP

Instead of soda water, run an equal amount of coconut water through a soda siphon to add to a mojito recipe (see page 222).

YIELD Makes 20 fish sticks and 1½ cups sauce; enough for 4 servings

PREP TIME 15 minutes

COOK TIME 20 minutes

INACTIVE TIME 3 hours

gear

large bowl

gallon-size zip-top bag

small sheet pan (quarter sheet)

blender

small bowl

sheet pan with rack

Dutch oven or heavy-bottomed pot

candy thermometer

3 shallow bowls/plates

whisk

ingredients

FAUX FISH STICKS

Two 20-ounce cans young green jackfruit in brine, drained

10 pitted Spanish Queen green olives (or any other large green olive)

½ cup coconut milk

2 tablespoons dulse powder

1 teaspoon kosher salt

TARTAR SAUCE

½ cup fresh soy milk (page 171)

½ cup pickle brine

1 tablespoon Dijon mustard

1 teaspoon kosher salt

1 teaspoon xanthan gum

1 cup grapeseed oil (or another vegetable oil, but grapeseed is best)

¼ cup finely chopped dill pickles

the most dangerous catch: vegan fish sticks and vegan tartar sauce

(Hot "fish")

When I was in the fourth grade, I was put in all sorts of fun problem-solving extracurricular thingies like Odyssey of the Mind and Destination Imagination. If you have a kid, I'd highly recommend you explore these. Both programs teach kids creative problem solving, as opposed to book smarts. My high school Destination Imagination team went to the world finals, and we were a bunch of nut jobs. We're all well-adjusted now, but then, we were hellions. I remember very well the first day of the state championships being passed out in the back of the van, still drunk off gin and frozen berries (No mixers! But see? Problem solving!) when our coach (now my very good friend) socked me in the buttocks to wake me up.

No kick in the ass could wake me out of the rut that I had dug myself into when attempting to make an animal-less version of fish sticks. Plant fats and fish fats are similar; hence the use of avocado and coconut with fish. Seaweed and olives have a sea-like brininess. Flavor was not the issue. The problem was texture. A fish stick, when you break it in half, *flakes*. It is cooked, it is moist, it is tender, and it's *flaky*. Now riddle me this: what in the plant world is flaky when cooked? We tried layering vegetables (no, that's lasagna), using potato flakes (gross), reconstituting coconut (like eating wet cardstock), layering fresh coconut like sashimi (page 176; too costly), and even making a freaking *vauquelin* (a modernist microwaved dessert, semi-invented by Hervé Thís) of emulsified oil and soy milk (this led to the tartar sauce, but dipping cooked mayo in mayo is no good). After multiple days of trying to find flakiness, my culinary cohort Erin and I were crazed and cockeyed.

We decided it would be the last recipe we tackled, and I nicknamed it "The Most Dangerous Catch." A day before our final cooking day, I was chatting with my GF in the car about smoking vegetables in my new smoker (check the barbecue on page 102) and how I wanted to smoke jackfruit from Chinatown because it pulls apart like pulled pork when it's cooked for a long period. BOOM. Even if I cooked it for a short time, I knew the jackfruit's fibrous nature would lead to that elusive flaking. Lo and freaking behold, I welled up when I had the first bite. This recipe is not just passable as a fish stick, it will take down anything in the freezer section. Plus, we all learned something about our bountiful planet and the way things work. No Chinatown? Head to mailorder sources. (Same goes with dulse, a type of red seaweed found in the North Atlantic, and xanthan gum.)

Assemble the faux fish sticks. Finely chop the jackfruit by hand. Chop the vegan olives until almost pastelike. In a bowl, combine the jackfruit, olives, coconut milk, dulse, and salt.

DREDGE

¼ cup cornstarch

½ cup water

¼ cup rice flour

1 cup plain bread crumbs

1 teaspoon kosher salt

Vegetable oil, for frying

Xanthan gum

One time a bacteria called *Xanthomonas campestris* grew on some broccoli, and it was called Black Rot. Gross! It secreted something weird and slimy, like mucilage. Sooner or later someone figured out that you could get the bacteria to make that goo and then turn it into a powder (xanthan gum) that readily dissolved in water. People then figured out that xanthan gum is an awesome emulsifier—remember that diagram back on page 37? Xanthan gum and all emulsifiers are what I call "handholders." They hold one hand with watery things and another hand with fatty things and almost never let go. Sometimes xanthan gum also causes watery things to hold on to themselves, which creates thickening. I absolutely adore xanthan gum in my restaurant kitchen. It makes sauces shiny and salsas less weepy, and can turn oil and soy milk into mayo. In general, it rocks my world. Xanthan gum holds my hand very tight.

Transfer this mixture to a gallon-size zip-top bag. Squeeze as much air out as possible, then lay the bag flat and shape the mix, packing it tightly, into a 7 x 10½ x ½-inch-thick sheet. Place the bag on a small sheet pan and freeze until frozen solid, at least 3 hours.

Place the frozen bag on your cutting board. Keep the mix in the bag and, using your sharpest knife, cut the bag in half (from the base of the bag to the zipper), then each half into 10 strips. The zip-top bag adds pressure to the sticks to keep them together as you cut. Put the cut sticks back on the small sheet pan and return to the freezer until it's time to fry, at least 30 minutes.

Make the tartar sauce. Put the soy milk, brine, Dijon, salt, and xanthan gum in a blender and blend on high, then, with the machine still on, slowly stream in the oil.

Scrape this mix into a bowl or container, then fold in the pickles. Cover and refrigerate.

HOLD IT? If you aren't planning on frying any time soon, let the sticks refreeze a bit after the cutting, then transfer to a fresh zip-top bag and keep frozen for up to a week. Freezer burn is not cute on these things. The tartar sauce can be kept in the fridge, covered, as long as the expiration date on the soy milk. If you used fresh soy milk, it will keep in the fridge for up to 3 days.

Fry the vegan fish sticks. Preheat the oven to 250°F and place a sheet pan fitted with a rack inside. In a Dutch oven fitted with a candy thermometer over medium heat, bring the oil to 350°F.

Mix the cornstarch and ½ cup water together in a shallow bowl with a whisk. Line up a dredging station with the rice flour in a second shallow bowl, then the cornstarch slurry, then bread crumbs and salt mixed together in the third shallow bowl. Remove the "fish" sticks from the freezer in batches of four at a time. Dip the frozen "fish" sticks one at a time in rice flour, then into the slurry (make sure it's fully coated), then in the bread crumbs, shaking off excess between each dip. Place the breaded sticks directly into the oil and fry in batches, 4 at a time, until the outside is golden brown and the inside is hot, 2 to 3 minutes. Transfer the fried sticks to the sheet pan with the rack and keep warm in the oven until done.

PLATE IT! Spoon swoosh (drop a spoonful and swoosh it with the back of a spoon) some tartar sauce on a plate, then stack these guys like Lincoln Logs. Marvel at your inventiveness for just a moment, then devour.

BREAK IT: Oddly, this is also a recipe for vegan "pulled pork." Smoke the "fish" mix (omitting the coconut milk, dulse, and olives but adding some medium-firm tofu) for about 2 hours. Mash this all up and season with salt and pepper.

YIELD Makes about 8 servings

PREP TIME 45 minutes

COOK TIME 20 minutes

INACTIVE TIME 12 hours or overnight

gear

stand mixer with dough hook

blender

rubber spatula

fine-mesh strainer or chinois (see page 37)

large sauté pan

pasta machine/extruder (optional)

large bowl

large pot

trivet (see page 62)

ingredients

EGGLESS PASTA

2 cups all-purpose flour, plus a little more for dusting

2 cups semolina flour

SAUCE

4 ounces raw cashews, soaked in 3 cups water overnight in the fridge

1 cup water

1 tablespoon vegetable shortening

1 onion, finely diced (about 2 cups)

2 garlic cloves, minced

2 tablespoons pickle brine

1 tablespoon sriracha sauce

1 tablespoon Bragg Liquid Aminos

2 teaspoons kosher salt

1 teaspoon sweet smoked paprika

1 teaspoon mustard powder

vegan mac and cheese that is entirely homemade

(Light "meat")

My GF is what I call a "pro-veg opportunitarian," meaning that she eats animal products when the opportunity to try something new or delicious presents itself. Other than that, she stays pro-veg as often as possible. We both enjoy the challenge in creating a meatless meal, but also the satisfaction of saying we did it nicely. If you want, you can just toss some store-bought pasta in the vegan cheese sauce, but I like extruding the pasta or hand-rolling *pici,* as we do here; I think part of the fun of this dish is saying that you are capable of producing something that you ate out of a box in college from completely real—and vegan—ingredients.

Make the eggless pasta dough. In a stand mixer fitted with the dough hook attachment, mix both flours and 1¼ cups tepid water on the lowest speed until you've formed a cohesive mass, 4 to 5 minutes. Turn off the mixer and press the dough into the bits at the bottom of the bowl to integrate them. Turn the mixer on again to the lowest speed and continue mixing for another minute or until fully combined.

Remove the dough from the bowl. Knead 4 or 5 times by folding over twice then making a quarter turn. Wrap the dough in plastic wrap and chill for at least 10 minutes, or until ready to use.

Make the sauce. Strain the soaked cashews and discard the cashew water.

In a blender, blend the cashews with 1 cup fresh water until very smooth, like cream, 3 to 5 minutes.

Using a rubber spatula, push the cashew mixture through a chinois or fine strainer; discard the pulp. This yields about 1½ cups very viscous "milk." Do not wash the blender.

In a large sauté pan over medium heat, add the shortening, onion, and garlic and sauté until the garlic is aromatic, about 3 minutes. Add the pickle brine, sriracha, Bragg aminos, salt, sweet smoked paprika, and mustard powder. Stir in the cashew milk and heat through, until the onion has softened.

Return the mixture to the blender and blend on high until smooth. Transfer back to the sauté pan over the lowest heat if you plan to serve right away.

HOLD IT? Pasta dough can be held in the fridge for 2 days, or in the freezer for 1 month. The sauce will keep in the fridge, in a covered container, for 4 days.

Make the pasta. Following the manufacturer's instructions, run the pasta through a pasta machine/extruder to make little macaroni (I used the small macaroni press attachment for a KitchenAid on speed 2). Put the finished pasta in a bowl and toss it with a pinch or so of all-purpose flour to keep it from sticking to itself.

Alternatively, if you don't have pasta attachments or a press, you can make the dough into *pici* by hand (see illustration) on a cutting board. If you have kids, put them to work and tell them to make the smallest Play-Doh snakes possible.

Sprinkle the snakes with a few pinches of flour and let stand on the cutting board until ready to cook.

Bring a large pot of salted water to a boil. Carefully add your pasta to the water, and stir occasionally until cooked through but not too soft, about 4 minutes for the macaroni or 4 to 6 minutes for the pici. Drain well and add to the sauté pan with the warm "cheese" sauce, stirring gently to combine.

PLATE IT! This is the kind of thing that gets scooped from the pan in which it was cooked, so put it on a trivet and relive your college days, without the scorched coffee table.

BREAK IT: Truffle oil, which is very divisive in the culinary world, is one of my favorite add-ins (to mac and cheese and popcorn, but that's it). It is more aroma than flavor and would make this mac and cheese disturbingly good. Or instead, add a few grinds of black pepper—now you have vegan *cacio e pepe*!

gear

medium bowl

sheet pan

shallow pan

candy thermometer

wine cork or whole nutmeg

spatula with holes or fish spatula

wok or frying pan

ingredients

CHESTNUT "STEAK"

Four 5.2-ounce bags roasted and shelled chestnuts

7 shiitake mushroom caps

½ cup tamari sauce

¼ cup red wine vinegar

¼ cup packed light brown sugar

2 tablespoons plus 1 teaspoon Dijon mustard

½ teaspoon ground cayenne pepper

YUBA "CHEESE"

Fresh soy milk (page 171)

2 teaspoons nutritional yeast

1 teaspoon onion powder

½ teaspoon garlic powder

½ teaspoon paprika

¼ teaspoon freshly grated nutmeg

(continued on page 247)

chestnut "philly cheesesteaks"

(Dark "meat")

In the winter, I smell roasting chestnuts all over the streets of midtown Manhattan. I find them as intoxicating a smell as that of any competing shawarma stand (page 207). If a little roasted nut can compete with rotisserie lamb, I figured that roasting it with mushrooms, tamari, and mustard would transform it into a savory sandwich filling. Yuba, the skin that forms on cooling soy milk, is easily employed too. When I was experimenting with the hiyayakko recipe on page 171, I lifted off the skin of the soy milk and chucked it aside, where it looked like freshly melted provolone. So I flavored fresh soy milk with spices and nutritional yeast so its skin would have the taste, texture, and appearance of cheese. Thus a "cheesesteak" with neither cheese nor steak, but delicious.

Start the chestnut "steak." Preheat the oven to 250°F.

Thinly slice the chestnuts and mushroom caps into ¼-inch pieces.

In a medium bowl, whisk together the tamari, red wine vinegar, brown sugar, Dijon, and cayenne. Add the chestnuts and mushrooms and toss to coat. Pour the entire mixture on a sheet pan and roast until the chestnuts have absorbed some of the liquid, about 40 minutes.

Make the yuba "cheese." Put a sheet of plastic wrap on a flat surface.

Put 2 cups of the soy milk in a shallow pan along with the nutritional yeast, onion powder, garlic powder, paprika, and nutmeg. Set over low heat, attach a thermometer, and bring the temperature up to about 175°F. Turn off the heat and watch as a thin film, the yuba, forms, between 3 and 8 minutes. When the yuba will hold the weight of a wine cork or one whole nutmeg, use a corner of a spatula or fish spatula to loosen the yuba from around the edge of the pan. (If your cork or nutmeg falls through, fish it out, remove and throw away the torn yuba, bring the mixture back up to 175°F, and try again.) Use the spatula to gently and carefully lift out the yuba and transfer it to the plastic wrap. Cover immediately with another piece of plastic wrap. You are now making your very own yuba "singles." Repeat the process, reheating the milk and allowing the yuba to form, until it becomes too difficult to remove the yuba.

HOLD IT? The yuba can get weird and drippy and should be used as soon as possible, but may be held in the refrigerator, wrapped in plastic, for up to 4 hours. The chestnut mixture can be cooled, and kept, covered, in the refrigerator, for up to 2 days.

Assemble the sandwich. Preheat the broiler.

Place a wok or frying pan over high heat and add the oil. Add the bell peppers and onion and sauté until the onion is becoming translucent, 5 to 7 minutes. Add the chestnut-mushroom mixture (including any sticky or liquidy bits) and cook until hot and aromatic, about 5 minutes.

Meanwhile, toast your hoagie rolls under the broiler until golden. Carefully fill the hoagies with the "steak" and peppers, then top with the yuba "cheese."

2 tablespoons peanut oil

2 bell peppers, seeds and ribs removed, sliced

1 yellow onion, sliced

2 big hoagie rolls

The Joys of Leftover Soy Milk

The remaining soy milk (about 2 cups) can be used for the tartar sauce on page 181 or on a bowl of Cinnamon Toast Crunch, which is the best cereal for plant milks, in my opinion.

PLATE IT! I like to wrap these in parchment paper and then in foil, like we got them on the street, but you could slice them into multiple minis to feed a crew.

BREAK IT: Go for broke: Smoke the chestnuts after marinating, then top with vegan chili (page 175) and vegan cheese sauce (page 182) to make a vegan smoked chestnut-chili cheesesteak.

YIELD Makes 1 terrine:
8 servings

PREP TIME 10 minutes

COOK TIME 40 minutes

INACTIVE TIME 1 hour

gear

6-cup terrine mold or loaf pan

blender

deep baking dish

very small pot

small pot

stand mixer with whisk attachment or a hand mixer

ingredients

STRAWBERRY PURÉE

1 quart strawberries, hulled

1 tablespoon confectioners' sugar

½ teaspoon kosher salt

About 2½ cups sparkling wine

DURIAN PURÉE

1½ ounces freeze-dried durian

2¾ cups water

2 tablespoons confectioners' sugar

½ teaspoon kosher salt

Ice

7 teaspoons agar agar

"WHIPPED CREAM"

1 tablespoon cornstarch

1 cup plus 1 tablespoon almond milk

1 tablespoon confectioners' sugar

strawberry bellini and durian terrine

(DESSERT)

In the discussions of weird food, durian often gets a mention. It hails from Southeast Asia, and doesn't get a lot of plate time here in America. Why? It's hard to acquire here, and it gets a bad reputation for being funky and foul smelling. But I believe the durian can be used to provide complexity and richness to a dish that otherwise has none. Durian gets its funkiness from all sorts of compounds, but it gets the "eggy" flavor from sulfur. Paired with sparkling wine (or in this case, a Bellini—fruit purée mixed with sparkling wine), which also contains sulfites, and has a layered complex flavor, and strawberry, which has a more straightforward and sweet profile, the durian becomes almost creamy, with an egg-custard-like flavor. A terrine (as opposed to a tureen) is a rectangular or oval mold for making multilayered or sliceable foods. Dairy is often a star ingredient in dessert terrines, in the form of whipping cream and actual custard—but durian is, of course, entirely vegan, and we use agar agar to firm up the layers in a vegan-friendly way. Rather than going to Chinatown for a fresh durian, I copped some freeze-dried (the BEST way to start eating durian) on the Internet.

Place a 6-cup terrine mold in the freezer to chill.

Make the strawberry purée. Pulse the strawberries, confectioners' sugar, and salt in a blender and blend until smooth. Transfer to a measuring cup and fill with sparkling wine to make 2 cups. Whisk to combine, then transfer to a vessel to hold. Measure out an additional 2 cups sparkling wine and reserve.

Make the durian purée. Place the durian, 2¾ cups water, the confectioners' sugar, and salt in a blender and blend until smooth, then transfer to a container.

Assemble the terrine. Set the terrine mold in a deep baking dish, and surround the mold with ice. Add water to the ice until just under the top of the terrine.

In a very small pot, mix ½ cup of the strawberry purée with 1 teaspoon agar agar and whisk to combine; let sit for 4 minutes. Place the pot over medium heat, whisking, and bring to a simmer, then remove from heat and stir in ½ cup sparkling wine. Pour this mixture into the chilled terrine mold. It will set in 3 to 4 minutes. Once set, proceed to the next step.

Rinse out the pot and mix 1 cup of the durian purée with 1 teaspoon agar agar and whisk to combine; let sit for 4 minutes. Place the pot over medium heat, whisking, and bring to a simmer, then remove from heat and gently and slowly pour it over the strawberry layer. (Don't pour too quickly or in one spot as this may puncture the first layer.) Allow to set, 3 to 4 minutes.

Repeat the steps above, creating alternating strawberry/wine and durian layers, until the supplies have been exhausted.

Cover and transfer the terrine mold to the fridge for at least 1 hour.

Make the "whipped cream." Make a slurry with the cornstarch and the 1 tablespoon almond milk.

Add the remaining almond milk and the confectioners' sugar to a small pot and bring to a simmer over medium heat. Add the slurry to the pot and cook until thickened, about 5 minutes. Transfer this to a stand mixer fitted with the whisk attachment, or use an electric hand mixer, and beat until cooled, about 10 minutes. The consistency will be frothy, like the head on a freshly poured soda.

HOLD IT? Both the terrine and the cream can be held in the fridge, covered, for up to 2 days. The colors may bleed a little, but I think that looks just as cool.

Unmold the terrine. Carefully dip the outside of the terrine into a sink or baking dish filled with hot water for about a minute. Slide a knife around the outside of the terrine. Place a plate or tray on top of the mold, then invert to unmold.

PLATE IT! Carefully slice the terrine with a sharp knife, then use a spatula to transfer to a plate. Add the "whipped cream" with a spoon and serve.

BREAK IT: If you were to put a bunch of cilantro leaves on a rack and spray them with simple syrup, then allow the sugar solution to dry, you'd have candied cilantro. This is a good idea to add an herbaceous punch to this dessert.

LAW
OF
CHEESE
FRIES

sharp meets mellow

Cheese fries are a buddy cop movie in your mouth. The desk-working potato is paired with a trigger-happy sharp cheese. They couldn't be further apart, but by the end of this edible movie, the two are best buds, bringing out the best in each other. Culinarily, this law is about making sharp flavors shut up and wait their turn in the gustatory conversation. Sharp flavors are hard to describe, as they are experienced somewhere between your tongue and your nose. As opposed to spicy flavors, like that from chiles, sharp flavors are what I call "mustard agents." They aren't all mustards, but work in a similar way: they have bite and are pungent, like a wake-up slap to your senses. You'll be shocked at some of the places where you can find sharp flavors. Mustards and aged cheeses are pretty obvious, but a lot of the same sharp-producing compounds can also be found in cruciferous vegetables and radishes. Sharp flavors work best with one-note, "mellow" flavors. Cheese fries, one of my favorite guilty pleasures, is the perfect two-ingredient dish because the potato is brought to life with the assertive cheese, but has the ability to hush the sharpness of the cheese. *21 Jump Street.*

sharp meets mellow

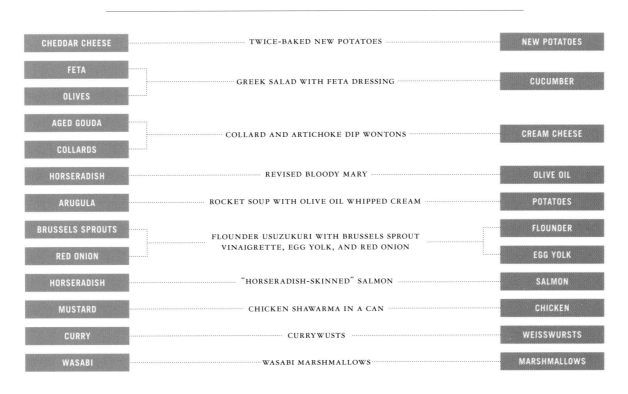

SHARP	DISH	MELLOW
CHEDDAR CHEESE	TWICE-BAKED NEW POTATOES	NEW POTATOES
FETA / OLIVES	GREEK SALAD WITH FETA DRESSING	CUCUMBER
AGED GOUDA / COLLARDS	COLLARD AND ARTICHOKE DIP WONTONS	CREAM CHEESE
HORSERADISH	REVISED BLOODY MARY	OLIVE OIL
ARUGULA	ROCKET SOUP WITH OLIVE OIL WHIPPED CREAM	POTATOES
BRUSSELS SPROUTS / RED ONION	FLOUNDER USUZUKURI WITH BRUSSELS SPROUT VINAIGRETTE, EGG YOLK, AND RED ONION	FLOUNDER / EGG YOLK
HORSERADISH	"HORSERADISH-SKINNED" SALMON	SALMON
MUSTARD	CHICKEN SHAWARMA IN A CAN	CHICKEN
CURRY	CURRYWUSTS	WEISSWURSTS
WASABI	WASABI MARSHMALLOWS	MARSHMALLOWS

YIELD Makes 20 to 30 little bites

PREP TIME 10 minutes

COOK TIME 45 minutes

gear

sheet pan

medium bowl

pastry bag with a large tip or
gallon-size zip-top bag

ingredients

POTATOES

2 pounds new potatoes,
scrubbed

3 slices cooked bacon

½ cup finely grated extra-sharp
cheddar

3 tablespoons unsalted butter,
at room temperature

2 tablespoons sour cream

GARNISHES (OPTIONAL BUT
AWESOME)

Extra grated cheese

One 2-ounce bag potato chips
(the wackier the flavor, the
better)

2 tablespoons minced fresh
chives

twice-baked new potatoes

(Canapé/snack)

Who knew that the humble new potato could be turned into shell casing for
a bullet of flavor? In this powder keg, the surly nature of the cheddar cheese
roughhouses the creamy new potatoes, not to mention some butter and sour
cream. These little bombs of sharp versus subtle are a perfect snack or party treat.
Bacon shrapnel provides some flavor backbone but minimal textural resistance,
so I like to top mine with more cheese, some potato chips, and fresh chives.

Make the potatoes. Preheat the oven to 400°F.

Place the potatoes on a sheet pan and roast dry until easily pierced with a
fork, about 30 minutes. Let cool slightly until easy to handle.

Cut each potato in half. Trim a slice from the bottom of each half so the
halves can stand up on their own. Chop the scraps and place in a medium bowl.

Working over the same medium bowl, use a ½ teaspoon to scoop out most of
the inside of each potato half and place the insides in the bowl of scraps. Place
the shells, cup side up, back on the sheet pan. Finely chop the bacon and add
it to the bowl of potato scraps. Mix in the cheese, butter, and sour cream until
combined.

HOLD IT? You can keep the hulled potato shells and potato mixture, covered and refrigerated, for up to 6 hours.

Preheat the oven to 400°F.

Place the potato mixture in a pastry bag with a large tip or zip-top bag with
the corner cut off, and fill each potato shell on the sheet pan, like a little deviled
egg. Bake until golden, 15 to 20 minutes. If desired, top with more cheese, and
bake 5 minutes more, until melted.

If you like, stick a potato chip in each one and top with chives.

PLATE IT! Plate these guys on a long serving vessel. If you are really crazy, make them
the centerpiece in the rauchbier soup on page 92 and pour the soup around.

BREAK IT: A touch of balsamic vinegar will add a fruity and zippy note. It may seem
weird on paper, but salt and vinegar chips are the best chips.

gear

large salad bowl

whisk

small bowl

ingredients

FETA DRESSING

1½ ounces crumbled feta cheese

2 tablespoons red wine vinegar

1 garlic clove, minced

¼ cup olive oil

1 tablespoon roughly chopped fresh oregano

½ teaspoon kosher salt

Freshly ground black pepper

SALAD

½ medium red onion, diced

6 plum tomatoes (see sidebar), seeded and chopped

2 large hothouse cucumbers, seeded and chopped

1 cup pitted kalamata olives, halved

Why plum tomatoes?

You could use any ripe tomato, but I find that plums have a less watery texture and are better for chunky salads.

greek salad with feta dressing

(COLD APP)

The Greek salad is a perfect example of soft muted flavors (tomato, cucumber) wrestling around with sharp, briny bites of feta, onion, and olive. It's a winning combo, in theory. But I find that most restaurants and home cooks just cube or crumble their feta, which makes for a difficult "perfect bite," as you can get either a bite with no feta or too bracing an amount. Feta is what I like to call a "condiment food," which implies that it is good *on* or *with* something, as opposed to by itself. By breaking down the feta in the dressing, you don't have to search around your bowl attempting to skewer the perfect bite.

Make the dressing. Roll a towel in a ring and nestle the salad bowl into it to stabilize it.

Put the cheese, vinegar, and garlic in a salad bowl and, while whisking furiously, slowly stream in the oil. Add the oregano, salt, and pepper to taste and whisk to incorporate. The streaky emulsified dressing will look weird and curdy, like cheese-ghosts haunting your olive oil. Don't get spooked, just set it near your cutting board.

Make the salad. Soak the onion in a small bowl of cold water for 5 to 10 minutes; set aside. (Soaking cut onions takes some of the harsh bite out of them.)

Combine the tomatoes and cucumbers in the salad bowl. Add the olives to the bowl.

Drain the onions well, pat dry with a paper towel, and add to the bowl. Toss it all together!

HOLD IT? It's generally against salad laws to hold a salad in dressing, but I think this one actually benefits from up to an hour or two of "married life" with the dressing. Just give it a toss before you refrigerate.

BREAK IT: Find some halloumi—the grillable cheese of Greece—cut it into cubes and skewer it with pieces of tomato, cucumber, onion, and olive. Then grill it (for some bitter notes) and drizzle it with vinegar and olive oil for a Greek salad on a stick. Eat it while it's warm!

gear

food processor

rubber spatula

large bowl

small bowl

two sheet pans, one with rack

large Dutch oven or heavy-bottomed pot

candy thermometer

slotted spoon or spider

ingredients

8 ounces cream cheese

¼ cup mayonnaise

9 ounces frozen quartered artichokes, thawed

10 ounces frozen chopped collard greens, thawed (see sidebar)

3 ounces aged Gouda cheese, grated

Finely grated zest of ½ lemon

½ teaspoon kosher salt

5 to 10 scrapes of a whole nutmeg

One 12-ounce package wonton wrappers (48 pieces)

Vegetable oil, for frying

☞ **Tip**

Can't find frozen collards? You can use fresh. The freezing process actually tenderizes the collards a bit, so just chop and freeze your fresh collards before use.

collard and artichoke dip wontons

(Hot app)

The wonton skin is one of the most versatile party tools in my edible armory, as you can fill a wonton skin with almost anything to make individual hors d'oeuvres. Rather than having a cauldron of spinach and artichoke dip for your guests to hover around, this recipe makes for a fully self-contained and highly snackable dip-and-vessel-in-one treat. More stout and assertive than spinach, the collards stand up to the cream cheese and nutty aged Gouda.

Make the filling. Pulse the cream cheese and mayonnaise in a food processor until combined, scraping down the sides of the bowl once with a rubber spatula.

Put the artichokes and collards in a clean towel and squeeze out all the moisture. Add them to the food processor and pulse until roughly chopped but not completely smooth. Scrape the filling into a large bowl. Add the Gouda, lemon zest, salt, and nutmeg and stir to combine.

Fill a small bowl with water. Put a heaping teaspoon of filling in the middle of a wonton wrapper. Dab your finger in the bowl of water and trace it around the inside edges of the wrapper. Fold one corner of the wonton over to the opposite corner, and press the edges together to seal, making a triangle. Then fold the bottom corners up to make a little crown shape. Place the filled wonton on a sheet pan or plate. Repeat until all of the filling and wontons are used.

HOLD IT? Uncooked filled wontons will keep in the fridge, covered, for a day. Or they can be frozen for a month—put the sheet pan in the freezer until the wontons are frozen, then transfer them to a zip-top bag.

Fry the wontons. Preheat the oven to 200°F and place a sheet pan fitted with a rack inside.

Fill a Dutch oven halfway with oil, clip on a candy thermometer, and bring the oil to 350°F over medium heat.

Working in batches, carefully lower 5 to 6 wontons at a time into the oil with a spider, throttling the heat as necessary to maintain its temperature. Fry the wontons, flipping occasionally with the spider or slotted spoon, until golden brown and blistered, about 3 minutes. Land the cooked wontons on the rack on the sheet pan in the warm oven. Continue frying in batches until all are cooked.

PLATE IT! These are the kind of treat that I think merits being piled hot on a paper doily on a big platter. One of my favorite party moves is to hand a guest the ready-to-go platter and walk away. Eventually the dish gets circulated, and everyone has fun trying to hand off the responsibility of serving to the unexpecting.

CHEAT IT! You're always capable of doing less. Instead of using wonton skins and frying individually, put the filling in a baking dish and bake in a 350-degree oven until hot and bubbly, about 25 minutes. Serve with pita chips.

BREAK IT: Mixing in some uni with this would make for a wicked bite. I first had uni and artichoke at Bobby Flay's joint Gato. Here, the low-tide uni will be zipped up by the artichoke while it adds a whisper of funky to the cream cheese.

gear

vegetable peeler

airtight container, preferably glass

strainer

reserved vodka bottle

cocktail shaker

ingredients

INFUSED VODKA

One 1.75-ml bottle vodka

4 ounces fresh horseradish, peeled and thinly sliced

2 celery ribs, trimmed and sliced

2 jalapeño peppers, quartered

¼ cup kosher salt

¼ cup whole black peppercorns

Peel of 2 lemons

Peel of 1 lime

BLOODY MARY

ice

2 ounces infused vodka

8 ounces low-sodium tomato juice

2 dashes Worcestershire sauce

1 teaspoon olive oil

☞ Tip

Before you do anything with hot peppers, put your latex gloves on.

revised bloody mary

(Drink)

History can't agree on who invented the Bloody Mary, let alone what should be in it and how it should be prepared. By steeping the various flavorings in the vodka, the cocktail is closer in appearance to its original iteration in simpler times, while retaining the modern flavor profiles we've come to expect. The horseradish adds a sharp bite—it's tempered by the soft sweetness of the tomato, and eventually by the olive oil that we thicken it with. Simultaneously, by removing the solids from the cocktail, the result is siltless and easily consumed with a straw.

Make the infused vodka. Combine all of the ingredients for the infused vodka in an airtight container, preferably glass, and store for 3 days in a dark, cool part of your kitchen. Retain the vodka bottle. Strain out the solids and discard them, and return the infused vodka to the vodka bottle.

HOLD IT! Once the vodka is strained it can be kept indefinitely!

Make the Bloody Marys. For each drink, in a shaker filled with ice, combine 2 ounces of the infused vodka with the rest of the Bloody Mary ingredients.

Shake and pour into a tall glass. You can get as crazy as you want with garnishes, but I like my big things in simple packages.

BREAK IT: For an even more intense experience, try this with vodka's more aromatic cousin, gin.

gear

stockpot

blender

bowl

whisk, egg beater, hand mixer, or cream whipper with N$_2$O charge

ingredients

SOUP

2 tablespoons olive oil

1 onion, diced (about 12 ounces)

2 garlic cloves, minced

2 large potatoes, peeled and diced (about 1½ pounds)

1 quart vegetable stock, (or vegetable broth, and cut the salt by half)

5 ounces rocket (arugula)

2 teaspoons kosher salt

½ teaspoon freshly grated nutmeg

WHIPPED CREAM

1 teaspoon kosher salt

½ cup heavy cream

¼ cup olive oil

GARNISH

Finely grated zest of 1 lemon

rocket soup with olive oil whipped cream

(HOT SOUP)

In other parts of the world, *arugula,* which sounds like an old-timey horn, is called "rocket." Rocket is a much better name for the potent plant, as its sharpness is off the charts. Just as sharp cheddar is softened by the potatoes in cheese fries, the arugula is offset by the creamy, starchy components in this soup. With rocket (arugula) now being sold year-round in packages in stores, this makes for a great "in-between-winter-and-spring" soup. It would pair exceptionally well with a beer made for that season, like a Bière de Mars.

Make the soup. In a stockpot, heat the oil over medium-low heat. Add the onion and cook until translucent, stirring occasionally, 8 to 10 minutes. Add the garlic and cook for another 2 minutes. Add the potatoes and stock and bring to a boil. Reduce the heat to a simmer and cook until the potatoes are tender and cooked through. Add the rocket (arugula) in batches and cook until wilted. Carefully transfer the hot soup to a blender, add the salt and nutmeg, and blend until smooth.

Make the whipped cream. Place the salt and cream in a bowl and begin whipping the cream slowly with a hand mixer, whisk, or egg beater. When the cream has reached soft peaks, fold in the oil until incorporated. Alternatively, place the cream, olive oil, and salt in a whipping canister and charge with one N$_2$O charger.

HOLD IT! Transfer the soup to a covered container, cool, and store in the fridge for up to 3 days, or freeze indefinitely. The whipped cream can be kept in the charger for up to 1 week.

Heat the soup until piping hot and transfer to a tureen or vessel from which the soup can be ladled or poured.

PLATE IT! Divide the soup among six bowls and top with some whipped cream and lemon zest.

BREAK IT: Remember that arugula salad we did on page 32? The duck would be awesome here, adding some richness to balance the sharp arugula. Just cook it separately, cut into cubes, and add to the bowl.

YIELD Makes 4 small servings

PREP TIME 10 minutes

COOK TIME 20 minutes

INACTIVE TIME 15 minutes

gear

small pot

slotted spoon or spider

medium bowl

blender

nutmilk bag, chinois (see sidebar page 37), or fine-mesh strainer

small bowls

small pot

sharp thin knife

ingredients

VINAIGRETTE

8 Brussels sprouts, quartered, (about 6 ounces)

¼ cup olive oil

Juice of ½ lemon (about 2 tablespoons)

1 tablespoon soy sauce

2 teaspoons fish sauce

½ medium red onion, thinly sliced from root to end

4 large eggs

¾ pound (12 ounces) flounder fillet (see sidebar)

flounder usuzukuri with brussels sprout vinaigrette, egg yolk, and red onion

(COLD FISH)

This recipe is brought to you by sulfur! Some people think sulfur stinks, but sulfur is our friend, and it's delicious, at least in small quantities. Sulfur tastes sharp, and in this particular recipe it's all over the place: the hard-boiled egg yolk, the onions, and the Brussels sprouts. Usually flounder is like an uptight businessperson—conservative, mild-mannered, almost boring—like the potato in cheese fries. Nine to five, that's just fine for flounder.

In this recipe, though, it cuts loose with sulfur, like a recovering corporate accountant fleeing to Burning Man. Literally, cutting loose, as in *usuzukuri*: a Japanese technique of slicing raw fish as thinly as possible, so that a patterned or colored plate can be seen peeking through the nearly translucent flesh.

Make the vinaigrette. Bring a small pot of water to a boil. Prepare an ice bath in a medium bowl.

Blanch the Brussels sprouts for about 1 minute, then shock in ice water. Drain the cooled sprouts, then transfer them to a blender with the oil, lemon juice, soy sauce, and fish sauce. Blend on high until smooth, 2 to 3 minutes. Push the mixture through a nutmilk bag, chinois, or fine-mesh strainer; discard the pulp and reserve the liquid.

Prep the red onion. Soak the onion slices in a bowl of cold water for at least 15 minutes to chill out the strong flavor. Drain and pat dry.

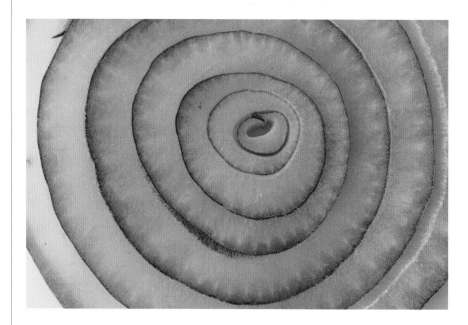

Prep the egg yolks. Place the eggs in a small pot and cover by at least 2 inches with cold water. Bring the water to a boil over high heat, then turn off the heat and let the eggs sit in the water, uncovered, for 5 minutes. Drain the eggs, run under cold water until they are just cool enough to handle, then drain again. Peel the eggs while they are warm, and then allow to cool completely in cold water.

Remove the egg yolks, saving the whites for another use (chop them up and sprinkle them on top of the arugula soup [page 201] or the ramen [page 120]). Mash the egg yolks in a small bowl with a fork until crumbly and fluffy.

HOLD IT! The vinaigrette, onion, and egg can be kept in the fridge for up to 3 hours. Buy the flounder the same day you plan to serve the dish, and keep it in the fridge, tightly wrapped in plastic.

Prepare the fish. Along the shortest side of the flounder, use a sharp, thin knife to cut very thin pieces at an angle in one long fluid motion, making strips about the size of an average Band-Aid. Keep them thin, and don't push them off the knife once you've sliced them as the weight of the slices will apply gentle resistance to the next slice.

PLATE IT! On four pretty patterned or colored plates, lay the onion slices down first, followed by the flounder. Do not overlap the flounder, but keep it touching ever so slightly. Using a spoon, drizzle the vinaigrette over the fish, filling in some of the spaces between the slices to make little pools of sauce. From very high up above the plate, sprinkle the egg yolk like snow.

BREAK IT: My chef buddy Nick Subic once made a bizarrely good dish of cocoa nibs, flounder, and blueberries. I think those things would work remarkably here, adding crunch, roasty-toasty flavors, and some sweetness and acidity. The best part about usuzukuri is that it's a nicely constructed canvas of raw fish for whatever your tongue desires.

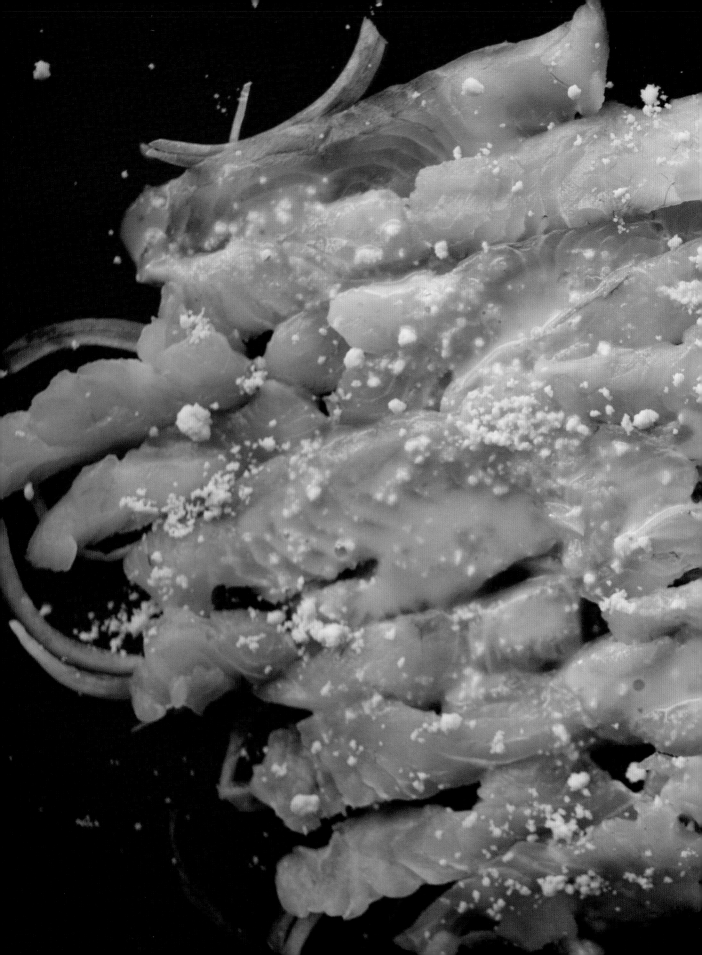

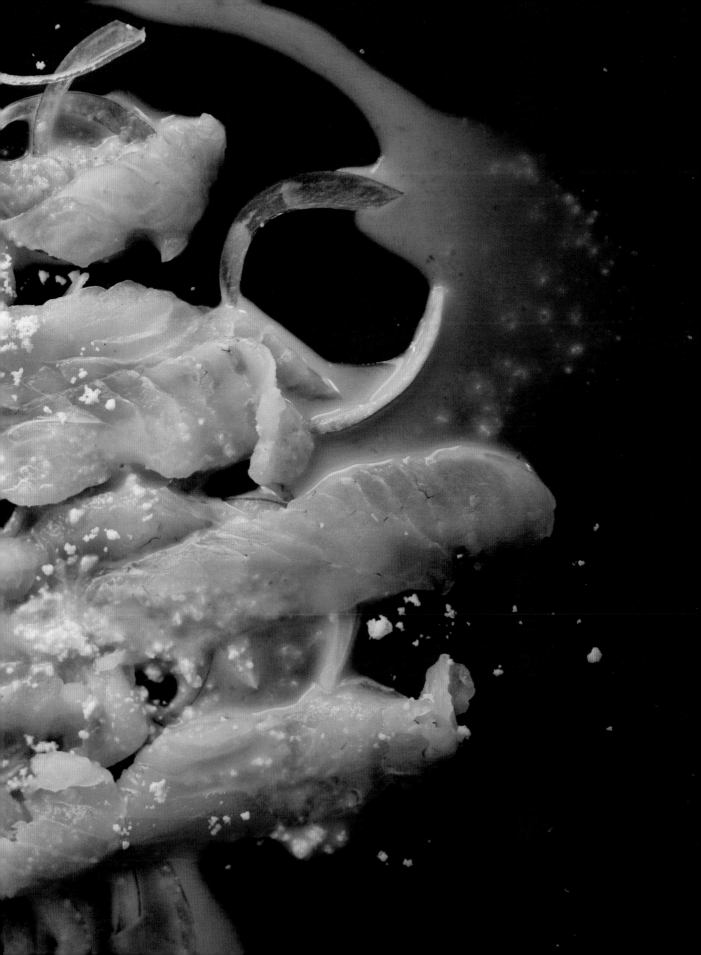

YIELD Makes 4 servings

PREP TIME 10 minutes

COOK TIME 40 minutes

gear

small bowl

cast-iron skillet

spatula or fish spatula
(see sidebar page 99)

ingredients

HORSERADISH TOPPING

¼ cup mayonnaise

1 large egg white

¼ cup peeled and freshly grated
horseradish (about a 1-inch
piece) or ¼ cup jarred grated
horseradish, drained well

1 teaspoon kosher salt

SALMON

2 tablespoons vegetable oil

1½ pounds skin-on salmon,
pinbones removed, cut into
4 equal fillets

Kosher salt

"horseradish-skinned" salmon

(HOT FISH)

Unless it's smoked or raw, salmon can be pretty mundane. In this dish, I use the sharp punch of horseradish like an old-fashioned alarm clock. It wakes up not just you, but the salmon as well. The fun part about this recipe is that the horseradish gets hidden under the crispy skin of the fish, like the *S* under Clark Kent's suit. And speaking of super, you should be eating salmon skin. It is the most delicious part of the whole fish, and if you do it right, it's better than a cracklin' of chicken skin any day.

Make the horseradish topping. Combine all the ingredients for the topping in a small bowl and set aside.

HOLD IT! The horseradish topping will keep in the fridge, covered, for 2 days.

Cook the salmon. Preheat the broiler. Preheat a cast-iron skillet with the oil over medium-high heat.

Liberally season the skin side of the fillets with salt. When the skillet is very hot and the oil is rippling, carefully place the salmon in the skillet, skin side down. Sear the salmon without moving it for about 4 minutes.

Remove the skillet from the heat and gently and evenly apply the horseradish topping to the raw side of the fillets. Carefully transfer the skillet to the broiler. Broil until the top is golden brown and bubbly, about 5 minutes.

PLATE IT! Transfer the salmon fillets to a cutting board, skin side down. Carefully slide a spatula (a fish spatula would be great; see page 99) between the skin and the flesh of the fillet, separating them. Transfer each fillet to a plate, and place the salmon skin, crisp side up, on top of the horseradish sauce. Now the horseradish is a secret! Aren't you creative?

BREAK IT: Roasted or poached pears would provide a great textural and flavorful counterpoint to the rich salmon and bitey horseradish.

YIELD Makes about 6 small sandwiches

PREP TIME 30 minutes

COOK TIME 2 hours

INACTIVE TIME 2 hours to overnight

gear

food processor with blade attachment

nonreactive bowl or gallon-size zip-top bag

small pot with lid

2 empty 28-ounce cans with lids, labels removed, cleaned

baking dish or sheet pan

probe thermometer

ingredients

CHICKEN SHAWARMA

1½ pounds boneless, skinless chicken thighs (6 to 8 small thighs)

½ cup plain Greek yogurt

2 tablespoons honey (see Tip)

2 tablespoons Dijon mustard

1 tablespoon olive oil

1 tablespoon mustard powder

1 teaspoon garlic powder

1 teaspoon kosher salt

1 large egg, beaten

AMBA

2 tablespoons vegetable oil

1 tablespoon whole mustard seeds

3 not-quite-ripe bananas

1 teaspoon kosher salt

2 tablespoons honey (see Tip)

1 tablespoon Dijon mustard

1 tablespoon rice wine vinegar

Sandwich-style white bread, for serving

chicken shawarma in a can

(Light meat)

I'm a huge fan of all things nerdy, in case you couldn't tell already. My GF calls me her man-child, as I'm still really into most of the things I was into when I was twelve. So after seeing the post-credits shawarma scene in *The Avengers*, a movie that I, as a lifelong comic-book junkie, had been anticipating for years, I wanted to make my own gringo-nerd version of shawarma. Instead of slices of meat, I use ground chicken, and instead of layering it on a skewer, I season it with honey and mustard and pack it into a can to bake which gives it the form of the meat that spins on the stick. (If you want, you can even make my very gringo rotisserie; see page 208.) Serve with white bread and banana amba (a punchy condiment normally made with pickled mangos) when your super-friends need to power up.

Marinate the chicken. Place the chicken in a food processor fitted with the metal blade and process until there are no large chunks left. Add the yogurt, honey, Dijon, oil, mustard powder, garlic powder, and salt and pulse until mixed. Place the mixture in a nonreactive bowl and cover, or in a zip-top bag and marinate for 2 hours to overnight in the fridge.

Make the amba. In a small pot over medium heat, add the oil and mustard seeds and toast them, shaking the pot constantly. The second the seeds start to pop, turn off the heat and cover.

Pulse the bananas and salt in the cleaned food processor until smooth. Add the banana mixture to the pan of mustard oil and put over medium-low heat. Add the honey, Dijon, and vinegar and stir until bubbling and thick, about 5 minutes. Transfer to a container and refrigerate for at least 3 hours.

Assemble the shawarma. Preheat the oven to 400°F. Let the chicken return to room temperature.

Add the egg to the marinated room-temperature chicken mixture and mix thoroughly with a wooden spoon. Pack the mixture into 2 cleaned 28-ounce cans and cover with the lids.

HOLD IT? This dish is best cooked to order. If needed, you can hold the amba and uncooked can of meat in the refrigerator until you are ready to use them; up to a day for the meat and up to 3 days for the amba. Before continuing, allow the can to come to room temperature.

Place the can of chicken onto a baking dish or sheet pan, and bake until a probe thermometer inserted into the middle of the chicken mixture reads 165°F, about 1½ hours.

After you remove it from the oven, let the meat cool for a few minutes in the can, then invert the meat on a serving plate. (See diagram on page 208 if you want to create a rotisserie.)

Always measure out the oil before the honey when both are called for in a recipe. That way you can measure the honey with the used oil spoon, making less of a mess and achieving a more accurate measurement, as the honey won't stick in the spoon.

PLATE IT! Serve your tower of meat with slices of white bread and smears of the amba.

BREAK IT: Amp up the Americana (and herbaceousness) by mixing in some of the Coolish Ranch powder on page 250. The herbs and buttermilk will temper the mustard flavors in the amba and chicken.

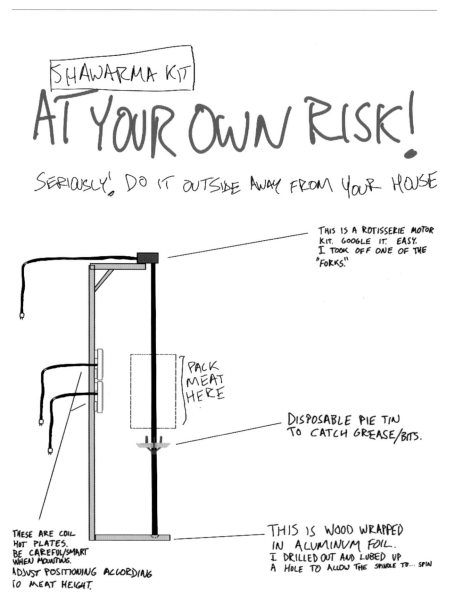

SHAWARMA KIT

AT YOUR OWN RISK!

SERIOUSLY, DO IT OUTSIDE AWAY FROM YOUR HOUSE

THIS IS A ROTISSERIE MOTOR KIT. GOOGLE IT. EASY. I TOOK OFF ONE OF THE "FORKS."

PACK MEAT HERE

DISPOSABLE PIE TIN TO CATCH GREASE/BITS.

THESE ARE COIL HOT PLATES. BE CAREFUL/SMART WHEN MOUNTING. ADJUST POSITIONING ACCORDING TO MEAT HEIGHT.

THIS IS WOOD WRAPPED IN ALUMINUM FOIL. I DRILLED OUT AND LUBED UP A HOLE TO ALLOW THE SPINDLE TO... SPIN

gear

medium pot

blender, spice grinder, or mortar and pestle

large pot

cast-iron skillet

ingredients

CURRYWURST SAUCE

1 whole cardamom pod, seeds removed from the pod, pod discarded

2 teaspoons whole cumin seeds

1 teaspoon whole coriander seeds

½ teaspoon ground cayenne pepper

½ teaspoon mustard powder

One 28-ounce can puréed tomatoes

¼ cup apple cider vinegar

One 1-inch piece fresh turmeric, peeled and thinly sliced, or 2 teaspoons ground turmeric

½ cup light corn syrup

2 teaspoons kosher salt

SAUSAGES

8 bratwursts

One 6-pack of your favorite light-colored German beer

2 tablespoons unsalted butter

8 crusty rolls or fries (optional; see recipe on page 226)

currywursts

(Dark meat)

I was a hellion when I was a teenager. I was in danger of failing to graduate and on a real course of adolescent self-destruction when my uncle gave me a CD compilation of tracks from Berlin's biggest music festival, LOVEPARADE. I was hooked immediately, on the squelch and soul, the pounding beats, and the way I could just *dance*. He told me that if I could make it through high school and wear the silly gown, he'd take me to LOVEPARADE. So, sure enough, in 2002, I was getting *schlüssel-ed* (that was my word—I think it means "key," but it was beer-speak for having had too much beer, to me) in Berlin, dancing around the Siegessäule and snacking on the most amazing (and only) street food I had ever had: currywursts. The super *scharf* (sharp, spicy) curry-flavored ketchup made the mild *weisswurst* dance in my mouth like an eighteen-year-old raver out of the country and drinking legally in the streets for the first time. Weisswursts are pretty tough to find in the U.S., so I sub in some very Midwestern bratwursts. This and a crusty roll to sop up the currywurst sauce might be delicious enough to keep your kids in school.

Make the currywurst sauce. Add the cardamom seeds, cumin, coriander, cayenne, and mustard powder to a medium pot. Over low heat, toast the spices until fragrant. Grind in a blender, spice grinder, or mortar and pestle.

Add the spices, puréed tomatoes, vinegar, and turmeric into the same pot and bring to a boil. Reduce the heat and simmer until thick, 25 to 30 minutes. Add the corn syrup and salt. Cook until thickened, glossy, and smooth, another 10 minutes. Reduce the heat to very low and cover to keep the sauce warm.

Make the sausages. Prick the sausages a few times with a fork. Pour 4 of the beers into a large pot and bring to a boil. Reduce to a simmer, and carefully add the sausages. If the sausages are not completely covered, add more beer. If there are extra beers, please enjoy. Simmer until the sausages are cooked through, about 10 minutes. Remove the sausages and transfer to a plate to cool.

HOLD IT! Hold the boiled sausages in the fridge for up to 2 days. Hold the curry ketchup sauce in the fridge for up to 1 week.

Preheat a cast-iron skillet over medium-high heat. Add the butter to the pan and swirl to coat. When the butter has melted, sear the bratwursts until golden brown and blistered on all sides (about 7 minutes).

PLATE IT! Resist the urge to put this in a bun. Serve with the warm sauce and a crusty roll on the side if you'd like, or some fries. This dish is sausage and sauce, and is not to be confused with a hot dog. You can look super-learned and well-traveled when you explain that to your friends.

BREAK IT: Cook down some sliced apples in the sauce, and watch as the sweetness and acidity play around with the spices. This would be a riff on Pork Chops and Applesauce, which falls under the law of PB&J.

YIELD Makes a lot of
marshmallows; more than an
average bag

gear

sifter or fine-mesh strainer

two 11 x 17-inch rimmed cookie
sheets

stand mixer with whisk
attachment

small saucepan

candy thermometer

rubber spatula

kitchen shears or pizza wheel

ingredients

¼ cup cornstarch

¼ cup confectioners' sugar, plus
more for dusting the shears

2 tablespoons black sesame
seeds

3 envelopes unflavored gelatin

1 cup ice-cold water

1½ cups granulated sugar

1 cup light corn syrup

½ teaspoon kosher salt

¼ cup wasabi powder

Butter- or olive oil–flavored
nonstick cooking spray

wasabi marshmallows

(DESSERT)

A few months after opening Do or Dine, I wanted to re-create a baked apple
dish, like my mother would make for me as a kid, complete with toasty marshmallows on top. But I wanted the marshmallows to grow up a little bit. Mild-
mannered marshmallows have a sweet, creamy and mellow flavor, so I knew
that mustard (or a mustard agent) would be the other side of the comestible
coin. Alton Brown has published the best recipe for plain marshmallows I've
ever seen, so I decided to doctor it for my needs.

Prep your pan. Combine the cornstarch and confectioners' sugar. Using a sifter
or fine-mesh strainer, dust half of this mixture on one of the cookie sheets, then
tilt to dust the four sides as well. Evenly sprinkle with half of the sesame seeds.

Make the marshmallows. Place the gelatin and ½ cup of the ice-cold water in
the bowl of a stand mixer fitted with the whisk attachment. Stir, and let sit for 5
minutes to allow it to bloom.

In a small saucepan fitted with a candy thermometer, combine the remaining
½ cup water, the granulated sugar, corn syrup, and salt over medium-high heat;
do not stir. Cook until the mixture reaches 235° to 240°F, 8 to 10 minutes, then
immediately remove from the heat. (Do not exceed 240°F.)

Turn the stand mixer with the bloomed gelatin and water on low, and carefully and slowly stream in the hot sugar mixture by pouring it down the inside of
the bowl. Once all of the sugar mixture has been incorporated, add the wasabi
powder, still mixing on low. Once incorporated, turn the stand mixer to high and
beat until fluffy, shiny, and just warm (feel the outside of the bowl), an additional
10 to 12 minutes.

Once the mixture is done, scoop it into the prepared pan. Lightly spray a rubber
spatula and use it to gently spread the marshmallow as evenly as possible. Lightly
spray the bottom of the second cookie sheet with the cooking spray and firmly
press it onto the marshmallows to even them out, then remove it. Evenly dust the
top of the marshmallows with the remaining confectioners' sugar–cornstarch mixture and sesame seeds. Let set, covered with plastic wrap, for at least 4 hours.

HOLD IT? Keep the marshmallows in an airtight container for up to 2 weeks.

Dust a pair of kitchen shears or a pizza wheel with confectioners' sugar and
cut the marshmallows into your desired size.

PLATE IT! These guys are fun little treats on their own, but you can also use them in a
s'more, or melt them over yams or apples, or even float them in a cup of cocoa.

BREAK IT: The same recipe and method here can be used with almost any powdered
ingredient (instead of wasabi) to achieve different flavors for use in your own creations—just be thoughtful as some powders are much more potent than others. For
example, adding some curry powder and putting these little guys on that banana split
(page 134) would be BONKERS. If you want to make a more traditional, kid-flavored
marshmallow, add a packet of powdered drink mix.

LAW OF LEMONADE

sour meets sweet

O f all the laws, the law of lemonade is probably the easiest to execute. Find something sour and add something sweet. Chances are the sum will be more palatable than the parts. The Italians have a single word to describe this phenomenon: *agrodolce,* literally "soursweet;" the concept is used all over Italian cuisine.

Sweetness comes from sugars; sour flavors come from acids, often found in fruits or fermented products. Saliva production gets bumped up when we taste sour foods, and more saliva means more food can contact more taste buds. So even if a food isn't particularly mouthwatering, a dash of acid can make it so. Why don't we just bite into a lemon, then? Because it's not palatable. Sugar tones down the taste of the acid, allowing for palatability.

Lots of the ready-made foods we enjoy have some play of sweet and sour. Coca-Cola has phosphoric acid to balance the sugars. The Big Mac is slathered in a sweet and tangy special sauce. The reason Big Food makes so much food that falls under the law of lemonade? It's one of the easiest ways to make something taste good. So while most every recipe has some sort of acidic component, in the recipes ahead, acid is the gear that makes it *go.*

sour meets sweet

LIME ZEST	LIME ZEST FRENCH TOAST STICKS	CHALLAH
GRAPEFRUIT	GINGER-BRÛLÉED GRAPEFRUIT	SUGAR
PICKLE JUICE	SPEED-PICKLE-BRINED CHICKEN NUGGETS WITH HONEY DIPPIN' SAUCE	HONEY
LIME / LEMON	THREE SWEET-AND-SOUR COCKTAILS YOU SHOULD KNOW	SUGAR
VINEGAR	CCF HOT AND SOUR SOUP	SUGAR
PASSION FRUIT	BURRATA WITH TROUT CAVIAR, PASSION FRUIT, VANILLA, AND DATES	DATES
MALT VINEGAR	CORRECTED FISH AND CHIPS	WHITE MISO
ORANGE	"ORANGE BLOSSOM" CHICKEN	MILK
YUZU	YOLO BURGER	KETCHUP
LEMON	LEMON-APPLE HAND PIES	APPLES

YIELD Makes 4 servings

PREP TIME 5 minutes

COOK TIME 25 minutes

gear

whisk

baking dish

2 sheet pans with racks

blender, spice grinder, or mortar and pestle

large sauté pan

fine-mesh strainer

ingredients

FRENCH TOAST

1 cup heavy cream

2 large whole eggs

2 egg yolks

¼ cup sugar

1 teaspoon kosher salt

¼ teaspoon pure vanilla extract

¼ teaspoon angostura bitters, about 5 dashes

1 teaspoon ground allspice

One whole loaf challah bread

2 tablespoons unsalted butter

LIME ZEST SUGAR

½ cup sugar

Zest of 3 limes

lime zest french toast sticks

(Canapé/snack)

Syrup tends to sog out whatever it touches—it also compounds the sweetness of the toast. Here, I make a zippy limed-up confectioners' sugar to offset the sweetness with a puckery sourness. The French toast is made out of challah. Already a supereggy, fluffy, and slightly sweet bread, it just needs a simple custard to bring it full circle. Instead of using a medley of ground spices, we rely on allspice and a few dashes of bitters, a combination of many spices and herbs in liquid form.

Start the French toast. Preheat the oven to 250°F.

Whisk together the cream, whole eggs, egg yolks, sugar, salt, vanilla, bitters, and allspice in a baking dish. Make sure the custard is very well combined and the eggs are well beaten.

Slice the whole challah loaf into thirds horizontally, then into 1½-inch diagonal strips. Place the strips in a single layer on a sheet pan fitted with a rack and toast until the exterior of the bread feels stale and dry, 10 to 15 minutes. Allow the sticks to cool.

Dip the sticks into the custard, let sit for a minute, then flip and let sit for a minute on each of the other 3 sides as well. Lay the sticks back on the sheet pan fitted with the rack to let the excess custard drip off, about 10 minutes.

Make the lime zest sugar. Combine the sugar and lime zest in a blender, spice grinder, or mortar and pestle. Grind until the consistency of confectioners' sugar, stopping to scrape down the sides, about 3 minutes.

HOLD IT? The soaked sticks can be held in the fridge, covered, for up to 12 hours. The sugar can be stored at room temperature for up to a week.

Cook the French toast. Place a clean sheet pan fitted with a clean rack in the oven. Preheat the oven to 250°F.

Melt the butter in a large sauté pan over medium-low heat. Once the butter is foaming, place some of the sticks in the pan without them touching. Cook until dark golden on one side, then flip and repeat on the other 3 sides. It doesn't take long to cook, so be mindful. I like my French toast with a little scorching, but that's up to you. Transfer the finished sticks to the sheet pan fitted with the rack to keep warm, and repeat the process with the remaining uncooked sticks.

PLATE IT! Stack all of the cooked French toast sticks like edible Lincoln Logs. Place the lime zest sugar in a fine-mesh strainer and dust the sticks like it's the most magical Christmas morning. Without syrup, the sticks can be eaten with hands, and make for an optimal buffet item.

BREAK IT: If you have leftover Jerk Chicken from page 279, pull the meat and keep it warm. Cut the bread into standard sandwich slices, then prepare the French toast as directed but using coconut milk instead of cream. Assemble into Jerk French toast sandwiches.

YIELD Makes 4 servings

PREP TIME 10 minutes

COOK TIME 5 minutes

gear

food processor or spice grinder

small serrated knife or grapefruit knife

sheet pan

ingredients

½ cup sugar, plus additional as needed

One 1-inch piece fresh ginger, peeled and minced

2 grapefruits

ginger-brûléed grapefruit

(COLD APP)

My grandparents have sent me Pittman and Davis grapefruits every holiday season since I can remember. When I was a kid, I put sugar all over them. As adults, my girlfriend and I have them all winter long, first thing in the morning, with a cup of toasty genmaicha tea. One morning I wanted to fancy hers up a bit, and brulée some sugar on top like at those fancy brunch restaurants that charge $6.00 for half a grapefruit. I looked in the pantry and realized I had no sugar. Crankily, I pushed everything out of my way in the pantry, convinced it had gotten pushed to the back. I didn't find it, but I did see a tin of candied ginger. In the bottom was residual ginger-flavored sugar. I spooned it on the grapefruit, torched it off, and was blown away. Using fresh ginger to make ginger sugar gives even more of a punch.

Some folks could get a little wound up about me putting a grapefruit in the "sour" section of the book as opposed to the "bitter" section. Calm down, everyone. Grapefruit might be a little bitter, but it's mostly tangy. If you want to try a bitter fruit, munch on a bergamot and get back to me—you'll find that grapefruit hardly bitter at all. It's tangy. And with tangy, we like sweet.

Make the sugar. Combine the sugar and ginger in a food processor or spice grinder and blend until fine and uniform. If the mixture appears wet, add a little more sugar. This isn't really an exact science because the wetness of ginger varies.

Prep the grapefruit. Halve the grapefruits horizontally. Cut a bit of the bottom off of each half so it sits flat. Using a small serrated knife, slice around each of the segments. Press out the excess liquid on top using paper towels.

HOLD IT! Keep the grapefruits refrigerated, uncovered, for up to 6 hours. Keep the sugar sealed in a dry place for up to 3 days.

Broil the grapefruit. Sprinkle ginger sugar generously over the top of the grapefruits and press down to pack tightly. Put the grapefruits on a sheet pan, place under the broiler, and broil until the sugar is bubbly and caramelized, checking every minute.

PLATE IT! These are best served each in a deep bowl with a grapefruit spoon, one of my favorite utensils. Crack up the sugar like you would before eating a crème brûlée and devour!

BREAK IT: Add some smoked paprika and/or cayenne to the mix to spice this up. Then mix any leftover juice from your bowl or grapefruit skin to make a "Mutt" to serve on the side. (This is my term for any riff on the Greyhound, which is grapefruit and vodka.)

YIELD Makes about 40 nuggets

PREP TIME 10 minutes

COOK TIME 15 minutes

INACTIVE TIME 20 minutes
with cream whipper, or 6 hours
without

gear

whisk

.5-liter cream whipper with two
N$_2$O cartridges (optional; I like
iSi brand)

small bowl

Dutch oven or heavy-bottomed
pot

candy thermometer

shallow bowl

spider or tongs

ingredients

CHICKEN

2 large chicken breasts (about
1 pound total)

1 cup favorite pickle brine

¼ cup confectioners' sugar

1 tablespoon kosher salt

DIPPIN' SAUCE

1 tablespoon pickle brine

¼ cup honey

NUGGETS

1 cup all-purpose flour

1 teaspoon freshly ground black

2 tablespoons kosher salt

1 tablespoon paprika

¼ cup granulated sugar

2 teaspoons garlic powder

3 tablespoons pickle brine

Peanut oil for frying

speed-pickle-brined chicken nuggets with honey dippin' sauce

(Hot app)

I have a giant beer stein engraved with "J\$." Somewhere along the line, J-Money, or even J-Mun, became my nickname. I would wager it's related to my compulsion to force everyone around me to get on my level of bon-vivantness, generally by blowing a ton of money on edible extravagance. These chicken nuggets—quickly marinated in pickle juice in a cream whipper—are inspired by the "family party platter" of chicken nuggets I ordered for my first prom date. We sat in tux and dress in the fast-food joint. I had purchased hideously gaudy goblets from the Goodwill and asked the staff to fill them with Sprite. It was a very humble beginning to my habit of over-the-top dining, but certainly one of my most memorable meals.

Make the chicken. Butterfly the chicken breasts by cutting them horizontally into two flat, uniformly thick pieces per breast, then cut into even 1- to 1½-inch nuggets.

In a measuring cup, whisk together the brine, confectioners' sugar, and salt.

If you have a cream whipper, load the chicken and brine into the charger. Charge with two cartridges of N$_2$O, one after the other, then put in the fridge for 20 minutes while you assemble the rest of the ingredients. (The cream whipper infuses the marinade into the chicken so it does not need to sit for long.) Alternatively, if you do not own a cream whipper, you can marinate the chicken in a bowl in the refrigerator for 6 hours.

Make the dippin' sauce. Whisk the honey and pickle brine together in a small bowl.

HOLD IT! Hold the marinating chicken in the fridge for at least 20 minutes and up to 6 hours.

Fry the nuggets. Fill a Dutch oven halfway with vegetable oil, clip on a candy thermometer, and bring the oil to 375°F over medium heat. Line a plate with paper towels.

Combine the dry ingredients for the dredge in a shallow bowl, then add the pickle brine. Using your hands, mix together the dredge until it's the consistency of semi-wet sand.

Drain the chicken in a colander, discarding the marinade, and put the chicken in a bowl.

Shake the excess brine off each piece of chicken, dredge the chicken pieces on all sides to coat well, then put them on a plate to hold.

Fry the nuggets, 8 to 10 at a time, so the oil temperature doesn't drop (throttling the heat as necessary to maintain a constant temperature of 375°F), and cook until the coating is dark and crispy and the center is cooked through, 2 to 4 minutes. Transfer the cooked nuggets to the paper towel–lined plate to drain. Continue cooking the nuggets in batches.

PLATE IT! I'd put all the nuggets on a platter, surrounding a central vessel of dipping sauce.

If you are going to have these as a meal, spoon the sauce on the plate, and gently rest the nuggets on top, so as not to sog out the entire nugget. Pair with fountain Sprite in a goblet you found at the Goodwill.

BREAK IT: Now that you know how to speed-brine, the question is what can be speed-brined with what. Immediately, I would think cranberry juice–brined turkey nuggets dipped in creamy mashed potatoes, but that's just the first thing that came to mind. If you wanted to go spicy, you could use some of the brine from the jalapeño carrots on page 264.

PREP TIME 10 minutes

SHAKE TIME 1 minute per cocktail

---

gear

muddler

cocktail shaker

---

caipirinha

MAKES 1 COCKTAIL

1 whole lime, cut into 8 pieces

2 teaspoons confectioners' sugar

2 ounces/¼ cup cachaça

Ice

---

mojito

MAKES 1 COCKTAIL

1 lime, cut into 8 pieces

1 teaspoon light brown sugar

2 ounces/¼ cup rum

8 to 10 fresh mint leaves

Ice

2 ounces/¼ cup soda water

---

whiskey sour

MAKES 1 COCKTAIL

Ice

2 ounces/¼ cup rye or bourbon whiskey

1 tablespoon fresh lemon juice

2 teaspoons confectioners' sugar

1 egg white (optional)

Dash of Angostura bitters (optional)

three sweet-and-sour cocktails you should know

(DRINKS)

Why should you know about these three cocktails? Because they teach you a lot about balancing sweet and sour, and actually make for great inspiration when you go to create your own dishes. These cocktails are listed from lightest to richest in flavor.

Caipirinha. When I was vacationing in Brazil, I ditched most of my gear at my *pousada* (kinda like a B&B but often with more rooms) and packed my backpack with limes, a bag of confectioners' sugar, and a bottle of cachaça. Everywhere I went I had a friend, so long as they had ice.

Muddle the lime and confectioners' sugar in the bottom of a shaker. Add the cachaça and a scoop of ice and shake until cold. Pour the contents (including ice and limes) into a short glass and serve.

Mojito. One of my first fancy bussing jobs was at a place called Roccoco, in Hagerstown, Maryland, my hometown. A super-learned cat named Malcom Norred wrote the recipe for a mojito on a receipt for me, even though I was only seventeen—I was advanced for my age, and he recognized that.

This mojito mixture (minus the ice and soda water) can be cooked briefly to burn off the alcohol, cooled, and folded into the sour cream in the Cuban[2] Chimichanga recipe (page 132) in lieu of the braising liquid.

Muddle the lime and brown sugar in the bottom of a shaker. Add the rum, tear in the mint, add a scoop of ice, and shake until supercold. Pour the contents (including ice and limes) into a tall glass and top with soda water.

Whiskey Sour. To be a well-rounded human, or at least to be my friend, it is a requirement that you drink whiskey. This is a nice baby step in that direction. Some people are squeamish about drinking egg white, but it creates a highly drinkable texture with a foamy head on top of the cocktail. Try using the cocktail recipe (minus the egg white) instead of the lemon juice in the Lemon-Apple Hand Pies (page 233) for a more adult-oriented treat.

Fill a shaker with ice. Add the whiskey, lemon juice, and confectioners' sugar and shake until cold.

Add the egg white, if using, and shake super-super-duper vigorously, until frosty and frothy. Strain into a glass. Watch as the head forms on top. Add a dash of Angostura bitters if you like. Fancy bartenders often drag a cocktail straw through the bitters to make swirly patterns.

BREAK IT: Bitters come in all manner of flavors, and every one of these cocktails can be modified with ease because of them. I think a spicy bitters would be good in all, but get crazy—add rhubarb bitters for acid, celery bitters for astringency, and so on.

gear

whisk

small bowl

large stockpot

ingredients

3 tablespoons cornstarch

¼ cup white vinegar

1 tablespoon vegetable oil

2 garlic cloves, grated

One 1-inch piece fresh ginger, peeled and grated

1 teaspoon white pepper

1 teaspoon onion powder

1 teaspoon ground cayenne pepper

2 quarts vegetable stock (or vegetable broth, and cut the salt by half)

10 ounces button mushrooms, thinly sliced

One 8-ounce can sliced bamboo shoots

3 tablespoons soy sauce

2 tablespoons sugar

1 teaspoon MSG (optional, see Tip)

1 teaspoon kosher salt

One 12-ounce package firm tofu, cubed

2 large eggs, beaten

☞ **Tip**

MSG is actually delicious. You can find it in Asian stores as well as Latin groceries, where sometimes it's called Aji No Moto.

ccf hot and sour soup

(Hot soup)

My GF and I are pros when it comes to staying in bed and watching Netflix while hungover. Our roles are clearly defined. I enter the wild and forage for Gatorades and coconut waters. I return, sometimes with straws. By this time, my GF has ordered CCF, or Crappy Chinese Food. But the crappy does not mean this is bad food. It's *great* food. We just needed a way to differentiate between this Chinese food, from the local take-out-only place, and the legendary places in Manhattan's Chinatown and Flushing, Queens. My GF rates a CCF joint based on its hot and sour soup. But when I started to develop this recipe, I realized that the crux of this soup is more based on a hell of an *aigre-doux* (sweet-sour) of a broth. I figured the local CCF joint doesn't use turbinado or ten-year-old balsamic, so I went with granulated sugar and white vinegar. These two create the perfect stage for a little cayenne to dance on. That said, the level of spice can be adjusted depending on your hangover. I tested this recipe on my actually hungover GF, and she approved, then went back to bed to watch *Orange Is the New Black*.

Whisk together the cornstarch and vinegar in a small bowl to make a slurry. Set aside.

Heat the oil over medium heat in a large stockpot. Add the garlic, ginger, white pepper, onion powder, and cayenne and sauté for a minute until fragrant. Add the stock, mushrooms, bamboo shoots, soy sauce, sugar, MSG if using, salt, and the cornstarch-vinegar slurry. Bring to a boil, reduce to a simmer, and cook until thickened slightly, 4 to 6 minutes. Add the tofu and cook until heated through, about 5 minutes. Using a wooden spoon, give the soup a healthy stir to set the broth in motion, then drizzle in the beaten eggs to make ghostly ribbons throughout the soup.

HOLD IT! The soup can be cooled and stored in the fridge, covered, for up to 4 days. Don't tell anyone, but sometimes I like to take a slug of it cold, straight from the fridge. It's like the CCF version of a Bloody Mary (see page 198).

This soup can take some abuse. If it thickens up too much, just add a little water. Reheat it on the stovetop, or in the microwave if you are too hungover.

PLATE IT! This soup is best enjoyed in a big deep bowl in bed, with your hungover partner.

BREAK IT: Strain off 6 ounces of the soup broth and shake over ice with a shot of vodka. Behold, the Asian version of the antiquated Bullshot (beef bouillon and vodka) cocktail.

gear

small microwave-safe bowl

ingredients

¼ vanilla bean

1 tablespoon olive oil

Nonstick cooking spray

8 pitted dates

1 passion fruit

One 8-ounce ball burrata

1¾ ounces salmon roe

burrata with trout caviar, passion fruit, vanilla, and dates

(Cold fish)

I am a huge Nintendo fan. I've played countless hours of Mario, Pokémon, and the like. Of all the games I've played, the series I've played the most is Smash Bros. In this game, four classic characters duke it out in an arena, often resulting in hilarity and chaos. This dish is Smash Bros. for your mouth. Ingredients of differing tastes, textures, and intensities do battle in a field of vanilla olive oil, which evokes sweetness, but is savory, complex, and deep. They go at each other with all their might. The sour passion fruit attacks the caviar's salt and the sweet dates with acid. The sticky date is protected by the fatty creaminess of the burrata. The burrata gets chomped as we crunch the passion fruit and search out the murky salinity of the caviar. It's impossible to decide a victor until you see what bite is left last on your plate, but I'd wager the last bite will be a perfect portion of all of the ingredients. This is a dish for people who can see the art in a good fight, not for people who use Pikachu's down and B move over and over.

Scrape the seeds out of the piece of vanilla bean, and discard the pod. Combine the seeds with the oil in small microwave-safe bowl. Microwave for 30 seconds.

Lightly spray a knife with nonstick cooking spray, then use it to dice the dates into small cubes.

Cut the passion fruit in half and scrape out the seeds; discard the skin. Set the seeds aside.

HOLD IT? The dates and oil can be left at room temperature, covered, for up to a day. The passion fruit seeds can be held in the fridge, covered, for up to 2 hours.

PLATE IT! This can be such a pretty dish, I try to have each serving look identical. Line up four plates. Quarter the burrata, being careful not to lose the creamy interior. Cut each of the quarters of burrata into 2 or 3 pieces.

Place the burrata sections on the plates. Next, divide the passion fruit among the four plates, placing it on top of some of the burrata and away from other pieces. Next, add the dates to the plate, in little piles, here and there. Add the roe in clumps, adjacent to or on top of the burrata. Finally, drizzle on the oil in a circular motion, like playing connect the dots.

BREAK IT: Adding more components to this dish will only make it more over the top. Use some cracked coffee beans for a bitter, toasty component, and cook some thyme with the vanilla bean to give it an herbal oomph.

YIELD Makes 4 servings

PREP TIME 20 minutes

COOK TIME 15 minutes

INACTIVE TIME 24 hours

gear

baking dish

large heatproof bowl

stockpot

rack or a sheet pan lined with paper towels

2 medium bowls

whisk

cream whipper plus N₂O charger

Dutch oven or heavy-bottomed pot

candy thermometer

2 sheet pans with racks

spider or tongs

ingredients

FISH

2 pounds cod fillets, skinned

1 pound white miso paste, at room temperature

CHIPS

4 pounds russet potatoes

1 cup kosher salt

BATTER

1 cup all-purpose flour

¼ cup rice flour

1 tablespoon baking powder

2 teaspoons kosher salt

1 cup light-colored beer

¼ cup vodka

1 tablespoon malt vinegar

corrected fish and chips

(HOT FISH)

An awesome plate of fish and chips with malt vinegar is one of life's great pleasures. Unfortunately, this dish is best consumed right out of the fryer basket, as the half-life of fish and chips is very short. Fish and chips is a great test of a cook, because it's all in the technique—therefore, fair warning, doing it right is a bit involved. Every plate begins with raw potatoes and raw fish. It leaps from the oil as crisp as it will ever be, and then rapidly descends into soggy entropy. As a consumer of fish and chips, I'm also guilty of contributing to its mushy decline, as I'm the guy who dumps malt vinegar all over it. The acidity of the vinegar coaxes out the sweetness of the fish, and plays a great foil to the glistening batter and chips. By bumping up the batter with a barrage of bubbles, putting a pellicle (that plasticene crust that forms on cured fish) on the pescado, putting the salt *inside* the chips with a salt water bath, and using malt vinegar powder instead of liquid, the mushy maladies of fish and chips have been corrected. My goal here was not to make a creative or "my spin on" fish and chips, but to make fish and chips that is as good on bite one as it is on the final bite, malt vinegar and all.

Marinate the fish. Rinse the cod, pat dry with paper towels, and portion into 8 pieces. Place the cod in a baking dish and gently and generously rub every piece with the miso. Wrap with plastic wrap, refrigerate, and allow to cure for 24 hours.

Prep the chips. Peel the potatoes. Slice off ¼ inch from both ends to square up the potato a little. Cut a ¼-inch slice off the side of the potato to keep it from rolling around. Cut each potato into ¼-inch slices, and then cut those slices into ¼-inch sticks. As you cut them, place the sticks in a heatproof bowl and add water to cover to prevent discoloration.

Once all the sticks are cut, drain the water into a stockpot, holding the potatoes back with your hands or tongs. Add the salt to the water, then bring to a boil over high heat. Pour the hot salted water over the potato sticks and let sit at room temperature until cool, about 30 minutes. Drain the potatoes, then set aside on a rack or sheet pan lined with paper towels.

Make the batter. Whisk all of the dry ingredients in a bowl, whisk the wet together in a separate bowl, and then whisk the wet ingredients into the dry. Pour the entire mixture into a cream whipper.

Prep the fish. Gently scrape the miso off of the marinated fillets (reserve the miso for up to 24 hours to add to ramen broth on page 120 or another cooked application if you want!). Rinse the fillets under cool water and land on a paper towel–lined plate. Gently pat dry. Chill the fish in the fridge until ready to fry.

HOLD IT? The cut potato can be held in water, covered, and refrigerated up to a day. The batter can be held, uncharged, in the charger up to 2 days. The fish, once rinsed, can be held in the fridge for up to a day.

TO FRY

½ cup rice flour

Vegetable oil, for frying

Malt vinegar powder, for serving (optional; available on the Internet)

Fry the chips. Fill a Dutch oven halfway with oil, clip on a candy thermometer, and bring the oil to 300°F over medium heat. Set up a sheet pan fitted with a wire rack.

Par-fry the dry potatoes in batches for 5 minutes, throttling accordingly to keep the temperature constant, then transfer them with a spider or tongs to the rack on a sheet pan. They will be softer and lightly colored.

Preheat the oven to 250°F. Once all the potatoes have been par-fried, turn the heat up to medium-high, and bring the oil up to 375°F, then reduce the heat to medium. Fry the par-fried potatoes in batches again until golden brown, 4 to 6 minutes. No need to salt these guys as the salt is inside them. Using the spider or tongs, transfer the twice-cooked potatoes to the rack on the sheet pan and keep in the warm oven until the fish is cooked.

Fry the fish. Keep the oil in the Dutch oven at 375°F.

Charge the batter in the charger with one charger of N₂O and dispense back into same bowl in which it was mixed. You should now have a superlight batter with four kinds of bubbles—beer bubbles, vodka evaporating bubbles, baking powder bubbles, and nitrous bubbles!

Put ½ cup rice flour on a plate next to the batter and fryer.

Lay 1 or 2 pieces of the fish in the rice flour, dust well, dunk in the batter, then drop directly into the oil and fry until golden brown, 3 to 5 minutes. Remove the cooked fish from the oil and transfer to the rack on a sheet pan in the oven with the chips to keep warm until all are fried. Continue dusting, dunking, and frying until all of the fish has been cooked.

PLATE IT! I love to serve these on newspaper, but people get weird about it. If you and your friends want the authentic experience, roll some newspaper into a cone and go to town. Otherwise, use parchment paper to absorb excess oil on the plate. Dust with malt vinegar powder, if you'd like. I like.

BREAK IT: Experiment with the miso rub. You can now impart almost any flavor to the fish, so why not amp it up? I'd head straight to kimchi juice (leftover from the sweet potato on page 268) for a funky and spicy take.

---

gear

small saucepan

gallon-size zip-top bag with
large bowl

roasting pan

probe thermometer

ingredients

6 navel oranges, about 1 pound

¼ cup kosher salt

2 tablespoons sugar

1 tablespoon whole black
peppercorns

2 bay leaves

1 cup whole milk

1 cup heavy cream

One 3½-pound whole chicken

"orange blossom" chicken

(LIGHT MEAT)

As a kid I hung out with some friends at an Exxon station that sold Hershey's ice cream (no affiliation with the chocolatiers). Hershey's was the regional creamery that made ice cream for retail scoop shops. My favorite flavor was "orange blossom," a mix of creamy vanilla ice cream and bright orange sherbet (others might recognize this combination from a Creamsicle). The play with sweet and sour inspired this roasted chicken recipe. Here the bird gets a dip in salt, acid, sweetness and fat, resulting in a deeply colored and supermoist bird.

Make the marinade. Zest and juice 2 of the oranges, then juice 2 of the remaining oranges and reserve the unzested, squeezed shells, refrigerated, until it's time to cook the chicken.

Add the orange juice, salt, sugar, black peppercorns, and bay leaves to a small saucepan and bring to a simmer over low heat. Allow to cool until just barely warm, then put in the fridge to chill completely, about an hour.

Combine the chilled orange juice mixture with the milk and cream. Set a gallon-size zip-top bag in a large bowl in the sink and put the chicken into the bag. Carefully pour the marinade over the bird, seal the bag, and refrigerate for at least 12 hours, turning the bird halfway through the marinating time.

HOLD IT? You can hold the chicken in the marinade for up to 24 hours.

Roast the chicken. Preheat the oven to 500°F.

Slice the remaining 2 oranges into ½-inch rounds.

Pull the chicken out of the marinade, and scrape away any excess aromatics; discard the marinade. Place the bird, breast side up, in a roasting pan. Stuff the chicken's cavity with the reserved squeezed orange shells, and arrange the sliced orange rounds around the chicken.

Roast the chicken for 20 minutes. Then, using a thick towel or pot holder to protect your hands, cover the pan with aluminum foil and reduce the oven temperature to 450°F. Cook the bird until the juices from the thigh run clear, about 1 hour more; the thigh meat should register about 155°F on a probe thermometer. (Bear in mind that the folks at the USDA specify 165°F.) Let the bird rest for at least 10 minutes before carving and serving. (Upon carving, you may notice a slight pinkness to the chicken. This is a natural reaction to the salt and sugar in our marinade. It's curing! The best indication of doneness is the feeling of the meat. If it feels rubbery and squishy, it's not cooked.)

PLATE IT! This chicken looks stellar on a big platter with the caramelized orange rounds surrounding it. This would be gonzo served with the butternut squash and orange soup on page 297 or the kimchi-loaded sweet potatoes on page 268.

BREAK IT: Much like a Sazerac cocktail (whiskey, absinthe, orange twist, bitters), a healthy does of anise would be great with the orange in this dish. Stuff some whole stalks of tarragon into the cavity halfway through the roasting, then lay some along the sides of the bird when serving.

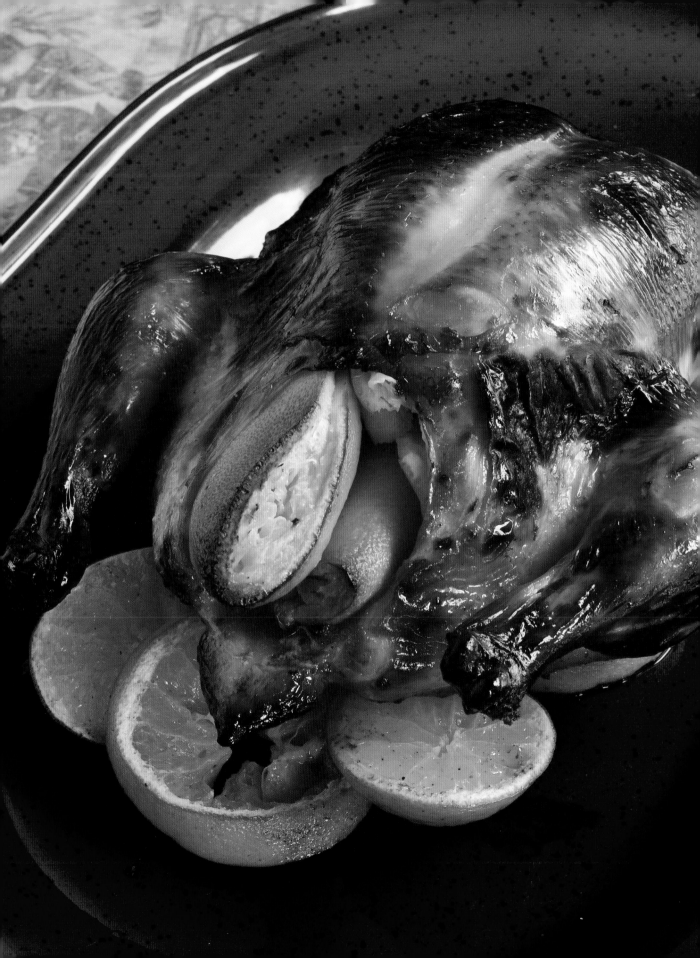

YIELD Makes 16 patties; 8 double decker burgers

PREP TIME 10 minutes

COOK TIME 20 minutes

gear

small pot

whisk

2 sheet pans

ring cutter or small glass

wax paper

small bowl

Dutch oven or heavy-bottomed pot

candy thermometer

large mixing bowl

kitchen scale

flat, hole-less spatula

meat mallet or tall pepper mill

ingredients

TOMATO DISKS (OPTIONAL, BUT WORTHWHILE)

One 12-ounce bottle V8 juice

1 teaspoon agar agar

SAUCE

½ cup mayonnaise

1 shallot, finely chopped

2 tablespoons ketchup

1 tablespoon yuzu juice (you can substitute lemon juice)

BURGERS

3 pounds ground beef (see Tip)

2 teaspoons fish sauce

2 teaspoons kosher salt

1 teaspoon freshly ground black pepper

Vegetable oil, for frying

yolo burger
(DARK MEAT)

The best burger in America is at Dyer's in Memphis, Tennessee. The secret? They smash the patties until thin, and then deep-fry them—but the oil is never discarded. Filtered, reserved, and topped off, the burger oil has been in the family for over a hundred years. It was transported in an armored car when they switched locations. Just imagine cooking garlic in oil every day for a hundred years, how perfumed and perfect it would be. Hence, Dyer's burger is a thing of miracles, and the closest a burger will get to being butter. In my version, I borrow their method, but add a melting tomato gel disk (because tomatoes are never in season and V8 has all of the vegetables!) and a splash of yuzu (the sour juice of a hyperaddictive citrus fruit from Japan) in my special sauce to balance out the sweetness in the ketchup.

Make the tomato disks. Whisk the V8 juice and the agar agar in a small pot. Bring to a simmer, then pour onto one of the sheet pans. Let set in the fridge until firm, 30 to 40 minutes.

Using a ring cutter or round glass, cut the firmed up V8 into 8 even disks, or cut into squares with a knife. Transfer the disks to wax paper, stack on a plate, and refrigerate.

Make the sauce. Put all the ingredients for the sauce in a small bowl and mix to combine.

HOLD IT? The tomato disks and sauce can be refrigerated, covered, for up to 3 days.

FOR SERVING

8 potato rolls (I like Martin's brand)

16 American cheese singles

Butter lettuce leaves

Pickle chips

☞ **Tip**

When it comes to ground beef for a burger, the fattier the better. Got a blend you like? Go for it.

Make the burgers. Preheat the broiler. Fill a Dutch oven halfway with oil, clip on a candy thermometer, and heat until the oil reaches 375°F.

Split open the rolls, place them on a sheet pan, and broil until toasted. Leave the buns on the pan and apply some sauce to each.

Place the ground beef in a mixing bowl and add the fish sauce, salt, and pepper. Combine until the seasonings are evenly distributed. Portion out the meat into 3-ounce balls using the kitchen scale. On a clean work surface, use a flat hole-less spatula and meat mallet or plastic-wrapped pepper grinder to flatten the portioned meat out as flat as possible without tearing: In your dominant hand, hold the spatula, and in your other hand, the mallet. Lay the spatula on top of the ball of ground beef. Using the meat mallet, strike the spatula, flattening the patty. Continue doing this around the edges to push the patty out to about 4 times the area. If the patty falls apart, just roll it back up and try again. Eventually you will be able to strike in one fluid motion, like the masters at Dyer's. It's not a science, it's an art.

Using the spatula, slide 2 patties, one by one, directly into the oil and cook until the middle puffs up slightly, about 1 minute. Land one patty directly on the prepared bottom bun and one off to the side. Lightly season each with salt and pepper.

Unwrap 2 pieces of cheese and, using tongs, hold one by the corner and very carefully dip it into the hot oil for less than 5 seconds. You run the risk of losing the cheese to breakage but it's safer than using your hands like they do at Dyer's. Lay the cheese on the first hamburger patty. Add the other cooked patty on top of the cheese. Repeat with the second slice of cheese to create a double-decker cheeseburger. Top the burger with a tomato agar disk, lettuce, and pickles. These aren't the kind of burgers you want sitting around. Serve them up like a short-order cook and push them out! Repeat with the remaining patties.

PLATE IT! These burgers are so fast food they don't need a plate. Lay them on sheets of parchment paper, and watch them get destroyed. Filter and save the oil for a hundred years! (See headnote.)

BREAK IT: The burger is a miracle, because a perfect burger makes a new canvas to paint upon. Want to add foie and jam (page 48)? Be my guest. How about curry and squid (page 277)? You betcha. Go crazy, and tweet me pics.

YIELD Makes 6 hand pies

PREP TIME 30 minutes

COOK TIME 25 minutes

INACTIVE TIME 1 hour

gear

large nonreactive bowl

large saucepan

food processor

shallow baking dish

sheet pan with a nonstick silicone baking mat or parchment paper

rolling pin

pastry wheel

small bowl

pastry brush

cooling rack

ingredients

FILLING

Juice of 2 lemons, about 2 tablespoons

4 Gala or Golden Delicious apples, about 2 pounds

1 cup sugar

1 teaspoon kosher salt

1 teaspoon ground cinnamon

1 tablespoon unsalted butter

CRUST

2¾ cups all-purpose flour

1 teaspoon kosher salt

8 tablespoons (1 stick) cold unsalted butter, cut into ¼-inch cubes and frozen

4 ounces vegetable shortening, about ½ cup plus 1 tablespoon, cut into ¼-inch cubes and frozen

½ cup ice-cold water

1 egg

lemon-apple hand pies

(DESSERT)

Most recipes for apple pie filling call for lemon in order to brighten up the appley flavor and boost the pectin (read: fruit glue) to thicken the filling. I read a blog post by genius food dude J. Kenji López-Alt (check him out, he's awesome) in which he describes making a pie filling without lemon, because he didn't want lemon flavor in the pie. Of course, me being me, I thought the opposite . . . why not add more lemon!? Let's make hot, semisolid cinnamon-apple lemonade encased in flaky pastry! Like an Applejack hot toddy!

I thought of my most gratifying pie experience and recalled Dale's Fried Pies in Knoxville, Tennessee. I hung out with Dale Mackey for my show *Rebel Eats,* but sadly the segment didn't make the cut. It was raining, cold, and Dale was a real good sport about the whole thing. Her pies are awesome, and come filled with craziness that I very deeply approve of (mac and cheese pie, curry pie, awesome fruit pie), and best of all, being fried hand pies, they are portable. Portability of quality food is a problem as old as food itself. The hand pie solves this, and also doubles as an edible hand warmer, something your doughnut will never do.

Make the filling. Place the lemon juice in a nonreactive bowl. Peel and slice the apples about ¼ inch thick and toss them in the lemon juice to prevent them from browning. Add the sugar, salt, and cinnamon, then toss with the apples.

Melt the butter in a large saucepan over medium-low heat, then add the apple mixture and cook for about 20 minutes, until the apples have softened and the liquid in the pan has thickened and darkened in color. Turn off the heat.

Add half of the apples and all of the liquid to a food processor and pulse until about the consistency of applesauce. Transfer this mix back to the pan with the remaining apples and stir to combine. Spread out on a shallow baking dish and allow to completely cool in the fridge. More surface area means less time needed to chill.

Make the crust dough. In a clean food processor bowl, pulse the flour and salt to combine. Scatter the frozen butter and shortening cubes around the bowl. Pulse the fats with the flours 5 or 6 times; they will be barely incorporated. Then, while pulsing the processor, use the emulsion tube to very slowly add the ice water, 2 tablespoons at a time; check after each addition and stop adding water when the bits of dough can be pinched together between your fingers. (The dough will most likely not need as much water as this recipe calls for because your flour might be more damp than my flour.) Press all the bits of dough together in the bowl, forming a ball, then tightly wrap the dough with plastic wrap. Chill the dough in the fridge for at least 30 minutes.

HOLD IT? You can hold the pie filling and dough for up to a day, covered, in the fridge.

Make the pies. Preheat the oven to 425°F. Line a sheet pan with a nonstick silicone baking mat or parchment paper. Lightly wet a work surface, then lay 2 long sheets of plastic wrap down, side by side, with about an inch of overlap. Now you don't have to flour your work surface and you don't have to dust flour off of everything.

Cut the dough in half. Rewrap one half, and place it in the fridge. Place the other half on the plastic wrap, and cover with another layer of plastic, pressing the dough down flat with your palm.

With a rolling pin, roll the dough (still between the two sheets of plastic wrap) into a rectangle about 7 x 18 inches. Remove the top piece of plastic wrap and place about ¼ cup of the filling about 2 inches from the short side of the dough closest to you, shaping the filling into a rectangle. Lift the closest edge of the bottom piece of plastic wrap and pull up and away from you to fold the top of the dough over the filling, making sure to pass the filling by about an inch, to allow space to seal. Cut/seal the seams on the three open sides with a pastry wheel, fork, or the back of a knife (be careful!). Trim and discard any excess dough, or lump it all together, and make a "cinnamon pig." Continue to make two more pies. Lay the three finished hand pies on the prepared sheet pan.

Roll out, fill, and cut/seal the other half of the dough into 3 more hand pies, using the rest of the lemon-apple mixture.

In a small bowl, beat the egg very well with a fork. Generously brush all the pies with the beaten egg, brushing carefully to coat to the edge. Poke 3 slits in the top of each pie with a sharp knife.

Bake until the tops are golden brown and the filling is set, about 25 minutes. Transfer the pies to a cooling rack until just warm enough to handle.

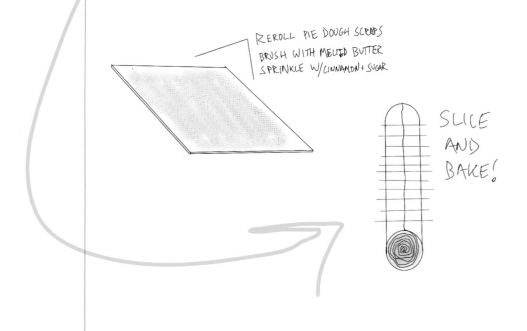

REROLL PIE DOUGH SCRAPS
BRUSH WITH MELTED BUTTER
SPRINKLE W/ CINNAMON + SUGAR

SLICE AND BAKE!

Hand pie extra credit

If you want to be awesome like Dale (see headnote), go ahead and make this pie dough, then put the leftovers of one of my other recipes in it instead of the Lemon-Apple recipe above. Mac and cheese on page 182, the lamb (off the bone) and carrots on page 45, even a slice of the chocolate cake from page 283, all chilled down first, would work great, but get creative: anything that is cold upon insertion and not too saucy could be the next big thing.

PLATE IT! Oh man, oh man, you could have so much fun. These guys might be nice wrapped in foil and eaten on a walk on a cold morning or evening. Or, if you wanted to, you could top these with ice cream. Traditionalists would say vanilla, but I think a scoop of chocolate might be insane—even more insane if you used the chipotle chocolate from page 134.

CHEAT IT! You can use this same filling with store-bought pie crust—just unroll it and cut it into squares as described above.

BREAK IT: Wisconsonians have a weird apple pie custom that breaks the law nicely. Add a slice of cheddar cheese before removing from the oven to give the pie some sharpness. To go even further, panfry a slice of scrapple and place it on top of the cheesy pie.

STEP YOUR GAME UP

Try replacing the lemon juice with a whiskey sour (minus the egg white; see page 222) for a more adult-oriented treat.

LAW
OF
PESTO

herbs meet fat

My mother told me the etymology of the word *pesto* after I asked about the mortar and pestle on the pharmacy sign. *Pesto* comes from the same root word as *pestle*, which was traditionally used to crush up herbs and nuts in the mortar for medicinal reasons. The law of pesto is about herbs, and the way they play with fats. Herbs make rich foods seem lighter, greener, and fresher. Pesto is mostly a sauce of fats (pine nuts, cheese, oil) but thanks to an herb, basil, pesto is rarely described as rich or heavy. This is the incredible "lightening" power of herbs. If there was one thing I could recommend to any cook to step up their cooking game, it would be to learn more about herbs. Parsley shouldn't just be chopped up and thrown on top of a dish "for color." Like all other foods (and herbs), it has its own flavor identity, and when it is recognized and utilized, it can do so much more. Herbs are flavor grenades: intense, pungent, and fresh-tasting.

herbs meet fat

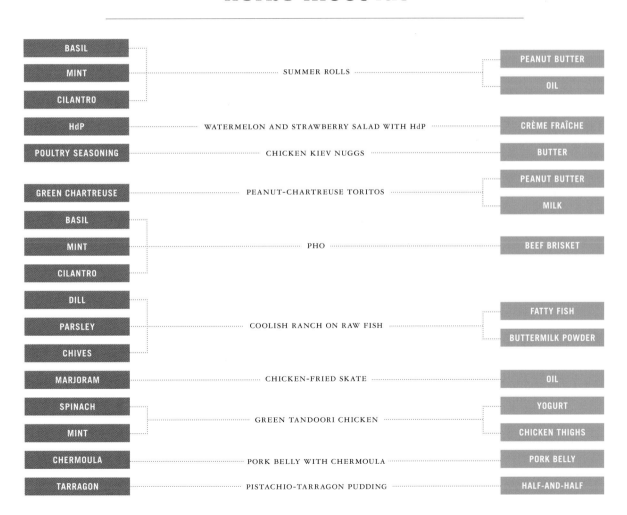

YIELD Makes 16 rolls

PREP TIME 15 minutes

COOK TIME 15 minutes

INACTIVE TIME about 4 hours

gear

small saucepan

whisk

sheet pan

Dutch oven or heavy-bottomed pot

candy thermometer

large pot

shallow bowl

fine-mesh strainer or chinois (see sidebar page 37)

large bowl

ingredients

SAUCE

1 tablespoon rice wine vinegar

1½ teaspoons hoisin sauce

1½ teaspoons tamari sauce

2 tablespoons peanut butter

3 tablespoons water

TOFU

One 12-ounce-pack firm tofu

Vegetable oil, for frying

VERMICELLI

About 8 ounces rice vermicelli

1 tablespoon grapeseed oil

summer rolls

(Canapé/snack)

Summer rolls, the leaner, cleaner alternative to spring rolls, are the kind of thing that when I see them, I want them, no matter the season. They are portable, pretty darn healthy, and have an addictive texture. The balance of semi-chewy rice paper and noodles along with the crisp veggies and toothsome tofu keep me coming back for bite after bite. By freezing the tofu, we expel a fair amount of water, which makes for a crisper exterior upon frying. The herbs are like a breath mint for your soul on a hot summer day, and the peanut sauce gives the dish some depth and spice, serving as an ideal dressing to what is essentially a hand-held pasta salad. I prefer tofu because I think it's fun to have a totally vegetable-based snack (and I usually share with my GF, who always wants tofu). If tofu isn't your bag, you could add precooked shrimp. If you are feeling especially crazy, substitute some of the lobster salad from page 298 for the tofu.

Make the sauce. Combine all the ingredients for the sauce in a small saucepan and simmer over low heat, whisking until the peanut butter has dissolved. Set aside to cool.

Prep the tofu. Cut the tofu in half horizontally, and then each half into quarters. Cut each of the quarters into 4 strips. Arrange the tofu strips in a single layer on a sheet pan and freeze until frozen solid, about 4 hours.

Defrost the tofu strips, and press with paper towels to extract as much moisture as possible without breaking them.

Fill a Dutch oven halfway with oil, clip on a thermometer, and bring the oil to 350°F over medium heat. Add the tofu strips and fry until golden, about 3 minutes, then transfer to paper towels to drain.

Prep the vermicelli. Bring 8 to 10 cups water to a boil in a large pot. Reserve about 1 cup of the hot water in a shallow bowl or plate.

Turn the heat off under the pot, drop in the noodles, and let soak until pliable, about 4 minutes for most types. Drain the noodles in a fine-mesh strainer, gently rinse with cold water until cool. Drain very well, then place in a bowl, drizzle with the oil, and toss to coat.

Make the rolls. On sheet pans or a clean work surface, divide the tofu, noodles, and vegetables into 16 equal piles. This may seem tedious now, but it will speed up the assembly process later on and provide a uniform filling amount.

Soak 1 sheet of rice paper in the reserved hot water and allow it to become pliable, about 45 seconds. Carefully remove the sheet from the water, and pull off onto a clean work surface. In your mind, draw a square in the rice paper; this is the fill zone. Spread the noodles out first along the lowest line of the fill zone. Next, nestle 2 of the tofu blocks into the noodles. Next come the veggie sticks, which should sit in front of the noodles. Add a healthy sprinkle of each of the herbs. Fold in the left and right sides along the fill-zone lines, then, starting from the bottom, carefully lift the bottom edge up, and pull gently so as to tightly wrap the filling. Continue making the rolls with the remaining ingredients, transfer to a platter, and cover them with plastic wrap until it's time to serve.

ROLLS

1 hothouse or seedless cucumber, finely julienned

1 yellow bell pepper, cored, seeded, and julienned

1 medium carrot, peeled and julienned

16 rice paper wrappers

¼ cup chopped fresh Thai basil

¼ cup chopped fresh mint

¼ cup chopped fresh cilantro

HOLD IT? These rolls can be held for up to 6 hours, refrigerated, wrapped in plastic.

PLATE IT! If I were taking these on the road, I'd shove some of that peanut sauce into a little squeeze bottle (like a hair color bottle—clean, obviously—from a beauty supply store) and leave the rolls whole so the herbs and veggies don't dry out.

If I were serving these to guests, I'd cut the rolls in half to expose all the pretties we put inside, and serve with the sauce in little ramekins.

BREAK IT: Instead of tofu, add chilled cooked mackerel or sardine fillets (see page 150). Their natural oils will lube up the interior nicely, while giving the herbs another fat to brighten.

PREP TIME 15 minutes

COOK TIME 15 minutes

gear

colander

large bowl

airtight container

small bowl

melon baller

ingredients

HdP

One ¾-ounce container fresh rosemary

One ¾-ounce container fresh thyme

One ¾-ounce container fresh lavender

One ¾-ounce container fresh oregano

One ¾-ounce container fresh marjoram

One ¾-ounce container fresh savory

SALAD

⅓ cup crème fraîche

½ teaspoon kosher salt

3½ pounds seedless mini watermelon

1 quart strawberries, hulled

What to do with extra HdP!

HdP is a workhorse. It's great on popcorn, stirred into soups, sprinkled on top of pizza, or even mixed into the burger on page 231 to French it up.

watermelon and strawberry salad with hdp

(COLD APP)

HdP is my shorthand for "Herbes de Provence." Generally HdP is a blend of dried herbs one might find in the south of France. Lavender is added to the mix in America—I kind of enjoy that we take the liberty to make up our own herb blend and label it as the regional specialty of another country. *Trés Américain.* In this recipe, HdP and a little salt turn what could be a fruity dessert into an awesome summer salad.

Make the HdP. Put the herbs in single layers between sheets of paper towels and stack on a dinner plate.

Cook the bundle in the microwave at half power, in 2-minute bursts, for a total of 15 minutes. The point of going in bursts is to create a gradual dehydration by allowing it to cool for just a moment in between. The herbs should now be fully dried.

Dump all the herbs into a colander set in a large bowl and let cool. Using your hands, rub off all the leaves from the stems by rubbing the mass of herbs in circles on the base of the colander. This will crumble the herbs—that is OK. The stems will stay in the colander and the leaves should fall through. Pick out and discard any small stems that slipped through into the bowl. Store the herb mix in an airtight container.

Prep the salad. In a small bowl, combine the crème fraîche, salt, and 1 tablespoon of the HdP. Let sit in the fridge while prepping the fruit.

Using the melon baller, create as many watermelon balls as you can, and place them in a colander to drain.

Place the hulled strawberries in the colander. Discard any excess liquid or use it to make a quick marg like on page 296. Mix the fruit and the dressing together, tossing gently.

HOLD IT? The HdP will keep, covered, at room temperature for a month. Store the prepped watermelon and strawberries in the colander, covered, in the fridge for up to 6 hours. The dressing can be kept in the fridge, covered, for up to 3 days.

PLATE IT! This is the kind of guy that looks great in an opaque bowl, with a big spoon in it. (Clear bowls are good for undressed salads, but nobody wants to look at a pool of pinkish [but delicious] liquid at the bottom of a bowl.) This would be a great summer salad with the F-Yeah Barbecue (page 102).

BREAK IT: Instead of crème fraîche, use half sour cream and half blue cheese to make a creamy, funky salad, elevated by sweet strawberries and herbs.

YIELD Makes about 25 nuggs

PREP TIME 20 minutes

COOK TIME 20 minutes

INACTIVE TIME 2 hours

gear

mixing bowl

whisk

pastry bag or gallon-size zip-top bag

sheet pan or plate

food processor or spice grinder

small baking dish or shallow bowl

2 sheet pans, one with a rack

Dutch oven or heavy-bottomed pot

candy thermometer

ingredients

HOTEL BUTTER

8 tablespoons (1 stick) unsalted butter, at room temperature

1 tablespoon panko bread crumbs

1 tablespoon kosher salt

2 teaspoons poultry seasoning

CHICKEN NUGGS

1 cup panko bread crumbs

½ teaspoon kosher salt

1¾ pounds ground chicken, or boneless, skinless chicken breast

2 eggs, beaten

Vegetable oil, for frying

chicken kiev nuggs

(HOT APP)

Hotel butter—a delicious amalgam of butter and chopped soft herbs, traditionally used to melt slowly over a seared steak or crusty roll—is solid proof that herbs and fat are best friends. But sadly it has fallen out of fashion, and with it one of the greatest applications of hotel butter ever made: the Chicken Kiev—pounded chicken cutlet wrapped around a log of straight hotel butter, then breaded and fried, so when you cut into it melted hotel butter dribbles out. No better reason to invent the Chicken Kiev Nuggs: tiny bites of chicken with a self-contained butter sauce. To re-create fast-food flavor, I've opted out of using fresh herbs in favor of "poultry seasoning."

Make the hotel butter. Put all of the ingredients for the hotel butter in a mixing bowl and whisk until combined. Place the butter in pastry bag or zip-top bag. Snip the tip, and pipe onto a sheet pan or plate into long bars about a ¼ inch wide. Freeze at least 30 minutes until ready to use. Once frozen, break into 1-inch pieces.

Make the nuggs. Pulse the panko and ½ teaspoon of the salt in food processor or a spice grinder. The goal is to get the panko to about half of its original size. Transfer the salted crumbs to a baking dish or shallow bowl.

If using unground chicken, chop the breasts into chunks. Pulse in food processor until finely chopped.

Place a heaping tablespoon of the ground chicken in your palm and flatten it slightly. Place a 1-inch-long piece of frozen butter in the middle, then place an additional tablespoon of chicken on top and pinch the sides together to fully contain the butter. Transfer the nuggs to a sheet pan, then lightly press all the nuggs with a second sheet pan so they flatten slightly and resemble the nuggets we all know and love.

Lightly dredge each chicken nugg in the beaten eggs, let the excess drip off, then dredge it in the panko. Land the dredged nuggs on the sheet pan. Repeat with all the nuggs. Place the sheet pan with the nuggs in the freezer until frozen solid, about 2 hours. (If you don't have space in the freezer for a full sheet pan, place the nuggs on plates and stack.)

HOLD IT? You can transfer the frozen nuggs in this state to a zip-top bag and keep them frozen for up to a month.

Fry the chicken nuggs. Fill a Dutch oven halfway with oil, clip on a candy thermometer, and bring the oil to 375°F over medium heat. Preheat the oven to 200°F, and place an empty sheet pan fitted with a rack inside.

Working in batches, add the frozen nuggs to the oil and fry them until golden brown and cooked through, 4 to 6 minutes. Transfer each cooked batch to the rack on the pan in the oven until all the nuggs are cooked.

PLATE IT! Pile these bad boys up in a paper cup or fry boat.

BREAK IT: Make your own poultry seasoning using fresh herbs and the HdP method (page 243), but up the sage. Then use ground duck for a gamey version.

YIELD Makes eight 2-ounce servings

PREP TIME 5 minutes

COOK TIME 2 minutes

gear

blender

ingredients

½ teaspoon pure vanilla extract

1 cup whole milk

¼ cup creamy peanut butter

½ cup chartreuse

3 ounces ice cubes

peanut-chartreuse toritos

(Drink)

A *torito* is a tiny, potent cocktail that is designed to make you feel like a "tiny bull" upon entering social situations. At least that's what I like to think. It originated in Veracruz, Mexico, and can vary widely, generally family to family. My buddy German (the molé guy from page 72) made a batch of toritos before the dinner shift one night, perfectly placing the servers in that sweet spot right before the law of diminishing drunkenness kicks in. Tips were high, cheeks were rosy, and good times were had by all. Even though the drink is cold, I enjoy serving it on a frigid day, when the temperature of the drink is actually much warmer than the temperature is outside. In my recipe, I use green chartreuse, which allegedly contains over a hundred herbs. It's a bizarre take on the law of herbs and fats, but after getting acquainted with this drink, it's easy to ask for seconds or thirds.

Add the vanilla extract to a blender and swirl it around the interior, then pour it out.

Add the milk and peanut butter and blend until smooth, scraping down the sides once or twice.

HOLD IT! You can hold the peanut-milk mixture in the fridge, covered, until you are ready to serve, as long as the milk doesn't expire.

Add the chartreuse and ice, and blend until smooth.

PLATE IT! This should be served in little teeny tiny cordial glasses, if you are a real sophisticate, or in tiny Dixie cups, if you are a real fun person.

BREAK IT: Add just a tiny drop of fish sauce to each cocktail. It might seem crazy, but the herbs in the chartreuse will tackle the fishy flavors while the fish sauce's salt amps up the fats from the nuts.

YIELD Makes 6 big bowls
PREP TIME 10 minutes
COOK TIME 3 hours
INACTIVE TIME 2 hours

gear

pressure cooker (at least 8-quart capacity)

tongs

bowl

colander

large pots

ingredients

BROTH

4 pounds veal bones

2 tablespoons olive oil

2½ pounds oxtail

3 pounds flat-cut brisket

1 large yellow onion (about 1 pound), unpeeled and halved

4 ounces fresh ginger, about one 4-inch piece, halved lengthwise and unpeeled

16 cups water

1 star anise pod

1 cinnamon stick

2 teaspoons whole black pepper

2 teaspoons whole coriander seeds

5 whole allspice berries

2 tablespoons kosher salt

2 teaspoons fish sauce

pho
(HOT SOUP)

The first time I had *pho,* a Vietnamese soup often served for breakfast, was with my boss from Sushi JeJu, Brian Yoo (see page 154). Once I worked hard enough to be on his innermost team of minions, he invited me to eat beef noodle soup with him and the rest of the sushi chefs. I had no idea what I was getting into, other than beef, noodles, and soup. He took me in his big truck out to Pho Duy on Drake Avenue in Fort Collins, Colorado. I ordered what he ordered, the number 10, large, which came with beef brisket and a pile of thin rice noodles in a heady, spice-infused broth. He showed me the method for doctoring the soup according to my liking, with fresh cilantro, basil, and mint, and bean sprouts, fish sauce, and sriracha. He made fun of me for not tucking the bean sprouts under the noodles—this cooks the sprouts and keeps the noodles from overcooking—and for sweating from my face as opposed to my neck (I guess that's a superstition for him). Anyhow, I fell in love with that $7 bowl of awesome, and the way I could use the herbs to temper the richness of the broth. The recipe below is a great starting pho with an intense broth made in the pressure cooker. If you are into fun cow parts (Navel! Tripe! Tendon!), those are also traditional in pho, and are usually included in the house special; if you like them too, add them in the secondary cooking of the broth.

Make the broth. Place the veal bones in a pressure cooker. Cover them with cold water and bring to a boil over high heat, uncovered, then discard the water, reserving the bones on the side. Scrub out the pressure cooker.

Add the oil to the clean pressure cooker and put over medium-high heat. Sear the oxtail in batches until deeply browned on all sides, 3 to 5 minutes per side. Reserve.

Sear the brisket until deeply browned on all sides, cutting it down to a more manageable size if needed, about 10 minutes.

Using tongs, put the onion halves face down on a gas burner and cook until very dark brown. (If you don't have a gas burner, use the broiler.) Char the ginger in the same way until very dark brown.

Add 8 cups water, the charred onions and ginger, star anise, cinnamon, black peppercorns, coriander, allspice, salt, and fish sauce to the pressure cooker with the meats and set over high heat. Lock on the pot's lid, and set to the highest pressure once it starts releasing steam. Drop the heat to low and cook at high pressure for 1½ hours. Transfer the whole kit to a sink and release the pressure while running cold water over the top. Once the steam is released, remove the lid. Remove the brisket from the broth and refrigerate. Remove the oxtails from the broth and pick the oxtail meat from the bones; put the bones back in the broth and refrigerate the meat.

Add 8 more cups water to the broth now containing the veal bones, oxtail bones, spices, and cooked vegetables. Pressure-cook the bones one more time using the same method and intensity, but cook for only 1 more hour. Release the steam, and allow to cool.

PHO

1 pound rice noodles

Bean sprouts (optional)

Basil sprigs (optional)

Mint sprigs (optional)

Cilantro sprigs (optional)

Lime wedges (optional)

Sliced jalapeño pepper
(optional)

Hoisin sauce (optional)

Sriracha sauce (optional)

───────

☞ **Tip**

Wondering what to do with the fat you've scraped off your stock? That's tallow, and it's delicious. Sometimes very awesome pho joints will serve it hot, on the side, for dipping the meat in, just for fat kids like me. It's not everyone's cup of meat, but it sure is mine.

Strain the broth into a container and discard all of the solids. Transfer the broth to the freezer if you have space or the fridge if you don't. Allow to chill until the fat has congealed, about an hour in the freezer, longer in the fridge. Scrape off the fat; reserve it for another use (see Tip) or discard.

───────

HOLD IT? The cooked meats and broth can be stored in the fridge for up to 5 days, or frozen for up to a month.

───────

Assemble the pho. Very thinly slice the brisket on the bias, and shred the oxtail with your fingers or two forks. Place in a 200-degree oven until warmed through, or microwave in 30-second increments until warm.

Place the gelatinized pho broth in a pot and bring to a boil over medium-high heat. Reduce the heat to medium-low and simmer while you prepare the noodles.

Bring a large pot of water to a boil. Place a colander inside a bowl in a sink. Place the rice noodles in the colander, and pour the boiling water over them, allowing them to soak and soften until opaque and just pliable, about 3 minutes. Rinse the noodles in the colander once under cold water to stop the cooking.

───────

PLATE IT! Divide the noodles among 6 bowls, and ladle over broth to cover. Add the meats and instruct your guests to add sprouts, herbs, lime juice, jalapeño, and sauces to their taste. Tell them to eat it while it's hot, making fun of them if they sweat from their face.

───────

BREAK IT: Leftover, cold, thinly sliced, rare steak au poivre (page 158) would be unbelievably delicious swimming in this broth. At most pho joints, they present you with rare steak to cook in the broth. Make it so.

───────

YIELD Makes ⅓ cup, which is a lot of ranch powder

PREP TIME 5 minutes

COOK TIME 20 minutes

gear

small pot

sheet pan with a nonstick silicone baking mat

blender or spice grinder

ingredients

COOLISH RANCH MIX

1½ cups water

½ cup white cornmeal

2 tablespoons buttermilk powder

1 tablespoon chopped dried chives

1½ teaspoons dried parsley

1 teaspoon kosher salt

1 teaspoon dried dill

1 teaspoon paprika

½ teaspoon MSG (see Tip page 223)

½ teaspoon garlic powder

1 pound sliced sashimi-grade raw yellowtail, salmon, mackerel, or other fatty fish (or a mix)

coolish ranch on raw fish

(COLD FISH)

In the earliest days of my restaurant, Do or Dine, we were approached by a start-up group called Underground Eats, which wanted to curate themed, exclusive dinners with a variety of different chefs, restaurants, and personalities around NYC. As this was to be Underground Eats's launch event, we wanted to make a once-in-a-lifetime experience. Together we created a menu that fused high cuisine with the flavors of bodegas—i.e., Brooklyn's corner stores. Bodegas sell snack foods and staples, and generally every Brooklynite has his or her favorite bodega, which is usually the one closest to them. I have become a connoisseur of bodegas, as no two bodegas are the same. Some sell plantains (Dominican- or Puerto Rican–owned). Some sell ginseng (Korean-owned). Some don't sell beer (Muslim-owned). Regardless, I always check the expiration date on whatever they stock, and I tend to favor ones that have a cat (no rodents). In planning the Underground Eats menu, I wanted to find the bodega version of fresh herbs. The closest I could find came in the form of Cooler Ranch! Doritos, specifically the "shake" at the bottom of the bag. I sprinkled this on raw yellowtail, which added salt, herbs, and fat all at once, and it was uncannily tasty. Here, I offer my recipe for ranch powder, with dried dill, parsley, and chives. This is delicious when sprinkled on top of a bowl of sushi rice (page 84) and raw fatty fish. This is also pretty bonkers on popcorn, or even—wait for it—corn chips when the bodega is out of Doritos.

Make the coolish ranch mix. Preheat the oven to 200°F.

Combine the 1½ cups water and the cornmeal in a small pot and set over medium heat. Bring to a simmer and cook until the mix is uniform in texture, developing an almost plasticlike sheen, 5 to 7 minutes, scraping the bottom to prevent sticking. Taste it—this is GRUEL! It will taste very bland, but the goal is to cook out the raw flavor of the cornmeal.

Pour the gruel onto a sheet pan lined with a nonstick silicone baking mat and spread out as thinly as possible. Place the sheet pan in the oven and bake until the entire sheet is dry and crisped, 15 to 20 minutes. Set aside to cool.

Crumble the sheets of dried gruel into a spice grinder or blender and grind until fine. Add the remaining ingredients to the ground cornmeal mix in the spice grinder or blender and pulse until incorporated.

HOLD IT? You can keep this in an airtight container at room temperature for up to a month.

PLATE IT! A little of this goes a long way—just a tiny dip for a piece of raw fish is enough to flavor the whole bite. Dip one side of each slice of fish into the ranch powder and fan out the slices on a serving platter.

Other Applications for Ranch Powder

Essentially what we've made is a "seasoned salt," like Lawry's. This is the kind of magic condiment that can turn a boring chicken breast into "woweezowee." Just use like you would salt, knowing that a little goes a long way. This would make a great gift to the domestically disadvantaged, or to college kids. College kids love ranch. It's awesome mixed with mayo for pasta or potato salad.

BREAK IT: Sharpen this up with some cheese powder instead of buttermilk powder. Cheese powder can be swiped from a package of boxed mac and cheese, or you can buy fancy cheese powders via the Internet. This won't be as good on raw fish, but it will be insanely good on popcorn, chips, or cooked meats.

STEP YOUR GAME UP

If you want to combine this ranch powder and fish with the nigiri method (see page 84), be my guest. Assemble the fish and rice without the wasabi, then dip the top of each assembled piece in the ranch powder. You can serve these on their own or alongside the everything bagel versions.

YIELD Makes 4 fillets; a light
meal for 2 or a hearty meal for 1

PREP TIME 10 minutes

COOK TIME 10 minutes

gear

sheet pan with rack

whisk

three shallow baking dishes
or bowls

cast-iron skillet

spatula or fish spatula (see
sidebar page 99)

ingredients

SKATE

4 skate wing fillets, skinned and
boned (which in this case means
the cartilage removed)

DREDGE

¼ cup all-purpose flour

¼ cup rice flour

1 tablespoon finely chopped
fresh marjoram

½ teaspoon baking powder

1 teaspoon kosher salt

½ cup whole milk

½ cup fish stock or clam juice

Vegetable oil, for frying

1 tablespoon finely chopped
fresh tarragon

☞ **Tip**

This dish should be served right when
it's prepared—skate can get am-
moniated quickly, so it's important to
prepare it the day you get it from your
fishmonger.

chicken-fried skate

(HOT FISH)

Skate used to get a bad rap, but in recent years all sorts of chefs are doing all
sorts of fancy things with it. But I think skate benefits from the simple Southern technique of "chicken frying," as in chicken-fried steak. Some people also
call it "country-frying." Regardless, it means dredging pounded cutlets of
your protein of choice in milk and then flour, panfrying them, and slathering
them with peppered-up gravy. Skate is pretty forgiving both in butchering and
preparation, but its mild flavor needs a gentle hand, or better, the soft caress
of herbs. Marjoram is like the Skipper to oregano's Barbie—just a little more
sophisticated, with some piney flavors; tarragon brings a punch of anise.

Prep the skate. Preheat the oven to 225°F. Place a sheet pan fitted with a
rack in the oven.
 Cut the fillets into similarly sized portions, scaling the larger ones down to
the size of the smaller. Don't fret if one is a little bigger than the other.

Prep the dredge. Whisk together the flours, marjoram, baking powder, and
½ teaspoon of the salt and divide between two baking dishes. In a third baking
dish or shallow bowl, combine the milk and stock.

Fry the skate. Heat ¼ inch of oil over medium-high heat in a large cast-iron
skillet.
 Dredge the skate fillets, one at a time, in the dry dredge, then one at a time
in the wet, and then into the second dry. Don't discard the wet or dry dredge,
because we are making gravy with it in a few minutes.
 Gently place a couple of the dredged fillets into the hot oil and fry for 2 to 3
minutes per side, flipping, or until the edges are golden. Do not crowd the skillet.
Using a spatula or fish spatula, transfer the fillets to the prepared sheet pan in
the oven to keep warm. Continue frying the rest of the skate. Transfer the final
round of skate fillets to the sheet pan, and turn off the oven.

Make the gravy. Drain out all but about 1 tablespoon of the oil from the skillet and discard. Reduce the heat to low. Whisk 1 tablespoon of the remaining dry
dredge into the fat in the skillet and cook for 1 minute, whisking. While whisking
vigorously, add the remaining wet dredge, the tarragon, and the remaining ½
teaspoon salt. Cook, whisking continually to work out the lumps, until thickened
to a gravylike consistency, an additional 1 to 2 minutes.

PLATE IT! This is an incredibly comforting dish but lighter than its steak counterpart. I
make this at the end of a long shift, and eat it out of a to-go container, slathered with
gravy, on public transit. If you don't have access to a restaurant to work in, put this on
plates with the gravy served on the side (see Break It). This is great with the crunch of
the Radish Caprese (page 61) or the heat of the Chilled Corn Soup (page 269).

BREAK IT: Replace the tarragon with cilantro and add some adobo sauce from a can
of chipotles to the gravy for a smoky effect.

YIELD Makes 4 servings

PREP TIME 15 minutes

COOK TIME 45 minutes

INACTIVE TIME 8 hours

gear

small pan

blender

gallon-size zip-top bag in a large bowl

rimmed sheet pan

probe thermometer

small pot

ingredients

MARINADE

1 medium yellow onion

1 tablespoon garam masala

1 teaspoon chili powder

17.6 ounces plain Greek yogurt

9 ounces fresh baby spinach

One 1-inch piece fresh ginger, peeled and finely chopped

2 garlic cloves, minced

1 tablespoon kosher salt

35 fresh mint leaves, about ¼ loose cup

4 pounds chicken pieces

1 tablespoon vegetable oil

green tandoori chicken

(LIGHT MEAT)

I love tandoori chicken, which is marinated in spices and yogurt and cooked in a hot clay oven. But sometimes I find that it can be a little bit heavy and not very complex in flavor. In my green version, the chicken gets a bath in spinach and mint, which brightens up the earthy spices, and is reminiscent of *saag,* a sort of Indian creamed spinach.

Marinate the chicken. Cut the onion into ¼-inch rings.

Over low heat in a small pan, toast the garam masala and chili powder, swirling the pan, until aromatic, less than 1 minute. Reserve.

Put the yogurt and spinach in a blender and blend on high until smooth. Add the ginger, garlic, toasted spices, salt, and mint and blend until smooth and incorporated.

Put the chicken, onions, and marinade into a gallon-size zip-top bag set inside a bowl, and marinate overnight.

HOLD IT! The refrigerated marinating chicken can only get better; marinate for up to 2 days.

Cook the chicken. Preheat the broiler on high. Grease a rimmed sheet pan with the oil.

Shake off and reserve excess marinade from the chicken and onions. Place the chicken pieces, skin side up, on the greased sheet pan. Try not to pack them too tightly or they won't brown well. Broil until the skin crisps slightly, about 8 to 10 minutes, then flip the pieces over and broil for another 8 to 10 minutes.

Reduce the oven temperature to 350°F. Add the onions to the pan and roast until the chicken juices run clear and the internal temperature is 155°F on a probe thermometer, about 25 minutes. (Bear in mind that the folks at the USDA specify 165°F.)

Place all the reserved marinade in a small pot over low heat and bring to a boil. Reduce the heat and continue simmering for 10 minutes; it will thicken slightly.

PLATE IT! I like to let people choose which parts of the bird they'd like to eat, so this is a good dish to pile on a platter, with the sauce on the side.

BREAK IT: Swap in quail for the chicken, as its assertive flavor will stand up against the herbaceous green tandoori. In addition, everyone can eat their own whole tiny bird, which is always fun.

IRON ME!

YIELD Makes 8 servings

PREP TIME 10 minutes

COOK TIME 6 hours 15 minutes

gear

baking dish

small pan

food processor

sheet pan

steak knives, for serving

ingredients

PORK BELLY

4 pounds boneless pork belly, sliced into 8 equal pieces

Fleur de sel, for finishing

CHERMOULA

1 tablespoon whole cumin seeds

1 tablespoon whole coriander seeds

1 teaspoon whole black peppercorns

2 lemons

1 bunch flat-leaf parsley (about 2.3 ounces), roughly chopped

1 bunch cilantro, roots removed but including stems (about 3.5 ounces), roughly chopped

1 teaspoon kosher salt

¾ cup olive oil

pork belly with chermoula

(Dark meat)

Pork belly was ruined by bacon (cured pork belly). Yes, bacon is wonderful, and we all love it. But it's not the only delicious way to eat pork belly. Belly isn't huge on flavor, so turning it into bacon helps; the smoke and the salt add depth, and the rendering process maximizes its fatty potential. That said, a long, slow, roast to crisp up the belly and a good, strong herbal component can also provide complex flavors and structure to the otherwise one-dimensional belly. Here I pair the belly with chermoula, which I think of as a North African pesto, generally containing herbs, spices, oil, and lemon juice. It can be thrown together in a variety of ways, so if you are missing something or a little shy on one ingredient, don't fret—in fact, I encourage you to doctor the chermoula to your specific liking.

Roast the pork belly. Preheat the oven to 225°F.
Lay the pork belly pieces in a baking dish, rind side up. Roast for 6 hours.

Make the chermoula. In a small pan, toast the cumin, coriander, and black peppercorns over medium heat until fragrant, swirling often to prevent burning. Add to a food processor and run on low to coarsely grind.

Zest the lemons into the bowl of the food processor, then add the juice, having first strained out the seeds. Add the parsley, cilantro, and salt and pulse to roughly chop.

With the food processor running, drizzle in the oil until pasty, pausing to scrape down the sides once. Transfer the chermoula to a container, cover, and let stand at room temperature for at least 1 hour.

HOLD IT? If you like, you can let the pork belly cool, then store in the fridge, covered, for up to 3 days; bring to room temperature before proceeding. The chermoula can be frozen indefinitely, or refrigerated (topped with olive oil to prevent browning), for up to a week.

After the 6 hours of cook time, increase the oven temperature to 500°F. Lay the pork belly pieces, rind side up, on a sheet pan, and blast in the oven for 15 minutes, or until the skin is visibly bubbly and crisp, like pork rinds.

PLATE IT! Spoon swoosh (drop a spoonful and swoosh it with the back of a spoon) out the chermoula. Add the pork belly on top of the swoosh, perpendicularly. Top the pork belly with a little fleur de sel. The pork belly can sometimes be a little tough on the exterior, so serve with steak knives.

BREAK IT: Smoking the pork belly before finishing it in the oven will make the herbs contend not just with the fat, but with the smoke as well. It will be a great match-up. You could also serve the gamey lamb breast from page 147 with this sauce, and taste as the herbs battle those funky flavors as well.

YIELD Makes 8 servings

PREP TIME 15 minutes

COOK TIME 10 minutes

INACTIVE TIME 3 hours

gear

3 medium bowls

medium pot

food processor

whisk

nutmilk bag, chinois (see sidebar page 37), or fine-mesh strainer

rubber spatula

ingredients

3 tablespoons water

3 tablespoons cornstarch

5 large egg yolks

1 teaspoon kosher salt

1 bunch tarragon, about 10 stems

1 quart half-and-half

9 ounces raw shelled pistachios

½ cup sugar

½ teaspoon pistachio or almond extract

pistachio-tarragon pudding

(DESSERT)

My grandmother used to make pistachio pudding, which happily reminded me of green slime, à la Nickelodeon. The pistachios' adorable green color certainly stands out, but so does their distinctive taste, which is fresh and light compared to other nuts. That freshness in the pistachio also welcomes herbs with open arms, a pairing that can be seen in pestos, crusts on seafood, or in this case, a revamp of Grandma's pudding. Tarragon, with its anisey-minty-sweet flavor, is just the herb for the job, and may make pudding chic once again.

In a medium bowl, combine 3 tablespoons water and the cornstarch and whisk to dissolve. Add the egg yolks and salt, then whisk very well until pale yellow. Set aside.

Tear the tarragon stalks in half, then rub them in your hands a little to bruise them. Add them to a medium pot and add the half-and-half. Set over low heat and bring to a simmer, then remove from the heat.

Meanwhile, pulverize all but 1 ounce of the pistachios in a food processor until very fine, scraping down the sides as needed. Roughly chop the reserved 1 ounce pistachios and set aside.

Add the pulverized pistachios and sugar to the half-and-half and whisk to fully incorporate the pistachio powder and dissolve the sugar. Return to the heat and simmer for an additional 5 minutes to infuse the flavors, then remove from the heat.

Pour the hot pistachio–half-and-half mixture through a nutmilk bag, chinois, or strainer into a bowl, reserving the infused half-and-half and discarding the tarragon and nut powder. Rinse the pot well and set aside.

Temper the egg yolk mixture by slowly streaming ½ cup of the hot pistachio-infused half-and-half into the eggs, whisking well to incorporate. Repeat, adding another ½ cup at a time to slowly warm the eggs, until all of the half-and-half has been incorporated; if you add too much at once or add it too fast, the eggs will cook and you will have pistachio scrambled eggs instead of pudding. Pour the entire mixture back to the clean pot, then add the pistachio or almond extract.

Set the pot over very low heat and cook, stirring constantly with a rubber spatula to scrape the bottom and sides of the pot, until the mixture thickens, then bubbles around the edges, 5 to 7 minutes. Stir in the reserved chopped pistachios for texture. Transfer to a bowl and gently press plastic wrap directly on the surface to keep a skin from forming, covering it entirely. Allow to chill in the refrigerator for 3 hours, or until cold.

HOLD IT? The pudding will keep for up to a week, covered, in the fridge.

PLATE IT! This pudding looks great spooned into martini glasses for a very late-'90s cruise ship feel. Otherwise, put it into individual bowls.

BREAK IT: Freeze the pudding in popsicle molds, then dunk into "Magic Shell"–type dark chocolate, then dust with unsweetened cocoa powder.

LAW OF GENERAL TSO'S CHICKEN

spicy meets sweet

eneral Tso's chicken, the bearer of the pepper symbol on the Chinese-American takeout menu, is a great example of how to mitigate heat. I've never had General Tso's Chicken that was so spicy I couldn't eat it. That's because of sweetness. Americans weren't so keen on heat until relatively recently, so I'd wager that back when Chinese food was being introduced to the U.S., an enterprising Chinese chef added a bunch of sugar to a hot dish to make it more palatable to his domestic audience.

Spiciness comes from chiles. Every recipe in this chapter will contain some sort of fruit that contains capsaicin, which produces the burn. To counteract, there will be sugar in some form. Sweet and heat is an unbeatable and addictive combo. Sweet Chili Doritos are on shelves, hot pepper jelly is spread on crackers throughout the South, and most sports bars peddle a sweet and spicy sauce on their wings (see how fruit can do it on page 44). Plus, spicy foods create endorphins, which make us feel euphoric. If there's anything I want my guests to experience other than satiety, it might as well be euphoria.

spicy meets sweet

JALAPEÑOS	JALAPEÑO-PICKLED CARROTS	CARROTS
JALAPEÑOS	NAKED ANGELS ON HORSEBACK	APPLES/CIDER
KIMCHI	KIMCHI-LOADED SWEET POTATOES	MAPLE SYRUP / SWEET POTATO
CHIPOTLE OIL / JALAPEÑO	CHILLED CORN SOUP WITH CHILE OIL AND HONEYDEW	CORN / HONEYDEW
OLD BAY SEASONING	SPICY MARYLAND CRAB SOUP	CRAB / CORN
SERRANOS	GRILLED SHRIMP AND PEACH SALAD WITH SERRANOS	PEACH
CURRY SPICES	RIESLING CURRY WITH SQUID	RIESLING
HABANEROS	JERK CHICKEN	SUGAR / BAKING SPICES
SALSA VERDE	DR PEPPER–BRAISED BEEF TONGUE TACOS WITH SALSA VERDE	DR PEPPER
HABANEROS	HOWITZER HABANERO CHOCOLATE CAKE	CHOCOLATE

YIELD Makes 1½ quarts pickles and brine

PREP TIME 15 minutes

COOK TIME 10 minutes

INACTIVE TIME 8 hours

gear

mandoline (optional)

nonreactive heatproof bowl or jar with lid

cheesecloth or nutmilk bag (optional; see page 311)

medium pot

ingredients

2 pounds carrots, peeled

4 jalapeño peppers, sliced

1 bay leaf

2 cups water

1½ cups white vinegar

1 cup packed light brown sugar

¼ cup kosher salt

 Tip

The strained brine can be used as the pickling liquid in the Speed-Pickle-Brined Chicken Nuggets (see page 220) for a spicy kick.

☞ **Tip**

Before you do anything with hot peppers, put your latex gloves on.

jalapeño-pickled carrots

(CANAPÉ/SNACK)

My buddy, co-chef, and co-owner of Do or Dine, George McNeese, is a pickle fiend. We regularly buy each other pickled vegetables and krauts, just to taste together. We are especially obsessed with the kinda sweet, kinda spicy pickled carrots that come in some brands of pickled jalapeños, but every can only comes with a few. By making them myself, I don't have to hoard them. I also get the benefit of the brine, which is a great chaser to a shot of whiskey.

Using a knife or mandoline, cut the carrots into ⅛-inch-thick coins and put in a nonreactive heatproof bowl.

Place the jalapeños and the bay leaf in some cheesecloth or a nutmilk bag, and tie it up to make a sachet. (This keeps the seasonings from floating around in case you decide to use the liquid for another purpose; see Tip.)

Put 2 cups water, the vinegar, brown sugar, and salt along with the sachet in a medium pot and bring to a boil over high heat. Reduce the heat and simmer for about 5 minutes, just to cook the jalapeños a bit.

Pour the hot brine over the carrots, cover, and transfer to the fridge to chill for at least 8 hours.

HOLD IT? This recipe holds for months in a covered container. I've never had pickled carrots go bad before I could eat them all.

PLATE IT! Jalapeño-pickled carrots can be used anywhere where a dose of sweet and spicy can add to the equation. Burgers, pizza, Mexican food, salads or if you want to get really crazy, chopped up in the tartar sauce for vegan fish sticks on page 180. These guys are awesome for out-of-hand snacking, or as an accompaniment to a meat or cheese plate (see page 91). These make a great gift, too, if you fancy up their glass container.

BREAK IT: Adding smoked beets to this mix will color the carrots, sweeten the brine, and add a smoky component not generally found in traditional pickles.

Pickling Other Things

So let's be clear. There are two types of pickling: quick-pickling (vinegar), which we've done here and on the grapes on page 114, and lacto-fermented pickling (salt water), which I'd like to leave for another cookbook and the pros. Salt water pickling produces lactic acid, but the process requires time and an oxygen-free environment. Vinegar-pickling uses acetic acid and can achieve a pickly product in a short amount of time without a special environment or specific temperature parameters; but note there is no fermentation involved in this process. Pretty much any vegetable or fruit will work with the quick-pickle method above. The flavors and possibilities are limitless. For example, you could substitute carrot juice for the water above, omit the jalapeños, and then pickle some jalapeños with sweet carrot juice, or you could make pickled blueberries, which are delicious on pancakes (see Law of Lemonade, page 213). Pickled cauliflower as a garnish for the Bloody Mary on page 198 is very tasty as well.

gear

microwave-safe bowl

blender

two ¼-cup capacity mini muffin pans

rimmed sheet pan

oyster knife with oyster box (see page 143)

small bowl

slotted spoon

ingredients

SAUCE

3 Granny Smith apples, peeled, cored, and chopped, about 1 pound 2 ounces

Juice of 1 lime (about 1 tablespoon)

1 knob celeriac (about 1 pound 4 ounces)

One 12-ounce bottle hard cider

3 tablespoons honey

2 teaspoons kosher salt

2 jalapeño peppers, seeds and ribs removed, diced

BACON CUPS

18 slices bacon

OYSTERS

2 dozen oysters

naked angels on horseback

(COLD APP)

Devils on Horseback—a sweet stuffed date wrapped in bacon and baked—is a great dish, and it follows the law of PB&J very nicely. Its sibling, Angels on Horseback—oysters wrapped in bacon and baked—is much lesser known and, in my opinion, rightfully so. I feel like some chef somewhere made it because some chef could, not because it was particularly delicious. The problem is that the delicate oyster cooks much faster than the bacon, which results in crispy bacon and a rubbery overdone oyster, or limp bacon and a juicy oyster: to cook one perfectly means to cook the other imperfectly. But my secret to a perfect oyster is to not cook it at all. Here I use muffin pans to make tiny bacon cups, perfect for cradling a raw oyster. Instead of the classic tomato-based cocktail sauce, I top them with a more complex sweet and spicy sauce of apples, celeriac, sweet hard cider, and jalapeño.

Make the sauce. In a microwave-safe bowl, toss the apples with the lime juice to prevent the apples from browning.

Cut off the woody top, excess roots, and base of the celeriac. Remove the skin, using a paring knife. Chop the celeriac to about the same size as the apples. Add the celeriac, cider, honey, and salt to the apples and stir to combine. Place a sheet of plastic wrap tightly over the bowl, and poke a few holes in it with a knife to allow steam to escape. Microwave on high for 10 minutes. Drain off the liquid and discard. Transfer the mixture to a blender, add the jalapeños, and blend until smooth. Refrigerate the sauce until cold, about 2 hours.

Make the bacon cups. Preheat the oven to 350°F.

Cut the bacon strips into two shorter halves. Set aside 24 of the half-pieces of bacon. Cut the remaining 12 halves in half again (so you end up with 24 quarter slices).

XRAY BACON CUP ASSEMBLY

That oyster liquor would turn the Bloody Mary on page 198 into something wild. When made with clam juice they call it a Caesar . . . so maybe we'll call this a Cleopatra. Also, you could replace the fish stock in the skate recipe (page 253) with the oyster liquor, or add it to the clam chowder instead of the clam juice.

☞ **Tip**

Before you do anything with hot peppers, put your latex gloves on

Wrap the half-size bacon strips around the inside of the mini muffin wells. Lay the quarter-size pieces down inside the ring of bacon and up the walls, covering the seam and the bottom, and letting the excess bacon drape over the lip of the muffin wells. Nest a second muffin pan on top, and press together firmly. Set the nested tins upside down on a rimmed sheet pan (this will let the bacon fat drain out) and bake for 25 minutes. Carefully remove the top pan and continue cooking until the bottoms are crisped, 6 to 10 minutes more. Remove from the oven and allow to cool on the pan, then transfer to paper towels to drain.

HOLD IT? The bacon cups can be kept in the fridge, covered, for up to 3 days. If they are coming from the fridge, allow the bacon cups to return to room temperature. The apple topping can be held in the fridge, covered, for up to 2 weeks.

Assemble the oysters. Using an oyster knife, with or without the oyster box (see page 143), shuck the oysters and liquor into a small bowl.

Using a slotted spoon, separate an oyster from the liquor, then place the drained oyster into a bacon cup. (See sidebar for ideas for the oyster liquor.) Top the oyster with a dollop of cold sauce.

PLATE IT! As the oysters are already in their own cup, simply arrange the cups in a single layer on any pretty plate or even a silver platter.

BREAK IT: White chocolate pairs well with briny things, like caviar and oysters. It works in the same way a white chocolate–covered pretzel does. Melt some chopped white chocolate in the microwave in 30-second spurts, then carefully dunk the bacon baskets into the white chocolate; allow them to drain and cool on a rack.

gear

sheet pan

food processor

clean kitchen towel

ingredients

6 sweet potatoes, scrubbed

One 16-ounce container kimchi

2 tablespoons sour cream

2 tablespoons maple syrup

18 slices American cheese
(white looks best)

**What to do with
kimchi juice!**

Kimchi juice is the kind of thing I wish they just sold in jars. Dashed on some pizza, used to deglaze a pan, or mixed into the Bloody Mary on page 198, kimchi juice delivers a salty, sour, and spicy punch all in one.

kimchi-loaded sweet potatoes

(HOT APP)

My buddy Sam Kim is a passionate food dude. He's eaten all around the U.S., and has introduced me to a lot of delicious stuff. He told me about a Korean practice of placing American cheese on a spoon and dipping it into spicy kimchi soup to melt, then eating it with some of the broth. I was completely baffled by both the technique and flavor until I tried it. The acid and spice of the kimchi are instantly tempered by the soft and round flavor of the American cheese. Any other cheese would simply be too much. In this recipe, I combine cheese and kimchi with two earthy sweets—maple syrup and sweet potato— which work as the Liston to kimchi's spicy Ali. Rather than blasting the sweet potato at high heat, we take a low-and-slow approach, which converts more of its starch into delicious sugars.

Bake the sweet potatoes. Preheat the oven to 300°F. Set a sheet pan on the bottom rack of the oven to catch any sweet potato drips. Roast the sweet potatoes directly on the top rack for 4 hours.

Assemble the sweet potatoes. When the sweet potatoes are almost done, drain the kimchi and reserve the juice for another use (see sidebar). Add the drained kimchi, sour cream, and maple syrup to a food processor and pulse until roughly chopped.

Using a knife, cut lengthwise about two-thirds of the way deep into each sweet potato. Using a clean kitchen towel, push the ends together to open the sweet potato up.

Place 1 slice of the cheese down into the cavity of each potato. Divide the kimchi mixture evenly among the 6 sweet potatoes, and top each with an additional 2 slices of the cheese.

Place the loaded potatoes on a sheet pan (the one from the oven is fine) and return the pan to the warm oven. Bake until the cheese has melted, about 10 minutes.

PLATE IT! Serve these on their own for a small meal or snack. You can even give it the ramen treatment, adding fun condiments like scallions, fish flakes, or seaweed. Or serve alongside the "orange blossom" chicken (page **228**).

CHEAT IT: If you don't have 4 hours to bake the sweet potatoes but still want to try this flavor combo, cut the potatoes into ¼-inch-thick sticks and toss them in a little olive oil. Bake at 425°F for 30 minutes, flipping halfway through. Then pile up the cheese and kimchi mixture and bake together like the best cheese fries ever made.

BREAK IT: Adding crisp bacon and chives would turn this into a Roy Rogers–style loaded potato, with the bacon adding a smoky component that will play nicely with the earthy-sweet sweet potato.

YIELD Makes 8 large bowls

PREP TIME 25 minutes

COOK TIME 45 minutes

gear

large stockpot with a lid

small bowl

large bowl

tongs

large skillet

slotted spoon

ladle

large bowl and ice for sink

blender

nutmilk bag or large coffee filter (see Tip)

melon baller

ingredients

SOUP

12 ears of sweet corn, shucked

3 tablespoons corn oil

1 large onion, diced

1 jalapeño pepper, seeds and ribs removed, minced

2 tablespoons sauce from a can of chipotles in adobo

One 13.5-ounce can unsweetened coconut milk

1 tablespoon kosher salt

CHIPOTLE OIL

1 ounce (about 8) dried chipotle chiles

½ cup corn oil

HONEYDEW

2 honeydew melons, halved and seeded

chilled corn soup with chile oil and honeydew

(COLD SOUP)

By borrowing a little from the law of guac (see page 167), I use coconut milk to give this summertime soup a creaminess and richness. The heat of the chipotle oil plays footsie with the sweet sweet corn, and then, just in case the heat gets intense, little pearls of honeydew work as a fire extinguisher. That chipotle oil is just a basic flavored/colored oil. You can use the process described in the recipe to infuse almost any flavor into an oil (see sidebar, page 271). This soup also gets a lot of its flavor from the bones of the corn, the cobs. I have served kids this same soup, but without the chile oil or honeydew, garnished with Cracker Jacks. Try it, they LOVE IT.

Make the soup. Chill 8 soup bowls. Bring 1½ quarts water to a boil in a large stockpot.

Using the blade of a sharp knife, cut all of the kernels off the cobs and transfer the kernels to a small bowl. Then use the back side of the knife to scrape the cobs. This is a task best done into a large bowl placed in your sink, unless you like liquid cornstarch all over your kitchen. Cut the scraped cobs in half.

Gently place the scraped cobs and the scrapings (reserving the kernels) into the pot of boiling water and cook, uncovered, for 15 minutes. Carefully remove the cobs with tongs and discard. Set the stock aside.

Meanwhile, heat 2 tablespoons of corn oil in a large skillet over high heat. Add 2 cups of the corn kernels and cook until slightly browned, 8 to 10 minutes. Using a slotted spoon, transfer the corn to the small bowl to cool. Cover, and place in the fridge.

Making flavored oils

Almost anything can be made into a flavored oil like we did here. My basic recipe is to add just enough oil to cover the flavoring agent in the blender, then blend until warm (seriously, the blender will heat the oil!), then strain through a nutmilk bag (my preference) or a coffee filter. This method could even be used with the lobster shells from page 298 to give something some extra color and a flavor bump.

Why cool it so fast?

An interesting note about spoilage. Corn is actually a grain, so this soup can ferment very easily, as it contains the beginnings of mash, which is the beginning of whiskey! Make sure you chill it down in the pot, then refrigerate it or freeze it right away.

☞ Tip

A chinois is good for straining large quantities of food from one vessel to the other, but you have to use a spatula or spoon to scrape and push the food through. A towel allows you to squeeze food through, and provides better filtration than a chinois and cheesecloth, but you risk ruining a towel and, if the food is hot, you could be burned. Cheesecloth, in my opinion, is only really good for making a custom-sized pouch of things that you want to submerge in a liquid (a sachet). The nutmilk bag filters as much as a towel and can be used as a sachet, but it isn't very large and can't be scraped, meaning you could burn your hands if the food is hot. A coffee filter has the most filtration, but is the smallest and can't be squeezed, meaning gravity will take its time. The bottom line is this: If you have both a nutmilk bag and a chinois, you don't need the rest.

Reduce heat to medium-low. Add the remaining 1 tablespoon of corn oil to the skillet. Add the onion and jalapeño to the skillet and cook until softened, about 4 minutes. Add the sauce from the chipotles in adobo, and toss the onion and jalapeño around in it until coated, and continue to cook until some of the mixture sticks to the bottom of the pan, about 4 minutes.

Ladle a bit of the corn cob liquid into the skillet, scraping the bottom of the pan to release the brown bits. Transfer the contents of the skillet and the remaining uncooked corn kernels into the large stockpot of corn stock. Cover, increase the heat to high, and bring to a boil. Reduce the heat to low and simmer for 15 minutes, still covered. Add the coconut milk and salt and stir to incorporate.

Set a large bowl or storage vessel for the soup in the sink. Working in batches, carefully transfer the soup to a blender and blend until smooth, then add to the vessel in the sink. Fill the sink with cold water and ice at least halfway up the sides of the vessel, and stir the soup in the vessel to chill rapidly. (See sidebar.) Once cool, transfer the soup to the fridge to chill further.

Make the chipotle oil. Combine the chipotle chiles with the oil in the cleaned and dried blender. Blend for 4 to 6 minutes at high speed. Pass the oil through a nutmilk bag or coffee filter into a quart container. If you use a nutmilk bag, this will take no time—using a coffee filter will take much longer. Using GLOVED hands, carefully squeeze the solids to remove the last of the oil.

HOLD IT? The corn kernels and soup will hold in the fridge, covered, for 2 days. Or freeze the soup and corn kernels. The chile oil will keep for up to a month in the fridge.

Prep the honeydew. Using the melon baller, create as many melon balls as you can from the honeydew, cutting off layers as needed to reach uncut flesh.

PLATE IT! Ladle the soup into the prechilled bowls. Divide the kernels among all of the bowls, placing them in the center of the soup. Add a few honeydew balls, then drizzle with chile oil.

BREAK IT: This would hop right over into Mexican territory with the addition of fully cooked ground chorizo crumbles. The spice will work in tandem with the sweetness of the soup, and the salty cured meat will liven up the rest.

YIELD Makes 8 servings

PREP TIME 15 minutes

COOK TIME 25 minutes

gear

large stockpot

ingredients

2 quarts beef broth

1 pound new potatoes (the three-color guys are awesome!), unpeeled, diced

4 carrots (about ¾ pound), peeled and diced

3 tablespoons Old Bay Seasoning

One 1-pound 12-ounce can diced tomatoes

2 cups corn kernels (about 3 ears' worth)

1 cup chopped fresh green beans

½ cup fresh or frozen and thawed lima beans

1 pound fresh lump crabmeat (canned, if you must)

1 cup fresh or frozen peas

spicy maryland crab soup

(HOT SOUP)

Where I come from, the classic recipe for crab soup is a couple cans o' Veg-All, a couple cans o' diced tomaytas, some beef broff, plenny o' ol'bay (McCormick's Old Bay Seasoning) an a big ol' pile o' crab. Although I see absolutely nothing wrong with the classic recipe, there is a lot to be gained if you use fresh or frozen vegetables, with the exception of tomatoes, which are sometimes sweeter in the can as they are picked in their prime. The best part of this dish is the textural medley that canned vegetables just can't bring to the table. Fresh vegetables work so well in this due to the law of General Tso's: the heat of the Old Bay coaxes more sweetness from the already-sweet fresh corn, peas, limas, and crab. Gon hon, get some.

In a large stockpot, bring the broth, potatoes, carrots, and Old Bay to a simmer over medium-high heat. Add the tomatoes with their liquid, corn kernels, and green beans, and cook until the potatoes are soft. Add the lima beans and cook for an additional 5 minutes.

Add the crab and peas and cook until just warmed through.

HOLD IT? I like to portion this into single-serving deli containers and freeze it indefinitely, then pull it out when I have a cold or am homesick, or just getting a case of winter. You can also refrigerate it for 3 days. If the soup is frozen or refrigerated, rather than reheating the entire batch, only reheat what's needed. The worst thing you could do here is overcook the vegetables, so anything past a simmer isn't a good idea.

PLATE IT! This is best served in a cup or bowl (it's always offered by the cup in Maryland) with Saltine crackers. I'm pretty adamant about using soup spoons—for all these little veggie nuggets, it's a must. Watch a Ravens game, pour one out for Poe, and devour.

BREAK IT: Place some tough meat like brisket or chuck in a slow cooker, cover with beef broth, and add the Old Bay from above. In about 6 hours, when the meat is fork-tender, transfer the whole kit to a stockpot and begin to make the soup. Now you have a meal-soup—Maryland Surf and Turf Soup.

gear

medium pot

slotted spoon

grill or grill pan

ingredients

1 pound (about 4) ripe but firm peaches

1 tablespoon olive oil

1 pound U16/20-size shrimp, peeled and deveined, tails still attached

1 to 2 small serrano peppers, sliced thinly (one is spicy, two is SPICY)

1 teaspoon fresh lemon juice

1 teaspoon fish sauce

½ teaspoon kosher salt

¼ teaspoon freshly ground black pepper

☞ Tip

Before you do anything with hot peppers, put your latex gloves on.

grilled shrimp and peach salad with serranos

(COLD FISH)

I'm obsessed with green papaya salads like I get at my favorite Thai joints. I wanted to make an American version that harnessed the potent "sweet meets heat" against the salty, funky fish sauce of the classic Thai dish. I drew inspiration from a trip I took to Georgia, where I ate Georgia shrimp and Georgia peaches. There was something about them, maybe even *terroir* (the flavor of the landscape in which the things grew) that made them a perfect pair. In this recipe, grilled peach does battle with potent serrano peppers, with shrimp serving as referee. This is a perfect dish to grill and then chill, or, if you'd like to cook it and eat it warm, it's just as good.

Prep the peaches. Fill a medium pot with water and bring to a boil. Score a small X in the bottom of each peach. Dunk each peach in the boiling water one at a time for about 30 seconds, then remove the peach with a slotted spoon. Once cool enough to handle, gently peel off the skins; they should slide off like silk pajamas.

Cut the peaches in half and remove the pits. Cut each half into 4 wedges. Place the peaches in a single layer on paper towels. If needed, refrigerate for up to 2 hours, if you aren't grilling immediately.

Grill the peaches and shrimp. Preheat a grill or grill pan over high heat. Brush the oil onto the grates.

Grill the peach wedges, flipping once, until nice grill marks appear on both sides, about 4 minutes per side. Put the peaches, with the burnt edges and all, into a serving bowl.

Grill the shrimp on the first side until the tail is pink, 2 to 3 minutes, then flip and cook until firm, another minute or two.

Add the grilled shrimp to the peaches. Add the serranos, lemon juice, fish sauce, salt, and black pepper to the bowl and toss to coat. Refrigerate the salad until chilled.

HOLD IT? The salad will keep in the refrigerator, covered, for up to 2 days.

PLATE IT! This is best served from a giant serving dish. Use a slotted spoon to serve, so the "juice" doesn't weep all over the plate.

BREAK IT: Cut back on the heat, replace with some cinnamon, and try this again in the fall with apples instead of peaches. While not as juicy and sweet, their crunch will be a great textural balance to the shrimp.

gear

colander

large Dutch oven or heavy-bottomed pot

grill or grill pan

mixing bowl

ingredients

CURRY

1 medium eggplant (about 1 pound)

½ cup kosher salt

2 tablespoons vegetable oil

1 medium onion (about 10 ounces), diced

2 serrano peppers, seeds and ribs removed, minced

2 medium russet potatoes (about 1 pound), peeled and diced

1 large carrot (about 8 ounces), peeled and diced

⅓ cup yellow curry paste

1 cup sweet white wine (I like German Rieslings, which have higher acid!)

One 25.5-ounce can unsweetened coconut milk

Vegetable oil or nonstick cooking spray, for greasing

1 green bell pepper (about 8 ounces), seeds and ribs removed, cut into ¼-inch strips

4 ounces snap peas, tips removed

½ head cabbage (about 12 ounces), sliced into thin ribbons

riesling curry with squid

(HOT FISH)

One of my favorite food scenes in a movie is from a Korean monster flick called *The Host* (not the teenybop film of the same name). A dopey guy whose dad runs a picnic stand is charged with cooking squid for picnickers, and gets reprimanded by his dad for stealing the tenth leg for snacking, which is allegedly the most special. But here in the U.S., squid is one of the most underappreciated creatures of the sea. It's abundant, delicious, and a textural blast. Squid come in many sizes and shapes, but for this recipe I use baby squid, which cook quickly and are quite tender with minimal cooking. Most curries use some kind of citrus to give the dish acid. I use German Riesling instead, which is still acidic but also rather sweet, and which tempers the heat of the curry spices. Unlike traditional curries, which have a gravylike texture, this is much lighter and more elegant, but still hearty and satisfying thanks to the bevy of vegetables.

Make the curry. Cut the eggplant into rounds. Liberally salt both sides of the rounds and place them in a single layer in a colander for 30 minutes. (This helps extract excess moisture, which can lead to bitterness and all sorts of other eggplant maladies.)

In a Dutch oven or heavy-bottomed pot set over medium heat, heat the oil. Add the onion and serranos and sauté until softened, about 6 minutes. Add the potatoes, carrot, and the curry paste. Cook for 8 minutes until the curry paste darkens slightly and aromatizes, stirring to coat the vegetables. Add the Riesling and coconut milk to the pot, and stir with a wooden spoon to scrape up any flavorful bits stuck on the bottom of the pot. Bring to a boil, reduce heat to medium, and simmer for 5 minutes. Then remove from the heat.

Preheat and grease a grill or grill pan over medium-high heat.

SQUID

2 pounds cleaned baby squid (or small regular squid)

2 tablespoons fish sauce

15 fresh basil leaves, cut into a chiffonade (see sidebar page 61)

───────

☞ **Tip**

Before you do anything with hot peppers, put your latex gloves on.

Rinse the eggplant under cold running water to remove the salt, then pat dry with paper towels.

Grill the eggplant until tender, about 3 minutes on each side. Transfer the eggplant to a cutting board. Carefully dice the hot eggplant and add it to the curry pot, with the bell pepper, snap peas, and cabbage. Simmer the curry over medium heat until the vegetables are just tender, about 5 minutes. (If you are planning on storing and serving this later, cook the vegetables a little less, so they don't get mushy when you reheat.)

Cook the squid. Meanwhile, working in batches, place the squid in a single layer on the grill or grill pan and cook, turning occasionally, until the pieces are opaque and have some nice grill marks. The tubes will firm up and the tentacles will contract; the tubes will need about 2 minutes on each side, the tentacles will need about 5 minutes in total.

Transfer the cooked squid to a cutting board and cut the tubes into thin rings. Transfer the cooked rings and tentacles to a mixing bowl. Add the fish sauce and chiffonade of basil and toss to coat.

─────────────────────────────

HOLD IT? Keep the vegetable curry in the fridge for up to a week. The squid mixture can only get better; up to a day in the refrigerator. Reheat the curry in a pot over medium heat and the squid by warming in a skillet over medium heat.

Or if you want to make the curry in advance, you can grill the squid while the curry is reheating.

─────────────────────────────

PLATE IT! Ladle the hot curry into bowls and top with the hot squid. Instead of eating a truckload of boring rice, the vegetables provide a multiflavor vessel for all that curry goodness.

─────────────────────────────

BREAK IT: If you were to add andouille sausage to this, you would have a sort of rice-less curry gumbo, which is hardly gumbo at all. Regardless, the cured sausage will bring out the sweetness of the Riesling, and coax more flavors out of the veggies.

YIELD Makes 6 servings

PREP TIME 10 minutes

COOK TIME 20 minutes

INACTIVE TIME 8 hours

gear

blender, spice grinder, or mortar and pestle

small pan

blender

gallon-size zip-top bag

large bowl

grill or grill pan

tongs

probe thermometer

ingredients

1 whole nutmeg

20 whole allspice berries

3 star anise pods

1 cinnamon stick

5 whole cloves

One 2-inch piece ginger

½ cup packed brown sugar

Juice of 1 lime

Juice of 1 lemon

2 habaneros, seeds and ribs removed, roughly chopped

2 garlic cloves, peeled and roughly chopped

1 tablespoon browning seasoning (optional)

1 tablespoon kosher salt

10 sprigs thyme

3 pounds chicken thighs, bone in, skin on

Canola oil, for greasing the grates or grill pan

☞ **Tip**

Before you do anything with hot peppers, put your latex gloves on.

jerk chicken

(LIGHT MEAT)

Living in Bed-Stuy, Brooklyn, has gotten me turned on to Caribbean flavors (check the Trinidadian scotch deviled egg on page 116). When I first moved here it felt like you couldn't go more than a couple blocks in the summer without seeing someone working an oil drum grill, smoke billowing as chicken fat hit the briquettes. But jerk chicken stays gratifying year-round. In the summer, the fruity heat of the habanero makes you sweat till you cool down, in the winter, the brown spices feel like you put on a cable knit. I wanted to make what I considered to be an authentic replication of what I eat on the street here, so I scoured the local markets. "Browning Seasoning," a combination of caramel coloring and concentrated vegetable flavorings, is optional in this recipe, and some cooks might give me flack for it, but to me, it's a vital part of the equation. I wouldn't drink Coca-Cola if it were clear, and I don't want my jerk chicken to be khaki.

Prep the jerk chicken. Combine the nutmeg, allspice, star anise, cinnamon, and cloves in a blender, spice grinder, or mortar and pestle. Grind until fine.

Place the ground spices in a small pan over low heat, moving constantly, until fragrant and toasty, about 2 minutes. Transfer the toasted spices to a blender.

Halve the ginger lengthwise, leaving the skin on, and place directly on a gas flame to char. If you don't have a gas stove, you can place it, cut side up, under the broiler. Once the ginger has blackened, roughly chop it and add it to the blender.

Add the brown sugar, lime and lemon juices, habaneros, garlic, browning seasoning if using, salt, and thyme to the blender and blend on high until smooth.

Put the chicken thighs in a gallon-size zip-top bag set in a large bowl. Add the marinade, seal the bag, and massage the thighs through the bag to coat completely. Rest the bag in the bowl, then transfer to the fridge to marinate overnight or at least 8 hours.

HOLD IT! The longer you marinate the chicken, the better it will be; up to 2 days in the fridge.

Grill the jerk chicken. Prepare a charcoal grill or preheat a gas grill or indoor grill pan over medium-high heat.

Grease the hot grates or grill pan with oil. Place the thighs, skin side down, onto the grill over direct heat or onto the grill pan. Cook until the skin releases itself from the grates, about 10 minutes. Using tongs, flip and continue to cook until the juices run clear or a probe thermometer reads 155°F, at least another 10 minutes. (Bear in mind that the folks at the USDA specify 165°F.)

PLATE IT! This chicken and the Grilled Shrimp and Peach Salad with Serranos (page 274) would be the best of buds.

BREAK IT: This would be crazy with a Coca-Cola brine. Mix Coke with salt and let the chicken sit in it for a day before marinating in the jerk rub. This will make for more caramelization and a gentle sweetness to counteract the heat in the marinade.

gear

stockpot

sharp knife or clean X-Acto knife (never used on anything other than food)

slow cooker (at least 8-quart capacity)

pot

large bowl

blender

strainer

medium saucepan

wok or large skillet

ingredients

TONGUES

Two 3-pound 6-ounce beef tongues (about 7 pounds total)

1 medium onion, quartered

4 garlic cloves, peeled and smashed

2 dried bay leaves

1 cinnamon stick

1 tablespoon whole cumin seeds

1 tablespoon kosher salt

1 teaspoon whole black peppercorns

1.25 liters Dr Pepper

2 tablespoons corn or vegetable oil

SALSA VERDE

1½ pounds tomatillos

3 jalapeño peppers

2 garlic cloves

1 teaspoon kosher salt

½ cup loosely packed fresh cilantro

dr pepper–braised beef tongue tacos with salsa verde

(Dark meat)

If you have not had beef tongue yet, you really should consider relinquishing your meat-eater's license. Beef tongue is one of the most delicious meats I've ever eaten. It's great thinly sliced and grilled quickly, but my favorite preparation is to braise it for hours in a flavorful liquid, then fold it up in a taco.

The first time I braised beef tongue was to impress the molé guy (see page 72), and he was pleased with the results. Since then, Dr Pepper is often my go-to liquid in braises and sauces. With twenty-three flavor components, it's clearly the chef of sodas and the soda of chefs, and when it's reduced, it becomes a lacquerlike sauce that's packed with *no se que es*. Only you will know that Dr Pepper is what gives the meat that sweet counterbalance to the spicy salsa verde. By wrapping the tacos in foil and storing in the slow cooker, you can make these ahead and snack on them all day.

Make the tongues. Fill a stockpot halfway with water and bring to a boil over high heat.

Rinse the tongues under cold water, then pat dry. Place the tongues in the boiling water and cook for 5 minutes. Remove the tongues and transfer them to a cutting board. While the tongue is still hot, carefully use the X-Acto, set on the smallest blade setting, or a sharp knife, to cut slits down the length of the tongues. Using these slits, grab ahold of the skin and peel it off. Use the knife to separate the skin from the flesh if you have to. (The process is sometimes a pain, and varies from tongue to tongue, but it will all be worth it in the end.) Discard the skin.

Place the peeled tongues in the insert of a slow cooker. Add the onion, garlic, bay leaves, cinnamon, cumin, salt, and black peppercorns and cover with the Dr Pepper. Put a lid on the pot and switch the slow cooker on low. Cook for 6 hours.

Make the salsa verde. Within the first 3 hours while the tongue is in the slow cooker, bring another pot of water to a boil. Fill a large bowl with ice and water to create a water bath.

Remove the papery "capes" from the tomatillos and discard.

Cut off the tops of the jalapeños, halve lengthwise, and remove the seeds and ribs. Finely dice 1 of the jalapeños and reserve.

Add the tomatillos, halved jalapeños, and garlic carefully to the water in the pot, so as to avoid splashing. Boil them until the tomatillos begin to rupture, about 10 minutes.

Drain the tomatillos, jalapeños, and garlic and add to the ice bath to shock them and stop the cooking. Once cool, drain them again and add to a blender with the salt. Blend until smooth. Add the diced jalapeño and cilantro to the blender and pulse until incorporated. Transfer the salsa to a container, cover, and refrigerate for at least 3 hours.

FOR SERVING

15 to 20 corn tortillas

Nappé Roots!

Nappé comes from the French verb *napper,* which means "to coat," as in having the ability to coat the back of a spoon, which is a consistency ideal for most sauces. It's really about viscosity—thick enough not to slide off of whatever it is you want it on. As an homage to the Nappy Roots, any time something reaches nappé consistency, I shout "Y'all Gone Up and Done It" from their album *Watermelon, Chicken, and Gritz.* This is a very good joke among very few people.

☞ **Tip**

Before you do anything with hot peppers, put your latex gloves on.

Make the cooking liquid. After 6 hours, carefully remove the hot beef tongues from the slow cooker. Allow the tongues to cool before covering and transferring to the refrigerator until cold, about 3 hours.

Strain the cooking liquid and discard any solids. Transfer about 1 quart of the braising liquid to a container; discard the rest. Cover and place the container in the freezer for 2 hours.

After 2 hours, remove the container from the freezer, scoop off the solidified fat, and discard it. Place a medium saucepan over medium heat, add the cold cooking liquid, and cook, stirring occasionally, until the liquid has reduced to a *nappé* consistency (see sidebar), about 2 hours; it will likely reduce to about ½ cup of thickened sauce.

HOLD IT? Allow the sauce to cool before transferring to a container and refrigerating. The meat, sauce, and salsa can be stored separately, covered, in the refrigerator for up to 2 days.

Assemble the tacos. Dice the cold tongue meat.

Heat the oil in a large skillet or wok over medium-high heat. Add the diced tongue and brown it, stirring occasionally, until heated through, about 6 minutes.

Add the reduced sauce and scrape up any flavorful bits stuck to the bottom of the pan with a wooden spoon; stir until hot. Transfer the meat and sauce to a bowl.

Meanwhile warm the tortillas by wrapping them in a moist towel and microwaving in 1-minute increments until warm.

PLATE IT! Set the cleaned slow cooker to the warm setting. Lay down squares of aluminum foil, with a tortilla on top of each. Add a scoop of tongue and a spoonful of salsa to each one. Carefully fold the tortillas, then the aluminum foil, and crimp the edges. Store the tacos in the slow cooker to keep them warm.

BREAK IT: You could smoke the beef tongue and baste it with Dr Pepper for a similar but smoked-out effect. Regardless, cool, cube, and reheat before topping with salsa.

---

gear

two 9-inch springform pans or cake pans

medium mixing bowl

whisk

large mixing bowl

stand mixer with whisk and paddle attachments

cooling rack

small pot

microwave-safe bowl

whisk

serrated knife

offset spatula

ingredients

CAKE

1½ cups unsweetened cocoa powder, plus a little more for dusting

2 teaspoons instant coffee granules

1 cup vegetable oil

1 cup heavy cream

½ cup sour cream

3 large eggs, lightly beaten

1 teaspoons pure vanilla extract

1 teaspoon bourbon

3 cups sugar

3 cups all-purpose flour

2 teaspoons baking powder

2 teaspoons baking soda

2 teaspoons kosher salt

howitzer habanero chocolate cake

(DESSERT)

My motivation for this recipe was entirely selfish. I was at Alex Guarnaschelli's cookbook release party and she served the chocolate cake from her book, and nobody would shut up about it, and rightfully so, because it was an absolute destroyer. It was perfectly Alex, and perfectly cake. So I immediately thought to myself, "Where's my bunker-busting chocolate cake recipe? When will I get to make it?" I knew from that moment that when I was presented with the opportunity to write a cookbook, I would create my very own Howitzer of a chocolate cake: a whiskey-coffee-chocolate behemoth, with white-hot (as in white chocolate, cream cheese, and habanero) frosting. As General Tso's chicken is to American Chinese food, I wanted this to be to cake: an explosion of sweet and heat. I knew also that I wanted a picture of a big slice of cake in the book, because cake makes people happy and happiness often leads to impulse purchases.

Make the cake. Preheat the oven to 350°F. Grease two 9-inch springform pans and dust with cocoa powder. (If you don't have two springform pans, use two greased 9-inch round cake pans and cut and grease a circle of parchment paper for the bottom of each pan.)

In a medium mixing bowl, gently whisk together the cocoa powder, 1½ cups hot water, and instant coffee until the cocoa and coffee have dissolved. In a separate, larger bowl, whisk together the oil, heavy cream, sour cream, eggs, vanilla, and bourbon. Gently whisk the cocoa mixture into the mixture in the large bowl and mix until all of the wet ingredients are blended.

Put the sugar, flour, baking powder, baking soda, and salt in the bowl of a stand mixer fitted with the paddle attachment and mix on low until combined.

With the stand mixer on low, slowly add the liquid ingredients to the dry ingredients in the mixer bowl. Mix until the batter is just smooth, scraping down the sides once or twice, about 2 minutes. Carefully divide the batter between the two prepared cake pans.

Bake until a toothpick inserted into the center of the cakes comes out clean, about 50 minutes.

Transfer the baked cakes, still in their pans, to a cooling rack. Once the cakes are cool enough to handle, remove them from the pans and let cool completely on the rack.

Make the frosting. Remove the stems, seeds, and ribs from the habaneros and discard. Finely dice the habaneros.

In a small pot over medium heat, melt the butter and add the habaneros. Cook until the butter begins to foam, 4 to 5 minutes. Remove the pot from the heat and allow to cool completely.

In a microwave-safe bowl, microwave the white chocolate chips at 50 percent power, stirring every 30 seconds, just until melted, about 2 minutes.

In the clean bowl of the stand mixer fitted with the paddle attachment, beat the cream cheese and salt on low speed until fluffy, about 2 minutes.

Add the cooled butter to the white chocolate and whisk to incorporate.

FROSTING

4 habanero peppers

16 tablespoons (2 sticks) unsalted butter

Two 11-ounce bags white chocolate chips

24 ounces cream cheese, at room temperature

½ teaspoon kosher salt

Crumb Coat

A crumb coat is basically a layer of primer paint for your cake. It suspends any loose crumbs in a thin layer of frosting and holds them there, and it makes a smooth surface for you to do your final frosting layer, crumb free.

☞ Tip

Before you do anything with hot peppers, put your latex gloves on.

With the mixer running on low, slowly and carefully combine the white chocolate mixture with the cream cheese and paddle until smooth. Refrigerate the frosting until ready to use, or you can use right away.

HOLD IT? The sour cream and baking soda will start making the batter rise right away, which will expand in a storage vessel, so once you mix the batter, you gotta bake the cake. The frosting can be refrigerated for up to 3 days.

Finishing the cake. Do not frost the cakes until they are completely—and I mean absolutely—cooled. If you frost when they are warm, your frosting will melt off.

Using a serrated knife, trim off the domed top of one of the cooled cakes so it's flat. Reserve the dome for snacking.

If the frosting has been chilling, put it in a stand mixer fitted with the whisk attachment and whisk it on low until light and spreadable, about 2 minutes. Reserve about a heaping ½ cup frosting in a small bowl for the crumb coat (see sidebar).

Put the trimmed cake, cut side up, on a large flat plate. Or, if you like, make a cake plate by tracing a circle around the bottom of your springform pan on a piece of cardboard and cutting it out; place the trimmed cake, cut side up, on the cardboard circle. Using an offset spatula, spread one-third of the frosting evenly over the top of the first cake layer. If some goes off the sides, that's OK, because we'll ice the sides as well.

Place the second cake on top of the first, dome up. (You could lop off the top of the dome, but I like the look of a rounded top.) Spread the ½ cup reserved crumb coat frosting all around the exposed cake in a thin layer. If possible refrigerate for at least 10 minutes.

Frost the entire outside of the cake with the remaining frosting.

PLATE IT! This cake should be cut into no more than 8 pieces and served to no more than 8 extremely awesome and deserving people. This is the kind of cake that makes bad days excellent again.

BREAK IT: Might as well go on ahead and "hot dog law" this with some bacon-bit sprinkles.

LAW
OF GIN
AND
TONIC

aromatic meets aromatic

G in and tonic is a magnificent creation: sour, sweet, and bitter all at once. But that is not what's important about a gin and tonic. What's important is its aromatic compounds. Aromatic compounds are things we "taste" with our nose, as opposed to our tongue. If you hold your nose and have a sip of a gin and tonic, you'll barely know the difference between it and a vodka soda. That's because gin gets its signature flavor from juniper, which is a very hard flavor to describe without smelling it. Juniper is something we taste with our nose: it tastes like pine smells.

The most outlandish culinary concoctions are validated by the invisible things our nose can see. In gin, there is a certain fresh, grassy, bright flavor that is echoed by the flavor of lime, particularly in the zest. What links them? Myrcene, a compound that only our nose can sense. Science has advanced far enough that we can prove this to be true, though our nose knew it all along. The following recipes use information gathered from the Volatile Compounds in Food database, which I highly suggest you check out online. It's amazing to learn what foods share compounds, and then develop your own recipes from there. Unlike the previous laws, this law isn't about the meeting between two or more opposing flavors. This is about using our schnoz to find the similarities between two seemingly disparate flavors. These dishes are all a little zany on paper, but you'll need just one bite, and sniff, to understand.

aromatic meets aromatic

JASMINE	JASMINE CHICKEN LIVER PÂTÉ	CHICKEN LIVER
PEAR	PARSNIP AND PEAR SALAD	PARSNIP
COCOA	ROASTED COCOA CAULIFLOWER	CAULIFLOWER
CUMIN	CARROT MARGARITAS	CARROT
CINNAMON		STAR ANISE
CLOVES	BUTTERNUT SQUASH AND ORANGE SOUP	CARDAMOM
CHAMOMILE	CHAMOMILE LOBSTER SALAD	ALMOND OIL
KIWIS	KIWI OYSTERS ROCKEFELLER	OYSTERS
MANGO	PORK TENDERLOIN WITH MANGO AND PINE	PINE
CLOVES	BANANA AND CLOVE BEEF TENDERLOIN	BANANAS
HOPS	BEER LOVER'S SUNDAE	PINEAPPLE

gear

small pot

slotted spoon

small bowl

sauté pan with lid

medium bowl

colander

blender

ingredients

12 tea bags jasmine tea

16 tablespoons (2 sticks) unsalted butter

2 bay leaves

1 pound chicken livers

1 yellow onion, halved and thinly sliced

2 teaspoons kosher salt

jasmine chicken liver pâté

(CANAPÉ/SNACK)

Remember when you were a kid and you thought that liver was gross because some cartoon kid didn't like it? Generations of people lost their appetite for something just because of seeing it be unpopularized on TV. When I get to make my food cartoon, the villains will inflict terror based on irrational fears of delicious things. Pâté is a good place to start loving liver, as the liver taste is a bit diluted with butter, onions, and other flavorings. Plus, jasmine tea is steeped in the butter to perfume the pâté with floral notes; coincidentally, both liver and jasmine contain indole, an aromatic compound, so they are both chemically and taste-wise a great match.

Snip off and discard the strings and tags of all of the tea bags.

In a small pot over low heat, melt the butter. Add 10 of the jasmine tea bags to the butter. Simmer on very low heat so that the butter doesn't brown, until it tastes jasmine-heavy, about 10 minutes. Remove the bags using the slotted spoon, squeezing them gently to extract the butter, then discard. Transfer the butter into a small bowl and place in the freezer to solidify.

In a large sauté pan with a lid, bring 2 cups water to a simmer. Once simmering, add the remaining 2 tea bags and the bay leaves. Turn the heat off and allow the tea bags to steep for 3 to 5 minutes; discard the tea bags.

Rinse the livers under cool water in a medium bowl until the water runs clear. With your fingertips, remove any membrane, dark black bits, or extra fat from the livers. None of these things will kill you so don't break your neck doing it, it just makes for a more even consistency in the end.

Add the sliced onions to the infused water in a single layer, then add the livers in a layer on top. Don't worry if the water doesn't cover everything fully. Cook over low heat, covered, until the onions are tender and livers are cooked but still light pink inside, 6 to 8 minutes.

Drain the livers and onions in a colander in the sink. Discard the bay leaves. Place the drained livers, onions, and salt into the blender, and blend until smooth.

Add the cold jasmine butter to the blender gradually, a few tablespoons at a time, and blend until incorporated, then repeating with a few more tablespoons, until all of the butter is incorporated.

HOLD IT? The pâté will hold in the fridge, covered, for up to a week. If you want to pour some rendered duck fat or bacon grease on top of the pâté to cover, you could keep it refrigerated for up to a month. It's nicest to serve this directly out of a pretty container. I like any sort of coverable ramekin. That said, you could use Dixie cups. No matter what, allow the pâté to return to room temperature.

PLATE IT! Serve this at room temperature with toast points.

BREAK IT: Serve this with some pickled carrots (page 264) to make this a little more banh-mi flavored.

gear

nonreactive bowl

vegetable peeler

chef's knife or mandoline with julienne attachment

mixing bowl

ingredients

¼ cup mayonnaise

Juice of ½ lemon

1 tablespoon Dijon mustard

2 teaspoons finely chopped dried rosemary

½ teaspoon kosher salt

1½ pounds (about 3 large) green Anjou pears

1 pound parsnips

Play the Mandoline!

The mandoline is an incredibly useful tool. It can turn 10 minutes of knife work into a 1-minute job. What I really love about mandolines is that they are precise. You can set a thickness and every cut will be the same. For someone who usually colors outside the lines, this is a priceless tool.

Always use the finger guard!

The mandoline is one of the most helpful kitchen tools, but also one of the most dangerous, if you get too confident. It does a great job of making thin, uniform slices and juliennes of foods, but it can also do that to your fingers and knuckles. I don't care if you are Daniel Humm, if you use a mandoline, use the finger guard!

parsnip and pear salad

(Cold app)

In most restaurant kitchens, everyone flips out over making sure everything has a ton of color, to the point of adding random herbs and microgreens, colored oils, and pepper dusts. So, being the contrarian that I am, I got to thinking about what foods contain the most flavor with the least color, and was drawn to the parsnip and the pear, which have naturally cream-colored flesh, and are practically incense for your mouth and nose. Parsnip and pear couldn't be further apart in terms of texture, which makes for a great juxtaposition as you chew, but their aromatic compounds line up like good kindergarteners.

Stir together the mayo, lemon juice, Dijon, rosemary, and salt in a medium nonreactive bowl.

Peel, core, and dice the pears, one by one, and transfer the pieces immediately to the dressing to prevent browning.

Using a sharp vegetable peeler, peel the parsnips. Using a sharp chef's knife, halve the parsnips, then very thinly slice with your knife or using a mandoline. Stack the slices and cut through to yield short matchsticks. Add to the dressing.

Chill, covered, until cold, about 1 hour.

HOLD IT? The dressed salad can hold in the fridge for up to a day.

PLATE IT! Serve this on a colored plate using a ring mold or biscuit cutter to form a pretty white puck, or next to a big piece of meat like the lamb shanks on page 45.

BREAK IT: Add texture, color, and a little bitter astringency with the simple addition of neatly diced celery.

gear

large mixing bowl

large cast-iron skillet

trivet (see sidebar page 62)

ingredients

¼ cup olive oil, plus more for drizzling

1 tablespoon unsweetened cocoa powder

2 teaspoons kosher salt

1 head cauliflower, leaves removed, stem trimmed flush with the head

roasted cocoa cauliflower

(Hot app)

Cauliflower is the ready-made canvas of the food world. The many nooks and crannies between the florets and its gleaming white palette are just asking to be covered with deliciousness. While cauliflower and other cruciferous vegetables in their raw states are often seen as sharp (see the Brussels sprout vinaigrette on page 202), when they are roasted those sharp flavors are muted and become toasty, more aromatically congruent to cocoa. Cocoa isn't generally thought of as savory, let alone a mate with cauliflower, but here it adds a rich and earthy aroma but no sweetness, as well as a pretty patina. You could cut the florets off the stalk after roasting, but I think it works best at a huge holiday dinner, carved tableside.

Preheat the oven to 300°F.

Combine the oil, cocoa powder, and salt in a large mixing bowl. Transfer as much of the mixture as possible in a container, but do not clean the bowl.

Place the cauliflower, floret side down, in the bowl. Drizzle half of the oil mixture down the stalk to season the interior of the cauliflower. Turn the cauliflower over and drizzle the rest of the oil mixture on top. Using clean hands, evenly distribute the oil mixture all over the top of the cauliflower.

HOLD IT! You can hold the uncooked prepared cauliflower, covered, in the refrigerator for up to a day.

When ready to cook, set the cauliflower, floret side up, in a cast-iron skillet. Bake the cauliflower until the stem is tender in the middle, about 1½ hours.

PLATE IT! Put a trivet down on the table and serve this right out of the skillet. Use a knife to carve off the florets at the table.

BREAK IT: Sweeten the chocolate with a drizzle of maple syrup or honey, and then cook this in a smoker. Or instead you could add some cayenne pepper and smoked paprika for a little zip and less smoke flavor.

YIELD Makes 1 cocktail and
1 batch of rimming salt (enough
for at least 8 cocktails)

PREP TIME 5 minutes

gear

small pan

blender, spice grinder, or mortar
and pestle

cocktail shaker

ingredients

RIMMING SALT

1 tablespoon whole cumin
seeds

Zest of 1 lime

1 tablespoon kosher salt

CARROT MARG

¼ cup carrot juice

2 tablespoons tequila

1 tablespoon fresh orange juice

Juice of ½ lime

Ice

Extra lime wedges, for serving

carrot margaritas

(DRINK)

The margarita is easily one of my favorite cocktails. It's kind of like Legos, in that as long as you play within the system of bricks (tequila, juice/acid, salt) you can create any flavor combination you want. Here I celebrate the aromatic similarity of carrot and cumin, which is a defining spice of Mexican food. Cumin is also an antioxidant, so this is the perfect cocktail for cheating on your juice cleanse (which I advocate, on occasion).

Make the spiced rimming salt. In a small pan over low heat, toast the cumin seeds until fragrant, about 1 minute.

Combine the cumin with the lime zest and pulse in a blender, spice grinder, or mortar and pestle until pulverized. On a small plate, mix the cumin–lime zest mixture with the salt until combined.

HOLD IT? The spice mix can be stored in an airtight container, at room temperature, for up to a week.

Make the drink. For each marg, place all the ingredients in a cocktail shaker with ice, then shake until very cold.

PLATE IT! Rub the rim of a glass with a lime wedge, then press it into a plate of spice-salt mixture to adhere the mixture to the rim of the glass. Fill the glass with fresh ice, then strain the cocktail into the glass. Serve after hot yoga for maximum effect.

BREAK IT: Freeze the carrot juice in advance to make super-frozen margaritas in a blender. This cumin salt would be bonkers if you used smoked salt. Purchase some, or just add some kosher salt to a pan the next time you smoke something.

YIELD Makes 6 servings
PREP TIME 10 minutes
COOK TIME 30 minutes
INACTIVE TIME 4 hours

gear

small pot

small bowl

whisk

fine-mesh strainer

shallow baking dish

blender, spice grinder, or mortar and pestle

large stockpot

blender

ingredients

MULLED WINE GELATIN

2 cups dry red wine

2 star anise pods

1 teaspoon whole black peppercorns

1 cinnamon stick

10 whole cloves

1 tablespoon balsamic vinegar

1 packet gelatin

SOUP

2 teaspoons whole fennel seeds

½ teaspoon whole cardamom seeds

1 butternut squash (about 3½ pounds)

2 tablespoons olive oil

1 yellow onion (about 12 ounces), roughly chopped

½ teaspoon cayenne pepper

3 cups fresh orange juice

2 cups vegetable stock (or vegetable broth, and cut the salt by half)

2 teaspoons kosher salt

¼ cup heavy cream

butternut squash and orange soup

(HOT SOUP)

The second the first leaf falls, I start depilling my sweaters and staring at the mulling spices. My go-to guys are cinnamon, cloves, star anise, and cardamom. They are seasonally predestined to pair with butternut squash, another fall workhorse. Also, the orange is aromatically similar to butternut squash, with its orange-colored, earthy-flavored carotenoids. (Don't believe me? Smell a freshly cut butternut squash and an orange side by side—it will be like playing the olfactory version of "Chopsticks" on the piano.) Aptly named, the butternut squash has a buttery texture when cooked through, and a nutty sweetness. In this soup, I use a toddy trick developed by my friend Erin Jamison, a mixologist at the Modern. She made a "jello" shot of whiskey, citrus, and spices, then poured hot water over for a self-mixing toddy. Here, mulled wine gelatin provides some acidity to the soup, and transforms from solid to liquid before the eyes.

Make the mulled wine gelatin. In a small pot over medium heat, combine 1 cup of the wine plus the star anise, black peppercorns, cinnamon, and cloves and bring to a boil.

Meanwhile, pour the remaining 1 cup wine into a small bowl with the vinegar, sprinkle over the gelatin, and whisk to combine.

Once the spiced wine mix comes to a boil, add the gelatin mixture, then bring back to a boil. Strain the wine mixture through a fine-mesh strainer and discard the spices. Transfer the liquid to a shallow baking dish, cover, and refrigerate until firm, 3 to 4 hours.

Make the soup. Grind the fennel and cardamom in a blender, spice grinder, or mortar and pestle until fine. Peel the squash, remove the seeds, and cut into 1-inch pieces.

Heat the olive oil in a large stockpot over medium heat. Add the onion to the pot and cook just until softened, 3 to 5 minutes. Add the spice mixture and cayenne and cook 1 to 2 minutes, or until aromatized. Add the squash, orange juice, and stock, cover, and simmer until the squash is very tender, 15 to 20 minutes.

Turn off the heat, then stir in the salt and cream. Working in batches, transfer the soup to a blender and blend until smooth.

HOLD IT? The gelatin will hold, covered and refrigerated, for up to a week. The soup will hold, covered and refrigerated, for up to 4 days.

Reheat the soup over medium heat until piping hot. Cut the gelatin into 1-inch cubes.

PLATE IT! Serve the bowls with 1 or 2 cubes of red wine gelatin in the center, then pour the hot soup around. Watch as the gelatin melts and swirls itself into the soup. Garnish with additional gelatin cubes to your liking.

BREAK IT: Salty meats or nuts would amp this soup up. Grab some seasoned nuts, pulse them in a food processor, and sprinkle them in. I've been known to cut Slim Jims into little pellets to add to dishes, and I think this soup is a worthy candidate.

YIELD Makes 4 servings
PREP TIME 10 minutes
COOK TIME 20 minutes
INACTIVE TIME 30 minutes

gear

medium pot

large bowl

4 disposable wooden chopsticks or skewers

large bowl with ice

kitchen shears

small pot

candy thermometer

whisk or food processor

ring mold (optional)

ingredients

LOBSTER

Six 4-ounce raw lobster tails

INFUSED OIL

4 chamomile tea bags

1 cup almond oil

MAYONNAISE

1 egg yolk

1 tablespoon white vinegar

1 teaspoon Dijon mustard

1 teaspoon lemon juice

1 teaspoon kosher salt

chamomile lobster salad

(COLD FISH)

I really didn't know about using chamomile outside of a tea bag until I saw a package of the dried flowers at my local market. I imagine if pillows had flavor they would want to taste like chamomile. The flavor is subtly sweet and mellow, and it works particularly nicely with shellfish. At my restaurant, one of the first dishes we did was called "Mussels, Relaxed," which was made with chamomile-infused wine. Here, we infuse almond oil with chamomile, which makes for a one-two punch of soft floral flavors; this will do all sorts of ballet moves in your mouth when combined with some sweet lobster tail meat. You could serve this lobster salad on a potato bun as a sandwich or as an accompaniment to a surf or turf (I like to pair it with the Banana and Clove Beef Tenderloin on page 304).

Cook the lobster tails. Bring a medium pot of water to a simmer. Fill a large bowl with ice and water to create an ice bath.

Insert a disposable chopstick along the inside of the back of the lobster tail, starting at the end of the tail and pushing it through to the thickest part. (This will keep it from curling while it cooks.)

Put the lobster tails, thick side down, in the pot of hot water and cook until the shell is bright red and the meat is opaque, 3 to 4 minutes.

Shock the tails in the ice bath to stop the cooking and cool.

Using kitchen shears, cut up the middle of the top of the shells. Pull out the meat, and transfer to a cutting board. Cut the meat lengthwise, then into bite-size pieces. Cover and chill in the refrigerator.

Make the infused oil. Snip off the strings and tags from the tea bags.

In a small pot with a candy thermometer, heat the oil to 200°F. Remove from the heat, add the tea bags, and allow them to steep for 10 minutes. Remove the tea bags, carefully pinching them between two spoons to extract any oil, and allow the oil to stand until it is at room temperature.

Make the mayonnaise. Set a bowl on top of a rolled-up towel so it doesn't go flying while you whisk. Whisk the egg yolk, vinegar, Dijon, and lemon juice in a large bowl until pale yellow and frothy, about 1 minute.

While whisking the yolk mixture furiously, add the chamomile oil, a few drops at a time, continuing to stream it in until all of the oil is emulsified and incorporated. Add the salt and whisk to incorporate. Transfer to the fridge to chill for at least 30 minutes.

Alternatively, you could use a food processor. Put the egg yolk, vinegar, Dijon, and lemon juice in the bowl and run it until it's splashing everywhere inside the food processor. Use the emulsion tube to stream in the oil. Add the salt last and pulse to incorporate.

HOLD IT? The cooked lobster meat can be stored in the fridge, covered, for up to 1 day. The mayo can be stored in the fridge, covered, for up to a week.

Assemble the salad. Add the mayonnaise to the lobster meat, a little at a time, until it's the consistency you'd like. I like mine heavily dressed as a side dish and lightly dressed as a sandwich. It's all in your hands. (This recipe will make more than enough mayonnaise for the lobster—save the rest for your next batch of tails, or try it on a ham sandwich.)

PLATE IT! If serving this dish as a salad, pack the dressed lobster into a circular mold to give it a nice form. If you are going to rock this as a sandwich, I'd put it on a toasted potato roll (preferably Martin's brand).

BREAK IT: Surf and turf works here because the rich beef complements the delicate lobster, and vice versa. I see no reason why you couldn't make a Double-Down of seared steak (page 74) and lobster salad, except that it's messy and hedonistic, which is also exactly why you should make a Double-Down of steak and lobster salad.

YIELD Makes 12 oysters

PREP TIME 15 minutes

COOK TIME 10 minutes

gear

oyster knife with oyster box (see sidebar page 143)

small mixing bowl

sheet pan

ingredients

2 peeled kiwis, diced, skin reserved

1 shallot, minced

¼ cup finely chopped fresh spinach leaves

1 teaspoon kosher salt

12 oysters, shucked, on the half shell, chilled (see page 143)

¼ cup panko bread crumbs

2 tablespoons unsalted butter, cold, cut into 12 pieces

kiwi oysters rockefeller

(Hot fish)

As stated in my recipe for Naked Angels on Horseback (page 266), I think the best way to cook an oyster is to not. How, then, could I possibly have a recipe for Oysters Rockefeller? Here, the oyster is just warmed, due to the insulating power of spinach and bread crumbs. Instead of herbs, I've augmented the classic recipe with kiwi, which shares some aromas with the oyster. The kiwi's astringent bite, sweetness, and sourness make it triply suited for an oyster, subbing in for horseradish, cocktail sauce, and mignonette, respectively; once you taste the two together, they meld on some sort of primordial level.

Prep the Oysters Rockefeller. Preheat the broiler.

Combine the kiwis, shallot, spinach, and salt in a mixing bowl and stir with a wooden spoon to mash slightly.

Put the oysters on a sheet pan. Add a scant 1 tablespoon of the kiwi mixture to each oyster, pressing gently to affix it.

HOLD IT? Shucked oysters should be used very soon after shucking. You can apply the mix to the shucked oysters, cover with plastic wrap, transfer to the fridge and store for up to 1 hour before you are ready to serve.

Cook the oysters. Divide the bread crumbs evenly over the oysters. Put 1 piece of the butter on top of the bread crumbs on each oyster. Broil until golden brown and bubbly, 6 to 8 minutes.

PLATE IT! Remember that kiwi skin we reserved? Cut it into 12 strips, and place the strips, green side down, on a plate. Put each broiled oyster in its shell on top of a strip of kiwi skin, using that fuzzy side to keep the oysters from sliding around as you carry and serve. My buddy Belinda (see headnote page 168) used to say "if it grows together, it goes together" and I would absolutely DESTROY these oysters if I were given a nice bottle of New Zealand sauvignon blanc to chase them down.

BREAK IT: We have a dish at Do or Dine that uses kiwi, duck, and fennel. The fennel and kiwi go together so harmoniously, I couldn't help thinking of replacing the spinach with shaved fennel. For bonus points, add a duck crackling or a strip of duck prosciutto.

YIELD Makes 6 servings

PREP TIME 10 minutes

COOK TIME 35 minutes

INACTIVE TIME 10 minutes

gear

blender

small pot

sheet pan with rack

mixing bowl

probe thermometer

ingredients

SAUCE

⅓ ounce white pine needles (see sidebar)

1 mango (about 12 ounces), peeled and diced

½ cup water

1 tablespoon kosher salt

PORK

2 pork tenderloins (about 2½ pounds total), trimmed (see page 307)

Fleur de sel

Olive oil

Pork Legalese

The USDA says pork is just fine at 145°F. If the government knows that overdone pork is a thing of the past, then you should too. I still like to live on the rebellious side at about 135°F, but to each his own.

White pine has long thin needles that are easy to pulverize. I'm sure any Christmas tree lot will part with some. Just make sure the tree wasn't sprayed with any chemicals. If you can't find white pine, try substituting fresh rosemary and mint.

pork tenderloin with mango and pine

(LIGHT MEAT)

Nothing says winter holidays like the scent of pine, so, inspired by a Douglas fir eau-de-vie beloved by my mixologist partner Luke Jackson, I wanted to figure out how to incorporate this super scent into a dish. I thought pork tenderloin, mild in flavor and lean as it gets, would be a nice backdrop. My family has a tradition of giving citrus or tropical fruits around the holidays, so mango, which shares some aromatic compounds with pine, is the perfect complement for this unusual but decidedly festive dish.

Make the sauce. Chop the pine needles as finely as you can. Combine the chopped pine needles, mango, water, and the salt in a blender. Blend until very smooth, about a minute.

Transfer the mango-pine mixture to a small pot. Bring to a simmer over low heat and cook until thickened slightly, about 10 minutes. Set aside and allow to cool to room temperature.

HOLD IT! Feel free to make the sauce in advance and store in the refrigerator for up to 3 days. Bring the sauce back to room temperature before proceeding with the recipe. The pork must be cooked to order.

Make the pork. Preheat the oven to 300°F. Line a sheet pan with parchment paper or aluminum foil and fit with a rack.

Place the tenderloins and mango pine sauce in a mixing bowl and flip to coat both tenderloins liberally with the sauce. Lay the tenderloins on the rack of the prepared sheet pan, pour over any remaining sauce, and cook until a thermometer reads 135°F in the thickest portion, 20 to 25 minutes (see sidebar).

Transfer the pork loins to a cutting board and allow to rest for 5 minutes. Using a very sharp knife, slice the pork into ¼-inch-thick rounds, being careful not to disturb too much of the sauce.

PLATE IT! Arrange the pork slices on a plate, following the curve of the plate, or present the slices on a long serving platter. If you've got some extra pine branches around, line the dish with them!

BREAK IT: As this sauce is very aromatic, it also works inside a traditional chicken Kiev. For inspiration, see the Chicken Kiev Nuggs on page 244.

gear

butcher's twine

8-quart pot (or larger)

BBQ thermometer

strainer

small pot

blender, spice grinder, or mortar and pestle

small bowl

whisk

extra-large cast-iron skillet

culinary torch (optional)

ingredients

MULLED WINE

1 bottle Cabernet Sauvignon

1 quart beef broth

¼ cup triple sec

1 teaspoon Angostura bitters

15 whole cloves

4 whole allspice berries

2 cinnamon sticks

2 star anise pods

1 teaspoon whole black peppercorns

1 teaspoon kosher salt

1 tablespoon unsalted butter

TENDERLOIN

Eight tied 6-ounce beef tenderloin fillets or about 6 pounds untrimmed/uncut beef tenderloin (see page 307 for directions for trimming)

banana and clove beef tenderloin

(DARK MEAT)

When I was in my early twenties, I thought beer had three flavors: light, dark, and Mike's Hard Lemonade. My eureka moment with beer (and the beginning of a lifelong affair) came with New Belgium Brewery's Abbey Ale. It's one of their oldest beers, and it's won them many awards. The aroma and flavors are distinctly of banana and clove, although neither is present in the beer. This is the magic of phenols! Having had at least a few kegs of Abbey in my life, I decided to apply the banana and clove combination to beef tenderloin, which is tender and lean, but lacking in the flavor department. My solution to this is to simmer the beef gently in spiced wine, then sear it to finish. The "brûléed" banana topping almost mimics the marrow texture that one would experience while eating a piece of beef on the bone, in its slickness and softness, while its rich caramelized fruit flavor adds some oomph to the beef. Providing the main perfume of the sauce are the cloves, which too often get lumped into the "fall spices" category. However, cloves grow in hot climates, just like bananas, so I think this dish is awesome on a summer night. With a beer, of course.

Make the steaks. Combine all the ingredients for the mulled wine, except the butter, in the very large pot. Place the "external" probe of a BBQ thermometer into the wine.

Over low heat, bring the temperature of the liquid to 150°F. Add the steaks and increase the heat to medium to bring the temperature back up to 150°F. Throttle the heat to keep it around 150°F. Insert the "internal" probe of the BBQ thermometer into one of the steaks, being cautious not to pierce all the way through. Keep the probe in the steak.

When the steaks' internal temperature reaches 130°F, about 20 to 30 minutes, remove the steaks from the liquid. Set the steaks aside to rest.

Bring the wine mixture to a boil, then turn the heat down and simmer until the mixture has reduced to about 1 cup, about 1 hour. Strain the liquid into a small pot, discard the solids, and reserve the liquid.

HOLD IT? The steaks can hold in the refrigerator, covered, for up to 12 hours; bring them back to room temperature before proceeding with the recipe. The reduced sauce can be covered and refrigerated for a day.

Add the butter to the sauce in a small pot over low heat. Whisk gently to thicken the sauce.

Make the bananas. Grind the cloves in a blender, spice grinder, or mortar and pestle until very fine. In a small bowl, combine the sugar, salt, and ground cloves.

Cut the bananas into ¼-inch slices.

If you have a culinary torch, preheat a cast-iron skillet over high heat. Add the tenderloins and sear on the first side until caramelized and slightly charred, about 2 minutes, then flip and remove from the heat. Arrange the bananas, overlapping in a shingle pattern, on the steaks. Liberally sprinkle the clove-sugar-salt mixture over the bananas. Use the torch to brûlée the sugar on the bananas until golden brown.

BANANAS

6 whole cloves

2 tablespoons sugar

2 teaspoons kosher salt

2 just under-ripe bananas, peeled and cut into ¼-inch disks

Alternatively, if you do not have a culinary torch, preheat the broiler to 500°F. Place the steaks in a single layer on a sheet pan. Arrange the bananas, overlapping in a shingle pattern, on the steaks. Liberally sprinkle the clove-sugar-salt mixture over the bananas. Broil the steaks until the bananas are golden brown.

PLATE IT! Drizzle the sauce on each individual plate. Place a steak on top of the sauce.

BREAK IT: Now that you know the flavors and how they work, make this into a tartare, using the recipe on page 88 as a guideline. Instead of red wine, consider red wine vinegar for an acidic component, add the spices, and fold in the banana at the last moment so as not to mash it.

Cleaning, trimming, and portioning tenderloin

I recommend buying a whole tenderloin because it's much more economical than buying individual fillets. It's also a heck of a lot of fun to take a massive piece of meat and trim it down to an elegant cut. The scraps can be ground and added to burgers (check the YOLO burger recipe on 231) or cleaned and used for tartare croquettes (see page 88).

Remove the whole tenderloin from its packaging over a sink or work bowl (lots of liquid will be in the packaging). Pat dry with paper towels. Working on a large cutting board, cut off the layer of thick fat on the bottom of the tenderloin, then remove the "chain" with your fingers and a fillet knife. Clean the meat from the sinew and reserve for another purpose, or discard it.

The cap is the large section wrapped around the tenderloin. It can be tricky to portion more than one steak from it, but I generally do it. Separate the cap from the rest of the tenderloin by pulling where you can and slicing where you can't. Set the cap aside.

Using your fingers and the knife, remove the external membrane and then the silverskin. The external membrane will feel almost slimy. You can pull it with your fingers to remove. The silverskin must be sliced off in strips. I like to use my knife to "start" it, then, holding the skin taut with my left hand, slide the blade under with my right hand, pushing the blade away from the meat. Discard the silverskin.

Tie off 8 equal portions of the tenderloin to make even, round portions. Tying slipknot-style knots is ideal for any protein tying. Cut the cleaned, trimmed, and tied tenderloin into 8 equal portions. The tail of the tenderloin can be used for other beef applications like the ones above, saved for a midnight snack, or simply cooked off for a kid or a very deserving dog. In my restaurant, that portion is often reserved for me; I eat it raw with just a little kosher salt. Cut the reserved cap into two more portions.

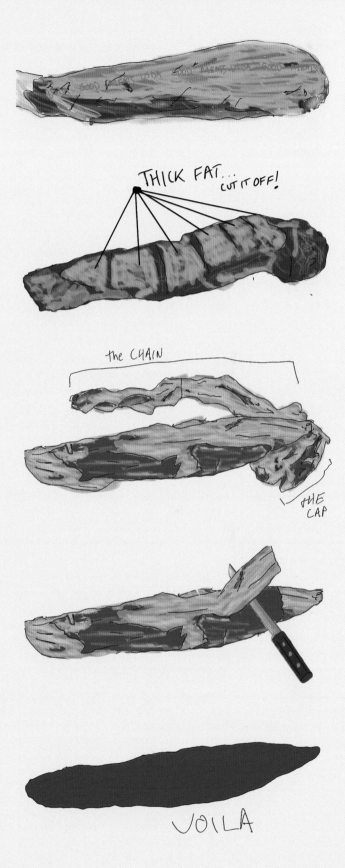

gear

small pot

medium mixing bowl

strainer

ice cream machine, insert bowl frozen ahead of time per manufacturer's instructions

freezer-safe container

food processor

heavy, high-sided pan

candy thermometer

whisk

ingredients

HOP ICE CREAM

2 cups heavy cream

¾ cup loosely packed Kent Golding whole hops leaves (Internet or home brew stores will have it—it's like the Ford Escort of hops; do not use hops pellets)

1 cup whole milk

½ cup sugar

2 teaspoons kosher salt

PINEAPPLE WHEAT BEER SORBET

12 ounces wheat beer, cold

1 cup crushed canned pineapple, drained

¼ cup sugar

Juice of ½ lemon

beer lover's sundae

(DESSERT)

Beer is one of my favorite things about being alive. I love exploring all of the varieties, styles, and flavors. Wheat beers are some of my favorites. They are crisp and summery, refreshing, and full of aroma. Hops, the plant that makes beer bitter, shares some smells with pineapple, which is also summery and refreshing. In this recipe, the two collide in the form of an ice cream and a sorbet. When one has both an ice cream and a sorbet on deck, it's practically license to sundae. Enter stout caramel, also made with beer containing hops, which will aromatically link itself back to the pineapple. The three play nicely in a huge mug, and for crunch, I add some of my favorite bar snacks: Cheetos and pretzels.

Make the hop ice cream. Put 1 cup of the cream and the hops in a small pot over low heat. Bring to a simmer, remove from the heat, and set aside to steep for at least 2 minutes.

Whisk the remaining 1 cup heavy cream, the milk, sugar, and salt in a medium mixing bowl until combined and the sugar has dissolved. (A lot of folks would tell you to cook this to dissolve the sugar, but then you'd have to wait for it to get cold again and I don't have patience for that—so just whisk it until it dissolves.)

Strain the warm hop-infused cream into the mixing bowl, pressing on the hops to extract all of the liquid. Refrigerate the mixture until chilled.

Put the chilled mixture into the bowl of an ice cream maker and process according to the manufacturer's instructions. Put the finished ice cream into a freezer-safe container and freeze for another 3 hours to harden.

Make the pineapple wheat beer sorbet. Place the cleaned ice cream canister in the freezer to chill again.

Pulse all the ingredients for the sorbet in a food processor until smooth. Refrigerate the mixture until chilled.

Put the chilled mixture in the bowl of the ice cream maker and process according to the manufacturer's instructions. Put the finished sorbet into a freezer-safe container and freeze for another 3 hours to firm up.

Make the stout caramel. Make sure you have all your ingredients ready and measured out, as this goes very quickly.

Put the sugar in a medium, heavy, high-sided pan over medium heat and clip on a candy thermometer. Once you see the edges beginning to brown and caramelize, stir once with a rubber spatula. Let the sugar continue to melt until there are no lumps. When the sugar is coppery brown and no hotter than 345°F, carefully add the beer; stand back, as the beer will bubble vigorously. Cook down the caramel to evaporate some of the liquid, whisking often, 5 to 7 minutes. Remove from the heat, whisk in the butter and salt, and chill.

HOLD IT? Keep the ice cream and sorbet in the freezer. Specially designed ice cream containers (or even reused old ice cream cartons) prevent freezer burn. Keep the caramel hidden deep in the fridge, as my first batch was "tested" by everyone who opened the refrigerator.

CARAMEL

1 cup sugar

½ cup room-temperature stout (measured from bottom of head)

6 tablespoons unsalted butter

1 teaspoon kosher salt

GARNISH IDEAS (OPTIONAL)

Whipped cream

Mini marshmallows

Salted peanuts

Pretzels

Cheetos

PLATE IT! Scoop like you've never scooped before. Warm up that caramel just a little in the microwave. Garnish to your heart's content—go wild; here, I just listed some of my personal favorites.

You could serve these in sundae glasses, but a beer mug is what we would do in my man cave.

BREAK IT: This ice cream and sorbet make a destroyer of a float in a mug of stout.

APPENDICES

GEAR

Gear costs money, and what with all the other things in the world, I can understand why kitchen gadgetry is not a high priority to some. I was complaining to a friend about the price of a deli slicer for my joint, and he said, "Deli slicers make flat-screen TVs" . . . I thought he had lost his marbles. But when I thought about it, he was right. Eating at home and cooking from raw materials is almost always cheaper/healthier/more emotionally satisfying than eating out. A piece of gear in your kitchen will produce countless things that you might otherwise spend money on without even thinking. Why buy a cake when you can make one? Why EVER would you get pot roast from a restaurant? By cooking at home, you save money, which you can use to buy a flat-screen TV.

Don't worry, I made a wish list for you, and it's only because I really want you to have a flat-screen TV.

- **The Rice Cooker:** My Black & Decker 3-cup rice cooker is perfect for my girlfriend and me. It is $13 at my local kitchen store right now. Rice cookers make perfect rice every time. In addition to saving you money and a headache, rice-cooker rice can be put on and left on the "keep warm" setting for hours, with little deterioration of quality. You need a rice cooker.

- **The Slow Cooker:** The slow cooker is like having a stay-at-home grandma. It cooks things all day or night, constantly regulating temperature. The slow cooker costs between $20 and $40, which I think is cheaper than a grandma. Slow cookers can be used to cook roasts, soups, and stews, but they also double as a warmer for serving food to the masses. For the price, nothing beats a slow cooker at turning tough meat into deliciousness. My favorite thing to do is put something in a slow cooker at night, and then have it for breakfast. It will make you dream differently, because you'll know there is goodness waiting for you in the morning.

- **The Pressure Cooker:** They should have called it a speed-cooker. It works by pressurizing a chamber, forcing a cooking liquid into something else. It can cook a whole potato in 15 minutes, and turn a tough cut of meat to a fork-tender jaw-dropper in 30. Pressure cookers range from $30 to $100 depending on size (I'd buy at least an 8-quart capacity), but they make up for it in their speed and function. The best broths, stocks, and soups are made in a pressure cooker.

- **The Nutmilk Bag:** Stop laughing. I recently discovered these $6 wonders and they have changed the way I do business entirely. These nearly unbreakable bags work like the cheesecloth of yore, but are reusable, cinchable, and finer than cheesecloth. My days of using cheesecloth, coffee filters, and strainers are coming to an end.

- **The Stand Mixer:** This is kind of like the Maserati of domesticity, but it's an important tool. A good stand mixer is at least $200. The stand mixer does what our body cannot. It can churn butter, knead dough, beat hot sugar into marshmallow fluff, and roll pasta in minutes. All of those things can be done by hand, but it hurts and takes time. The stand mixer is cheaper than a chiropractor.

- **The Cream Whipper:** I believe the ability to carbonate or charge a liquid with gas is important. Coke went flat? Charge it! You can make sparkling wine from still wine, make fluffy pancakes without a leavening agent, and yes, make whipped cream in just seconds! What they don't advertise on that $25 package is that the cream whipper works like a cold pressure cooker. The gas puts pressure on the contents, forcing flavors to marry quickly. Once you put fresh fruit and vodka into a cream whipper, you will never buy flavored vodka again. Chunks of meat can be speed-marinated and liquids can be rapidly infused. In a pinch, the cream whipper can turn meh into marvelous.

- **The Dutch Oven:** If you fry often or wish you could, I'd like to propose the idea of dedicating a Dutch oven or a pot with a lid exclusively to frying. When you are done frying, turn off the heat, move the oil to the back burner, and let it cool. Strain the cooled oil through a fine-mesh strainer. If you filter the oil, you can just store it, lidded and at room temperature, in the vessel. No need for a FryDaddy.

ENTERTAINING

There are three types of party people: the people who can throw a party, the people who can participate in a party, and the people who can do both. You probably already know which one of those three you are, but this chapter's goal is to give you everything you need to become the lattermost. These are the *entertainers*. An entertainer performs, and time and space is their stage. An entertainer parties by throwing parties. An entertainer knows when they are throwing a good party, and that makes them party even harder.

Throwing a good party is a necessary skill in the modern world. More than just an occasion, a good party serves as a mile marker in the timeline of life. People remember periods of their lives based on these markers. I've had people show up in my restaurant and talk about a party I threw a decade earlier, half a country away. That feels damn good. When people stagger up to you and say "killer party" with a grin, you'll get a high like none other. A good party brings people together who might not otherwise engage. When you step back from a great party and watch the mingle, it's like watching a plant grow in hyperlapse. You are creating life, sorta! What with the high stakes, it's no surprise that throwing an ideal party can be a little intimidating to the uninitiated. Luckily, you have the following tenets of entertaining.

the first rule of post-college parties

There is always food and drink. This is your only real job in killer party throwing. Everything else is just gravy. No matter your budget, you can host a party with plenty of food and drink.

If your wallet is tight, throw a less expensive party. You'd be surprised how far you can get with a handle of liquor in the freezer and a bag of chips and the collard and artichoke dip baked straight up in a baking dish (page 197). One might consider themselves a gourmet and a bon vivant, but Schlitz serves the same function as a craft brew at a party.

If there's no money at all, hold a BYOB potluck. Seriously. Everyone knows you don't show up to a potluck without a dish, and if a party is advertised as BYO, they can't complain about a lack of drinks. Put the preparedness on them, and don't feel guilty! After all, you are

volunteering your space and time to host them.

Once I've made a party budget, I look at my total and divide it in half. One half is the actual budget I use for planning the party; the other half I keep for "runs." If something runs out, or the food burns down the kitchen, there is still some cash to make a liquor or ice run, or order an unsliced pizza (if you cut a pizza into small squares on your own, you can feed more people, and they will eat less of it).

know why you are partying

Seems like a no-brainer, I know, but you'd be surprised how this one little thing can change your demeanor when you entertain. You are entertaining not because of an event or an occasion, but because you want to see people, and celebrate the good times. You want people to meet, mingle, and cut loose. The best Super Bowl parties have very little to do with what's going down on the field. A birthday party isn't so much about making someone's day the best ever, but about getting a group of people together to raise a glass to the beauty of one person's *entire life*. If you can't participate in the party because you're too busy worrying about coasters on the coffee table, the right music, or keeping your ex away from your current flame, you've missed the point. It's always about bringing people together, including you.

the show must go on

A good entertainer doesn't pull over the party bus when you get a flat tire. There are plenty more tires on a party bus anyway. Drive a party until the rims make sparks on the pavement of existence. How you handle the bumps in the road is where the magic happens. The first pants-off dance-off party probably started with spilled wine and white jeans. Furthermore, don't make the road too smooth for everyone else. For example, I never rent or buy chairs for a party. This is how you take the magical photo of grown adults sitting cross-legged on the floor enjoying their bowls of squid curry (page 277). I don't use glassware, and it's not because I am scared of having someone drop a Carrot Margarita (page 296) and break a nice glass, it's because I'd hate to be the guest who broke a glass and had to feel awkward.

Lastly, and I'll reiterate this, be sure there is enough food and drink. Food and beverage are the great unifiers, so no matter what happens, if there is food and drink, it's still a party. That means that the menorah can drip wax on the silk tablecloth, Johnny can cry on his

birthday, and the power can go out in the third quarter. You'll still have a party.

we get by with a little help

When you host a large gathering, it's helpful to have a copilot who is familiar with your party grounds and you in general. If you keep the paper towels in a weird place, this person should know. This person can do only 10 percent of the "work" for the party, but can take 50 percent of the load off of you. This tiny bit of help frees you up some from showing people where to put their trash or collecting coats. It's vital to the comfort and mental health of your guests that they see you having a good time as well. Enthusiasm is infectious, and I think it's best to infect by example. You can also use a copilot to do your bidding while you focus on keeping the food and drink flowing. Nobody's mingling? Ask your copilot to make a few introductions. Nobody dancing? You and your copilot can be the two that start to tango. Freeing yourself from these petty party problems can also give you an advantage in the kitchen. After all, you are . . .

cooking for them asses

I don't think it takes any particular planning to cook for six guests. That's a dinner party, and lots of recipes can be plated for six. A real party is much larger, and it involves some strategy. When you cook for the masses, there are three kinds of foods: scoops, build-its, and single bites. I'll describe those in detail. You can have just one category for a more restrained approach, or you can blow it out with a little bit of all three.

Scoops are vats of food that guests serve themselves, from a bowl of dip to a platter of fried chicken. This is the easiest way to get food to your guests, but the least elegant. That shouldn't keep you from making a charcuterie board (page 114) or a big vat of Greek salad (page 196). If you know your event and your crowd well enough, you'll know when to put out a tricked-out crowd-pleasing oyster Caesar (page 87) or when to get sophisticated and heady with a parsnip and pear salad (page 291). Or when to put out a handle of vodka and a bag of Doritos.

The easiest way to step up your scoop food game is to serve something hot. Hot food is a luxury! The slow cooker is the number one party tool for keeping things warm. One super dish served hot out of a slow cooker can make a party so much more. Even if it's just bean soup (page 66) or tongue tacos (page 281) wrapped in

foil and held in the slow cooker, people get jazzed for hot food.

The appeal of hot food is also shown in the popularity of outdoor grilling, which always makes for a great party. Usually, if you are grilling, you are preparing scoop food. It goes from a grill to a landing pad, and people scoop it up and put it on their plate. I implore you to cook as little food on the grill at a time as possible. Start with some veggies or a shrimp salad (page 274), take a breather, and then move on to jerk chicken (page 279) or grilled mackerel (page 154). Hell, I even do the big meats in spurts. Nothing's worse than having a ton of food on the grill while everyone stands around waiting, or worse, someone eating a cold burger or hot dog because all of the grilling took place at once. You can prolong the party and gauge your guests' needs in real time.

"Build-its" are the next level of party food. Here, you set up an array of parts that the guests put together themselves. A slow cooker of chili (page 175, for my vegan version) or even ramen (page 120) with an array of condiments is a good start. A BLT bar is my greatest invention. A great, drunken birthday party can be powered by BLTs. A DIY deviled egg setup (see page 116) is fun as can be. The advantage to this is that your guests can make their food to their liking, and the cooking is generally done far in advance. A "build-it" of drunk food might not work well at more somber events, or a family reunion. In this case, augmentation with scoops or single bites is advised.

"Single bites" is a less fancy wording than hors d'oeuvre, so that's what I say. They are the most time-consuming, but the most elegant of party foods, because they are tiny compositions. There is no work on behalf of the guest. You've already cooked it, put it together, and plated it. They just have to eat it. These compositions don't have to be complicated. It could be a toast with nut butter and bacon (page 28), or it could be a tiny doughnut piped with foie gras and jam (page 48). It could be a wonton filled with spinach and artichoke dip (page 197) or it could be a tiny spoon of burrata and caviar (page 225). The only downside of small bites is that there is generally a little advanced assembly required for you and/or your copilot—but this doesn't have to be a chore.

This leads me to the most important piece of party logic.

make a plan, maybe stick to it

Making a plan in advance is key. Before you even think of partying, you need to think of how you are going to attack.

First, decide on a theme. A theme is the word that you put before the word party on your invitation. It could be an elegant Super Bowl party or a Pan-Asian Thanksgiving.

The next step is to plan your invite list. Themes help decide who is coming to the party. If you say it's a tiki birthday party, lots of people will show up, because tiki is fun and pretty user-friendly. If you say it's Meat Madness Memorial Day, maybe your vegan friends won't show. The biggest parties aren't always the best, so plan your invite list to maximize fun, not size.

Next, plan a menu. If there's a glut of any one thing in your fridge, be sure to use it in your food. That's not being cheap, that's just making room for beverages and more food. Your guests don't know and don't care. The food is free to them, so if you need to use up late-season zucchini, do it. Again, a theme will guide the menu accordingly. Decide what style of party food you are going to have: scoops, build-its, single bites, etc. A combo of all three may seem like a little work, but your efforts will be rewarded. Make a list of components and ingredients you need to buy, but do your best to cut corners. People don't expect you to make your own salsa, or whip your own cream. Buy what you can, and make what you can't. Work backward from when your party starts to construct a timeline of which components of your party need to be cooked when. The more you can make in advance, the better.

Next, consider your service vessels. Most stores sell aluminum serving vessels, which while not beautiful, are cheap and disposable. Disposable serving gear/plateware is a necessity. I know it might not be the most environmentally conscious thing to do, but as long as you don't use it every day, I see no problem. Most disposable stuff is recyclable these days anyhow. The last thing you want is to break a wineglass or do dishes. Always party with paper or plastic.

Next, look at your party space and abandon functional fixity. An office trashcan is an upside-down chair. A coffee table is a sofa. A fish tank is just a piece of plywood away from being a killer serving table. A bathtub is the biggest cooler you never had to buy. You need to have a plan for where your food will be staged. Factor traffic flow. Walk into your party in your mind, and think about what the guests' needs will be. I don't put coats in a bedroom. I put coats as close to the door as possible so I don't have to fetch them later. Portable garment racks are cheap, and are generally designed to collapse and be stored for the next party. Your guests will probably want a drink, and they won't want to have to ask for one. Make signs. Seriously. The best parties are the ones where the guests don't have to think. I am also a big fan of making an off-limits area. This is where you store all the things that would ruin your day if they got red wine sprayed on them, or if your clumsy roomie from college knocked it over. It's also a good place for you and your copilot to formulate strategies or make out.

Lastly, once you've made the plan, don't be afraid to crumble it up and throw it away (unless it has vital times or recipes written on it). Once a party starts, a party has a mind of its own, and if you are so hell-bent on keeping it contained to the parameters on a piece of paper, you are hardly partying at all.

a final thought: the importance of music control

Whatever music you may like, be sure to hide whatever it is that controls it. Bluetooth does wonders for this. Tunes are the WMD of parties. Don't let them fall into the hands of the drunken.

PARTY GUIDE

scoop it up or build it out

snacks
Apricot and Habanero Wings
Cheater's Charcuterie Board
Collard and Artichoke Dip (don't wrap it in wontons, just heat and serve with pita or chips!)

salads
Radish Caprese
Smoked Oyster Caesar
Greek Salad with Feta Dressing
Grilled Shrimp and Peach Salad with Serranos
Chamomile Lobster Salad
Parsnip and Pear Salad

soups
Adzuki Bean and Kale Soup
Better Tomorrow Vegan Chili (make it into a build-it—put all sorts of accompaniments around the warm vat of chili!)
Smoked Gouda and Rauchbier Soup

hot meats
Chicken Shawarma in a Can Party
F-Yeah Barbecue (this can also be a build-it of sorts, if you put condiments in the vicinity of the meats, along with some bread to make sandwiches)
Currywursts
Riesling Curry with Squid
Jerk Chicken

desserts
Pistachio-Tarragon Pudding
Wasabi Marshmallows

go mini

Hazelnut Butter Toasts with Bacon (or replace the nut butters with Foie Gras Mousse from page 48)
Jalapeño Poppers with Blueberry Dippin' Sauce (drizzle the dippin' sauce on top)
Dixie Cup of Chilled Red Pepper Soup
Halibut Ceviche in Mini Mango "Tacos"
Foie Gras Doughnut Holes (cut the dough with a shot glass)
"Two-Pump" Crostini
Radish Caprese (skewer the components!)

Dixie Cup of Chilled Yellow Beet and Watermelon Soup with Turmeric Cream
Everything Bagel Nigiri
Steak Tartare Croquettes with Smoky Mayo (drizzle the mayo on top)
Smoked Cannoli
Mini Reuben Wellingtons
Salt Cod Scotch Deviled Eggs
Minted Sake Sea Shooters
Open-Faced Duck Salad Sandwiches
Lamb Breast with Coriander, Cumin, and Lime (cut the lamb smaller and skewer)
Guac Cornets
Coconut "Sashimi" (cut the strips into small rosettes, garnish with radish and plum, serve on a spoon)
Twice-Baked New Potatoes
Trout Caviar with Burrata, Passion Fruit, Vanilla, and Date (divide into very small portions and plate on spoons)
Naked Angels on Horseback
Kiwi Oysters Rockefeller
Lime Zest French Toast Sticks

themes

latin
Carrot Margaritas
Guac Cornets
Chilled Corn Soup with Chile Oil and Honeydew
Dr Pepper–Braised Beef Tongue Tacos with Salsa Verde
Chipotle Chocolate Ice Cream (see Banana Split for Sophisticates recipe)

caribbean
Mojitos
Corn Fritters with Curry
Halibut Ceviche in Mini Mango "Tacos"
Jerk Chicken
Howitzer Habanero Chocolate Cake

kid party
Speed-Pickle-Brined Nuggets with Honey Dippin' Sauce
Lime Zest French Toast Sticks
Twice-Baked New Potatoes
Chilled Corn Soup with Chile Oil and Honeydew (garnished with caramel corn, and the hot peppers left out)
Wasabi Marshmallows (made with powdered drink mix instead of wasabi)

izakaya party
Hand Roll Party
Minted Sake Sea Shooters
Collard and Artichoke Wontons

TEXTURE

One way to learn about texture is through onomatopoeia. Say "texture" real slow and deep like a Houston rap record and it sounds like the texture of molasses. Say it like a chipmunk and it sounds crunchy and sharp like potato chips. I love that damn word, *texture*.

Cookbooks love to talk about taste. Many will get specific and talk about sweet, sour, salty, bitter, even umami, and that is helpful. But when you get to the point when you are juggling flavors pretty well, there is another aspect of cooking that is also incredibly important, but is talked about much less: texture. Food without texture is not nearly as satisfying overall as food where texture has been considered. This is one of the reasons why hospital food (free of choking hazards) gets a bad rap. If texture weren't a big deal, we'd buy presogged cereal and sweetened cream instead of ice cream. Without texture, food would be grim.

Here is another way to think about it. Texture, in relation to food, is the way we experience "touch" in our mouths. As you chew, you are forcefully touching food. And it responds: some foods fight back, others cave. Your mouth doesn't even need to work for some foods to take the esophageal plunge. Some make noise and draw attention. Some refuse to take the plunge at all—but those are usually not edible.

Attempting to synthesize an entire sense onto a page without infinite time and a doctorate is a big task, but if you stick with me (that was a texture joke), you'll soon be adept in applying much-needed texture to your edible creations as much as correctly seasoning them.

---

finding texture

The fastest way to start really understanding texture is to listen to your food. Sometimes when our teeth push food, it breaks. When things break, they make a sound. The noisiest foods are the C foods: Crisp, Crispy, Crunchy. These foods all have some degree of "shattering" of the food involved. They don't melt like butter, or flake like fish. They don't grind down like a meatloaf. When your teeth strike them, they break into sharper, smaller pieces, rattled by the impact.

CRISP foods are the most quiet of the noisy three. Crisp foods are wet, and that moisture dampens their sound. Could you imagine biting into a stick of celery that sounded like a handful of Pringles? Of all the words you could use to rate romaine lettuce, certainly "crisp" would be in the top three. When lettuce loses its crispness, it becomes wilted and floppy. If I were a musician, I'd say "crisp" is like a cymbal hit with one of those fluffy drumsticks: distinct, but not hard.

CRISPY is crisp without the moisture to dampen the sound. It's dry as all get out, brittle and noisy. It's thin and tinny and sharp. Dried leaves are crispy, even though we don't eat them. The crispy coatings on fish. The crispy bubbles of skin on the wings on page 44 or the pork belly on page 257. It's fleeting and fragile, thin and lacy. It's the cymbals hit with penny nails.

CRUNCHY has some bass. It's low and rumbly. Crunchy foods, like carrots or nuts, break into large pieces as opposed to the broken glass of crispy foods. Crunchy foods might have some moisture to them, but mostly, they have a more flexible structure than crisp and crispy foods, which means less shattering upon dental impact.

There are other food textures that are less noisy. The following textures deal with the way foods disintegrate as we push them around the bouncy castle of our mouths.

Aside from fish, **FLAKY** things are generally crisp or crispy things that have been assembled by man, like puff pastry, pie crust, and wafer cookies. Flaking is what happens when food gets bounced around and our tongues can perceive layers. The food separates not just into pieces, but pieces of similar size on top or beside each other. That just blows my mind. Flaky things are generally tender, but not all tender things are flaky. Tender foods display little resistance in the bouncy castle that is a mouth. The way fish flesh flakes is the strangest of all textures to me. (See The Most Dangerous Catch, page 180.) No other foods "flake" like fish do.

CHEWY puts up a little bit of a fight, and then gives up or simply becomes flattened or stretched out enough to be swallowed. An oatmeal cookie just as easily sticks to itself again as it does break apart. This is chewy. Rubbery octopus can be chewy. We simply squish it until it's malleable to be folded up and sent down the hatch. When chewy goes too far it becomes tough; tough foods put up a fight and sometimes they win. We sometimes spit those things into our napkin.

Probably the rarest of all textures is **SNAPPY**. Most people don't even know this exists, but it exists in abalone, jellyfish, and cartilage. Snappy foods *shear* themselves. Our teeth pinch them until they snap, like silly putty being pulled too quickly. This is my favorite of all textures because it's so elusive.

Liquids get their textures from the speed at which they move. If you want to get technical, this is called viscosity.

Slow-moving liquids are often **STICKY**. Stickiness prolongs the time in our mouth, which can be a great thing. Too sticky, though, and we lose a tooth. My dad and I learned this from a cold Mary Jane's candy one day. To me, that candy is just a very, very slow-moving liquid. Fats move a little bit quicker. Fats are the best kind of guests in a mouth party. They hang out for as long as you'll have them. They take no offense when they are rinsed out by something acidic (wine, yay) or pushed away by something absorbent (bread, yay).

CREAMY LIQUIDS are these rich, gentle lingerers and we love them. They coat the mouth, and don't need to be roughed up and forced out like something sticky. When these liquids put up too much of a fight, fancy food people say they are cloying. Cloying foods are the worst guests at a mouth party: they don't know when to leave.

Then there are the **REFRESHERS**, the liquids that are fast and free of fats, but maybe contain some scrubby minerals or acids, like water or lemonade. They don't linger. They are refreshing because they don't hang out. They go down, you have some more, and they refresh your mouth. Refreshing, to me, is a texture because of the way your mouth is left feeling. It's the opposite of something cloying.

Lastly are the **FIZZY LIQUIDS**. Liquids with gas shoved in them are the most pleasing to me. Bubbles are just spaces of air, but these spaces transform your mouth into a veritable washing machine. There's a reason that bathtub stuff is called "Scrubbing Bubbles." Fizzy liquids are like using that canned air stuff for your keyboard, but on your taste buds: just compressed air in a palatable vessel that you use to clean your mouth crevices. To us humans, that is generally very enjoyable. Imagine if your toothpaste didn't foam! That wouldn't be very refreshing at all. And that would be a poorly textured toothpaste.

making texture

There are textures out there that are surprising, because they don't fall into the categories above, and with few exceptions, they are created by humans. If you see someone on some TV show making a foam, a gel, or a "sphere," don't get all tripped up in the "molecular gastronomy" jargon. They are just farting around with textures like the rest of us cooks.

Carrot foam, fish froth, and mustard air are all just liquids with a certain amount of air put in them. When a liquid is moving slow enough that it can hold bubbles of gas in place, it creates a foam. So why mess with foams? Because they play tricks on our tongue. Our mouth can be full of whipped cream but the taste is no more potent than a teaspoon of heavy cream. That's the power of gasses, and why you should be incorporating them into your cooking. In the old days, only things with fats or eggs could hold gas in them enough to create these foams. With modern additives and techniques, you can turn a carrot into a foam in no time. (Carrot foam—carrot juice plus gelatin in a cream whipper—would be especially amazing as an accompaniment to the Lamb Breast with Coriander, Cumin, and Lime on page 147.)

FOAMS aren't necessarily fizzy. Foams can be dense or thin, but they are essentially an array of bubbles, which are made of varying amounts of gas surrounded by tiny amounts of liquids. Large, wet bubbles make froths, which are a form of foam. Froths aren't very stable, and turn into a puddle quickly, but look nice when floating on top of another liquid, like a latte. That milk is frothy. Some foams are thicker, and more stable. They can be practically cut with a knife, and are like the foamy milk on top of espresso in a cappuccino.

"AIRS," which is a terrible name but what chefs are calling them, are the lightest and driest of all, holding their shape until just jostled. Imagine the foam on a freshly poured soda, but without the volatility—with the bubbles just hanging out, waiting to be disrupted. Airs dissipate quickly, as they are very dry and very gaseous. They are just waiting to break down into not much liquid at all. Airs are the toughest things to make, because it's like playing Jenga in a ratio of air to liquid.

There are also **SOLID FOAMS**, which really trip me out. A good example is the meringues in the dacquoise on page 77, where we made a network of liquid-cased air sacs, then cooked out the liquid and left behind a dissolvable solid (sugar) encasing the air. You don't have to cook foams to make this effect. Ice cream is essentially a liquid with air whipped into it, then solidified by freezing. Now imagine freezing so much that there was no liquid left. This is freeze drying, which makes crispy foams, and it's largely for astronauts.

Modern chefs like to play at making things that aren't normally crispy **CRISPY**. Like I described above, crispy things generally contain air somewhere. A potato chip is basically a series of solidified blisters in suspended animation. Steam from the cooking of the potato tries to escape—it expands, creating a blister. It either pops, or gets cooked in place—all that's left is a thin shell that once housed a tiny bit of liquid. Cooks do this by building a solid structure and filling it with air, or removing liquid to the point that the structure is brittle. Carrot chips? No way in hell a carrot is going to be crispy without the human hand. They just don't shatter enough on their own. Crispy things are generally very absorbent, which makes them nice scrubbers for fatty or sweet liquids. This is why we put those crispy onions on the swordfish on page 98: they provide a physical scrubber to move the fish oil out of your mouth. Imagine if you made the kale in the bean soup on page 66 into crispy chips that would soak up all that beany soup or shatter in the mouth.

GELS are kind of like foams except they replace liquids with solids and gasses with liquids. Gels act like solids, in that they retain their shape if left undisturbed but when broken down convert mostly to liquid. Think of it as a water balloon filled with water balloons. It's not going anywhere, until a pin or a tooth or any other pressure-exerting object comes to mess with it. Jell-O is the best example. Put Jell-O in a blender and you get liquid. Seems simple, but there aren't many foods that do that, which is why people either love or hate Jell-O. Another cool thing about gels is that they don't slide around and spread like your average sauce—they stay put! For this reason, chefs make sauces into gels for laser accuracy in plating and portioning. You could make the salsa for the escolar on page 43 into a gel by blending it up and adding a thickening agent like agar agar or gelatin. This would create a semi-solid that could be skewered with a fork or applied in pinpoint-sized dots to the plate (a bit OCD): a plate of red dots with a few white squares, closer resembling an abstract painting than a plate of fish and sauce. Because gels are so infrequently encountered in the culinary wild, they allow

us to create foods that fool the mind. What looks like a Hershey's Kiss could be gravy (the braising liquid from the lamb shanks on page 45), and vice versa. Using this sort of technique—which stimulates, tricks, and tickles the brain—makes cooking as much about being interesting as it is about being nourishing.

The last texture, and what I deem the epitome of modern technique, is the **SPHERE**. The sphere is a solid or a gel that encases a liquid. When we apply pressure to a sphere, it ruptures and releases liquid. Naturally, we experience this sensation in caviar, grapes, cherry tomatoes, and sometimes ravioli or dumplings, but we can create spheres out of almost any liquid or liquified ingredient. These little pops are a unique texture experience and can be used to liven up otherwise monotextured things. Imagine if you took some fresh oysters, blended them up, turned them to spheres, and put them in the oyster Caesar on page 87. Or made honeydew spheres for the corn soup on page 269.

go forth

With an experimental mindset and this book, you can take every recipe in the previous chapters and vary it using any of these textures and techniques. To start, note the different textures in the dishes you make. For example, how does a sticky sauce affect your dish versus a creamy one? How does a crispy element change a sandwich, and how does a crunchy one? Then, I recommend you find a recipe you are comfortable making, and intentionally trick out the texture a little. Try making one element that is normally one texture another texture—for example, roasting or deep frying can make certain vegetables crispy, or raw crunchy vegetables can be used as a garnish for a dish with those same vegetables cooked. Fry up some of the parsnips in the parsnip and pear salad, then top the salad with those. They will work almost like croutons, but are made of the salad itself! If you are curious about foams, gels, and spheres, just consult the Internet for help with the specifics. Most of the techniques and malleable recipes modernist cooks have come up with are available for free online, and it's generally pretty reliable. My favorite blog is khymos.org, which has an entire free cookbook on manipulating textures. Ingredients like agar agar and maltodextrin (turns fats to powders . . . so you could make bacon and lime "confectioners' sugar" to put on those French toast sticks on page 216!) are easily found on the Internet as well. Be creative and have at it!

VEGAN OR VEGETARIAN?

I live with and am in love with a semi-vegetarian. I myself eat vegetarian more often than most cooks. I have my own set of reasons for this, but I won't bore you with them. Your relationship to meat is your own thing, but let me tell you, a less-meat life is still a great life. All of the recipes below are proof!

LAW OF PEANUT BUTTER AND JELLY

Hazelnut Butter Toasts with Bacon and Jam: Omit the bacon or use a "fakon"-type substitute.

Arugula Salad with Pan-Roasted Duck and Figs: Cook mock duck according to its instructions, and use a plant oil to cook the figs.

Jalapeño Poppers with Blueberry Dippin' Sauce: Sometimes I think Tofutti tofu cream cheese is better than standard cream cheese. Shhh.

Chilled Red Pepper Soup with Cold Fried Chicken and Goat Cheese: Make the soup without the cheese or chicken; garnish with chopped roasted nuts and avocado instead.

Tomato Soup with "Grilled Cheese" Ravioli: Use a vegan cream cheese substitute.

Halibut Ceviche in Mini Mango "Tacos": Use the raw "fish" mixture from the vegan fish sticks on page 180 instead of fish.

Escolar with Strawberry Salsa: Use the "fish" mixture from the vegan fish sticks on page 180 instead of fish, but cut the mixture into cubes instead of sticks before panfrying in vegetable oil.

Apricot and Habanero Wings: This glaze would be awesome on grilled carrots!

LAW OF COFFEE, CREAM, AND SUGAR

"Two-Pump" Crostini: Use a butter substitute and mix it directly with the pumpkin pie filling.

Radish Caprese: Omit the mozzarella and add cubes of avocado—not visually tricky, but just as good!

Endive Gratin with Taleggio and Raisins: Omit the cheese and butter, and replace with a cheese substitute and vegetable shortening, respectively.

Chilled Yellow Beet and Watermelon Soup with Turmeric Cream: Put the turmeric in almond milk and whip until frothy!

Adzuki Bean and Kale Soup: Already vegan and vegetarian—it's good to go!

Octopus Tiradito: Instead of octopus rounds, you could roast slices of baby eggplant (leave the skin on for purple color).

Pork Tenderloin Molé Donburi: This dish would be awesome with tempeh instead of pork.

LAW OF BAGEL AND LOX

Everything Bagel Nigiri: Smoke plantains in the cold smoker, then slice thin and use to replace salmon.

Grilled Swordfish with Dill Pickle Emulsion and Onion "Chaw": Firm tofu will taste pretty good instead of swordfish!

F-Yeah Barbecue: Use a combination of jackfruit and medium-firm tofu instead of brisket.

LAW OF THE HOT DOG

Chilled Watercress Soup with Fried Bologna: Omit the bologna, but replace with thinly sliced veggie dogs.

Hand Roll Part: Don't use fish! Veggie hand rolls are awesome! Even better, use the tempura bit recipe to batter and fry the vegetables.

Banana Split for Sophisticates: Replace the ice cream with your favorite animal-free ice cream and the croissant with a giant vegan cookie.

LAW OF THE WEDGE SALAD

Cold Cantaloupe Soup with Peas and Mint: This will be great without the yogurt, just use a bit of almond milk, and mash the peas to make a paste!

Clam Chowder with Celeriac and Parsnip: This isn't a bad soup without the clams. I'd replace with seaweed!

Mackerel with Sweet Potato and Chimichurri: Add more dulse to the fish stick mixture (page 180), form it into patties instead of sticks, and grill, then sauce with chimichurri.

LAW OF GUACAMOLE

Every recipe in this chapter is vegan as is.

LAW OF CHEESE FRIES

Twice-Baked New Potatoes: Use vegetarian cheeses and "fakon" instead.

Greek Salad with Feta Dressing: Instead of feta, use salty, briny pulverized olives.

Collard and Artichoke Dip Wontons: Here you can substitute animal-free cream cheese and almond milk.

Revised Bloody Mary: All set!

Rocket Soup with Olive Oil Whipped Cream: Omit the whipped cream and drizzle with olive oil.

Flounder Usuzukuri with Brussels Sprout Vinaigrette, Egg Yolk, and Red Onion: Here the flounder can be replaced with strips of young coconut meat. Omit the egg yolk.

Currywursts: Use veggie dogs!

LAW OF LEMONADE

Ginger-Brûléed Grapefruit: All set!

Speed-Pickle-Brined Chicken Nuggets with Honey Dippin' Sauce: The speed brine process works well with mushrooms (or with any vegetable).

Three Sweet-and-Sour Cocktails You Should Know: Instead of egg white in the whiskey sour, mix in a tiny bit of cornstarch.

CCF Hot and Sour Soup: Omit the egg, stir in some crumbled tofu if you'd like.

Corrected Fish and Chips: Use the vegan fish sticks (page 180) instead!

YOLO Burger: Use the "mayo" base from the tartar sauce in the fish sticks recipe (page 180), then make the special sauce. Cook veggie patties with the same method!

LAW OF PESTO

Summer Rolls: Good to go.

Watermelon and Strawberry Salad with HdP: Use almond milk and lemon juice instead of crème fraîche.

Peanut-Chartreuse Toritos: Already vegan!

Pho: Instead of a meat broth, pressure cook carrots, celery, onions, mushrooms, and fennel to make a rich vegetable broth, and replace the meat with blanched vegetables or tofu.

LAW OF GENERAL TSO'S CHICKEN

Jalapeño-Pickled Carrots: Great as is.

Kimchi-Loaded Sweet Potatoes: Replace American cheese with vegan cheese.

Chilled Corn Soup with Chile Oil and Honeydew: Fine as is!

Riesling Curry with Squid: The squid is good, but the vegetable curry is great without it!

LAW OF GIN AND TONIC

Roasted Cocoa Cauliflower: Great as is!

Carrot Margaritas: Good to go!

Butternut Squash and Orange Soup: Use agar agar in the wine gel instead of gelatin.

ACKNOWLEDGMENTS

I was introduced to Will Schwalbe through my friend Lee Schrager. Will and his sidekick, Kara Rota, took me out for drinks as opposed to showing me their office. That was a good start. We drank bourbon, which was a smart move. If after two bourbons you don't feel attraction or revulsion to your company, you should probably have more bourbon. We talked about being a TV "culinary rebel," a restaurant cook, and just a guy who likes pizza and wings like any other guy. And there we determined that they, and others, were most interested in how I come up with the food I cook. The laws were born. During the process of making this book, Will and Kara have been more like cool guidance counselors and a lot less like red-checking pencil editors. I really didn't know people so kind, fun, and enthusiastic could exist (in the world of publishing).

Because I'm no good with paperwork, math, or negotiating on my behalf, my agent, Eric Lupfer, helped make this come to fruition. The best thing he did, though, was introduce me to Elinor Hutton, who has served as the "whip" behind this project. The "whip" was probably the toughest job of all, as it meant getting my text (and me) whipped into shape to send to the team at Flatiron. Ellie kept with me when I was sluggish, furthered my ambitions, and provided a really great brain to bounce ideas off of. She's also very funny and smart, and really gets what's going on in the world. That's a rare commodity. I owe Ellie a check for seven dollars and twenty-two cents, which is an inside joke. I also owe a huge amount of thanks to Elizabeth Van Itallie and her design for being the casing to this book's sausage. Without her, this project would be chopped meat.

And Daniel Krieger: the best photographer, period.

While I was on *Food Network Star,* there was only one person on the culinary team who wore the same chef shoes as I do (Dansko) and that was Erin Barnhart. Erin ended up working with me at Do or Dine, and on this cookbook as well. Erin has an incredible knack for organization and creativity, which don't often go hand in hand. Erin also served as the other paddle in the mental ping-pong of figuring out how to make fish vegan or how to proof doughnuts in a crummy Brooklyn apartment. She's a worthy opponent. Erin recorded everything I did as we developed and tested the recipes, which requires a keen attention to detail. She aced this. Best of all about Erin: she is the most positive person I know. It's hard to have a shit day with her around, even if everything is disasterfied (which it was, often). I owe Erin a nice meal that she doesn't have to help cook.

Thanks also to the recipe testers, who helped me fine-tune the recipes and told me when they were horse-hockey.

Throughout this entire thing, my partners Luke, Perry, and George have afforded me the time and peace of mind to get this book done. They deserve a vacation.

Lastly, my GF, Brooke Sweeten, who has put up with all of my culinary tantrums, a smelly kitchen, and dishes everywhere. I love her, and I owe her a boyfriend who isn't writing a book.

INDEX

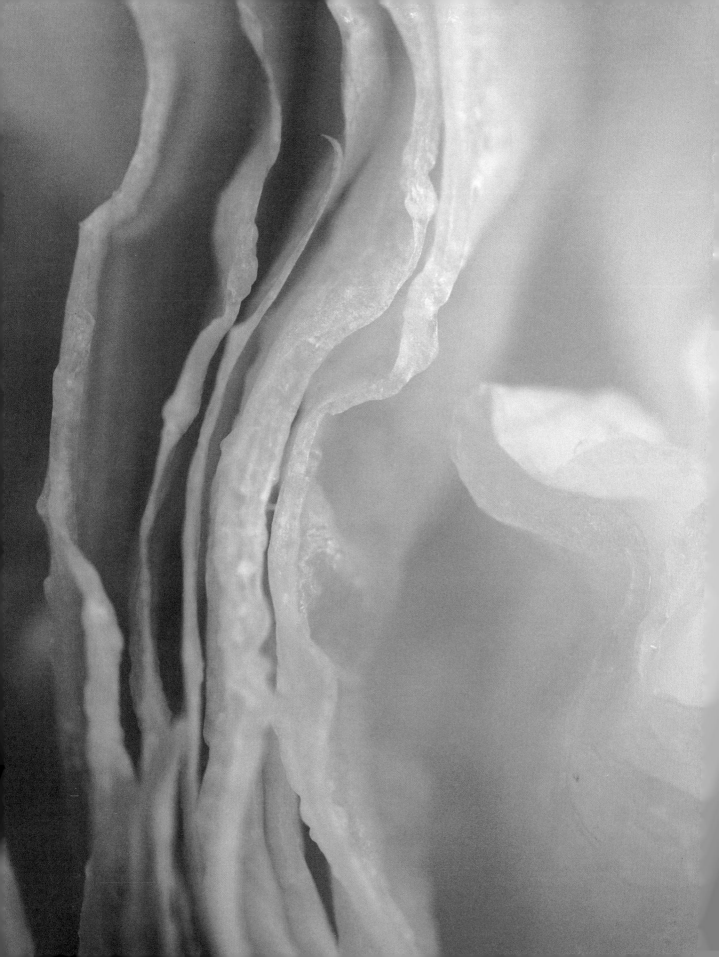